SOCIOLOGY
OF
AMERICA

AMERICAN STUDIES INFORMATION GUIDE SERIES

Series Editor: Donald Koster, Professor of English, Adelphi University, Garden City, New York

Also in this series:

AFRO-AMERICAN LITERATURE AND CULTURE SINCE WORLD WAR II—*Edited by Charles D. Peavy* **

AMERICAN ARCHITECTURE AND ART—*Edited by David Sokol* *

AMERICAN FOLKLORE—*Edited by Richard M. Dorson* **

AMERICAN HUMOR AND HUMORISTS—*Edited by M. Thomas Inge* **

AMERICAN LANGUAGE AND LITERATURE—*Edited by Henry Wasser* **

AMERICAN MUSIC—*Edited by Barbara Hampton* **

AMERICAN POPULAR CULTURE—*Edited by Marshall W. Fishwick and Larry Landrum* **

THE AMERICAN PRESIDENCY—*Edited by Kenneth E. Davison* **

AMERICAN RELIGION AND PHILOSOPHY—*Edited by Ernest R. Sandeen* **

AMERICAN STUDIES—*Edited by David W. Marcell* **

ANTHROPOLOGY OF THE AMERICAS—*Edited by Thomas C. Greaves* **

EDUCATION IN AMERICA—*Edited by Richard G. Durnin* **

HISTORY OF THE UNITED STATES OF AMERICA—*Edited by Ernest Cassara* *

NORTH AMERICAN JEWISH LITERATURE—*Edited by Ira Bruce Nadel* **

WOMAN IN AMERICA—*Edited by Virginia R. Terris* **

*in press
**in preparation

The above series is part of the
GALE INFORMATION GUIDE LIBRARY

The Library consists of a number of separate Series of guides covering major areas in the social sciences, humanities, and current affairs.

General Editor: Paul Wasserman, Professor and former Dean, School of Library and Information Services, University of Maryland

SOCIOLOGY
OF
AMERICA

A GUIDE TO INFORMATION SOURCES

*Volume 1 in the American Studies
Information Guide Series*

Charles Mark

*Associate Professor and Chairman
Department of Sociology and Anthropology
North Adams State College*

With the assistance of

Paula F. Mark
*Instructional Services Librarian
University of Massachusetts, Amherst*

Gale Research Company
Book Tower, Detroit, Michigan 48226

**Library of Congress
Cataloging in Publication Data**

Mark, Charles.
    Sociology of America.

    (American studies information guide series; v. 1)
(Gale information guide library)
        1. United States--Social conditions--1960-
--Bibliography. 2. Sociology--History--United
States--Bibliography. I. Mark, Paula F., joint author.
II. Title.
Z7164.S66M37 [HN59]   016.3091'73'092   73-17560
ISBN 0-8103-1267-0

CONTENTS

Contents

SUMMARY TABLE OF BIBLIOGRAPHIC ITEMS

	Item Numbers:			Items per Chapter:
Chapter 1:	1	–	22	22
Chapter 2:	23	–	121	99
Chapter 3:	122	–	250	129
Chapter 4:	251	–	326	76
Chapter 5:	327	–	379	53
Chapter 6:	380	–	428	49
Chapter 7:	429	–	526	98
Chapter 8:	527	–	619	93
Chapter 9:	620	–	665	46
Chapter 10:	666	–	758	93
Chapter 11:	759	–	842	84
Chapter 12:	843	–	911	69
Chapter 13:	912	–	983	72
Chapter 14:	984	–	1080	97
Chapter 15:	1081	–	1128	48
Chapter 16:	1129	–	1168	40
Chapter 17:	1169	–	1269	101
Chapter 18:	1270	–	1326	57
Chapter 19:	1327	–	1412	86
Chapter 20:	1413	–	1468	56
Chapter 21:	1469	–	1538	70
Chapter 22:	1539	–	1663	125
Chapter 23:	1664	–	1735	72
Chapter 24:	1736	–	1861	126

VITAE

Charles Mark received his Ph.D. in sociology from Charles University of Prague and taught in Europe, New Zealand, and since 1954 in the United States. He conducted comparative research in the developing countries of Africa and Asia. Besides articles and book reviews in American and foreign journals, his publications include RESEARCH STUDIES IN COMPARATIVE SOCIOLOGY, ANALYSIS OF AMERICAN LIFE, and OUTSIDE READINGS IN SOCIOLOGY AND ANTHROPOLOGY. In 1971 he founded the Department of Sociology and Anthropology at North Adams State College, North Adams, Massachusetts, and served as its first chairman. He is a member of the American Sociological Association, Eastern Sociological Society, and the International Sociological Association.

Paula F. Mark received her M.A. from the University of Otago, New Zealand, and her M.S. from the School of Library Service, Columbia University. Formerly the Director of Copiague Memorial Public Library in New York, she is a reference librarian in charge of instructional services in the library of the University of Massachusetts at Amherst.

FOREWORD

Charles Mark's SOCIOLOGY OF AMERICA inaugurates the series of guides to information sources in American studies. I believe it to be an excellent representative of what should prove to be an unparalleled and most valuable series of volumes covering the principal areas of study in American civilization as well as timely and important subjects such as the American presidency, Afro-American literature and culture since World War II, and women in America. These guides are intended to be of service not only to the undergraduate student in search of essential materials for course study, but also to more advanced scholars who may be in need of a tightly organized, up-to-date bibliographical guide to assist them in their research.

The twenty-four chapters of Professor Mark's book cut across the wide range of interest displayed in modern sociology, ranging from "Black America" to "Work and Occupations." The emphasis is always on the sociological study of American life, with the focus shifting from works concerned with the general aspects of American society to those that treat more specific matters.

Professor Mark's emphasis is quite properly, I believe, on works published after 1960; however, he has not neglected to include classics in the field, pioneering studies, or other works of substantial merit that were published earlier. He has also emphasized, again quite properly, the work of American sociologists without overlooking extremely significant work on America by non-Americans, if written in English or if existing in translation.

The annotations, so necessary, I think, to enhance the worth of any bibliography, are an especially valuable part of Professor Mark's book. They are clear and compact, but most important, they provide the reader with ready insight to what may be available in the literature.

I take genuine pleasure in introducing this scholarly and interesting volume which augurs well for the success of the entire series.

Donald N. Koster
Series Editor

PREFACE

This bibliography was prepared in 1973 and 1974 as a collection of works which focus on American society in general and on specific aspects of American life and culture in particular. Rather than being multidisciplinary, as many collections of work on American society tend to be, this selection concentrates on the sociological study of American life. The majority of the authors represented here, about 85 percent of the total, are sociologists, most of whom are present or past members of the American Sociological Association. Other social sciences such as anthropology, political science, psychology, history, and economics are represented through works which are often quoted in sociological literature. Most of the books listed in chapters 4 through 24 were first published since the end of World War II, the greater number of them after 1960. Earlier publications were included if they were cited as classics, pioneering studies, or works of special merit, but as a rule the more recent publications received closer attention.

The material from which listings were selected was obtained by a systematic search of volumes in sociological collections of several libraries. Besides footnotes, references, and lists of recommended titles in books and periodicals, other resources such as book reviews and book notes in journals, publishers' lists, and subject and author sections of library catalogs were consulted.

The selection was generally based on the following criteria, used singly or in combination:

1. The subject was American society and culture or some specific aspect of American life, rather than general sociology or sociological theory.

2. The author was a sociologist or one representing a related social science, who was often cited in sociological writings.

3. The work was reviewed in one or several sociological journals, especially in the AMERICAN SOCIOLOGICAL REVIEW, CONTEMPORARY SOCIOLOGY, the AMERICAN JOURNAL OF SOCIOLOGY, and SOCIAL FORCES.

4. Priority for inclusion in most cases was determined by frequency of citation and, in others, by the fact that the work represented an area of

study not covered by other selections.

5.   The work was substantial, or had special bibliographic value.

Through the application of these criteria, a file of about 9,000 cards yielded by the initial search was reduced to the number of entries listed here. The bibliography is thus fairly selective, and no complete enumeration of works by particular authors or on particular topics was attempted.

The system of classification of the material into chapters and sections was developed during the process of selection and essentially derived from the material itself. Any system of classification results in a certain amount of overlap. To minimize it, generally used categories such as social stratification, marriage and the family, deviance, and crime and delinquency were adopted for most chapters. However, concern with material specific to American society called for several additional chapters: "Black America," "Jewish Community," "Women," and "Youth." Where overlap occurs, it is dealt with by cross-references.

The bibliography consists of relatively compact units. Chapters range from about 40 to 120 entries, and most of them are divided into topical sections which average about 10 entries. Thus any section can be easily scanned. Chapters are designated by numerals and sections within them by capital letters. Each bibliographic item is listed only once and numbered consecutively from the first chapter. Entries within the sections are arranged alphabetically by the name of the first author or editor, or in the case of serial publications, by title. This order is used for the sake of convenience in locating entries and consequently does not reflect the relative importance of any publication. Where there are two authors or editors, both names are given in the text and in the index; where there are more than two, only the first author is listed.

The first two chapters are devoted to bibliographic resources, particularly those which deal with periodical literature, and to general reference works; specialized reference works are listed at the beginning of most chapters. The third chapter provides an annotated list of some 120 journals in which material on American society may be found. The entries which follow are limited to books, arranged in a sequence of related fields of sociological specialization. Chapters 4 through 8 present works which deal with American society as a whole, the population, and its spatial distribution in regions and in rural and urban communities. Chapters 9 through 13 cover the major segments of a socially stratified system and its divisions by race, religion, national origin, and social class, which find their most direct expression in the American occupational structure. The most intensively studied minorities, the Black and the Jewish communities, were assigned chapters separate from other ethnic and religious groups. Chapters 14 through 18 focus on the private sphere of life, emphasizing both the informal and formal process of socialization involving family, age, and sex roles, as well as educational and recreational concerns. Chapters 19 through 23 cover the structure of power relations in society, as reflected in formal organizations and the political system, and the processes of social conflict, reorganization, and disorganization. The final chapter lists selected works in American sociology, many of them theoretical, complementary to the previously listed monographs and empirical studies.

The study of social problems has not been confined to any one chapter, nor could it be, since almost any aspect of American life can be viewed from a critical or problematic perspective. Books which convey the whole range of social problems are included in Chapter 4, on American society, but works which deal with specific social problems are listed within the chapters to which they relate. For instance, the chapter on the urban community contains a section on problems of residential segregation; the chapter on Black America contains a section on racial conflict and discrimination; and the chapter on social stratification includes a section on poverty.

The emphasis in this bibliography is neither on theoretical sociology, nor on applied sociology and related fields such as social work, but rather on empirical studies, monographs, and research reports which provide sociological investigation and analysis of American life. The considerable literature on the theory and history of sociology and on methodology of social research has generally not been included here except for some items in the final chapter on selected works in American sociology. Equally, comparative and cross-cultural studies which are concerned, for instance, with population, the family, or the city in global perspective are obviously beyond the scope of this collection. Thus, this bibliography is sociographic and, as far as possible, specific to American society rather than formally sociological in an abstract sense; with few exceptions most of its works were authored by American sociologists.

Besides monographs and other works which deal with particular topics, this collection includes some texts and anthologies which are broader in scope. Such texts are useful for overall orientation in an area such as religion, family, or crime, and serve as a link between empirical and theoretical studies. Many of them list additional bibliographic material, as do anthologies, which often contain research reports and articles reprinted from journals. Where a varied collection of sociological journals is not available, an anthology provides at least some access to periodical literature. However, no attempt was made to list texts and readers in introductory or general sociology.

Annotations have been provided for almost 80 percent of the entries; they were omitted where the title, alone or with the subtitle, provided sufficient information about the nature of the work. The relative brevity of an annotation makes it no substitute for the more extensive book review which, for many of the items, can be located in a scholarly journal with the help of some of the indexes discussed in the first chapter.

It is hoped that this book will prove useful as a reference work in libraries in the United States and elsewhere and that it will aid the student who approaches the study of American society and culture from a sociological view point.

Preface

The preparation of the bibliography owes much to the availability of library resources at North Adams State College; the colleges of the Pioneer Valley, especially Amherst and Smith; and the University of Massachusetts in Amherst, where most of the work was done. A number of students assisted in the initial search; their assistance is gratefully acknowledged, as is the courtesy shown by the staffs of the libraries mentioned. Judith Mark and Vera Mark, graduate students at the University of Massachusetts, Amherst, participated in various stages of the preparation of the manuscript; without their help, publication deadlines could not have been met.

Chapter 1

INTRODUCTION TO RESOURCES

FOR SOCIOLOGY OF AMERICAN LIFE

Chapter 1

INTRODUCTION TO RESOURCES FOR

SOCIOLOGY OF AMERICAN LIFE

The study of American society, culture, and ways of life is a multidisciplinary endeavor shared by social sciences and humanities alike. Among the social sciences, especially anthropology, social psychology, and sociology, the interdisciplinary boundaries have sometimes become blurred because of the convergence of research interests. Anthropology, which traditionally specialized in the ethnography of native populations within and beyond the borders of the United States, has begun, in recent decades, to study certain aspects of modern American society such as the youth culture and minority groups, which were previously regarded as more purely sociological concerns. Psychology and social psychology have also investigated social and behavioral phenomena in the American context including the process of socialization, education, and family life. In several disciplines the focus on America is represented by an important field of specialization such as American history, government, literature, and folklore.

At least theoretically, sociology is in a central position to focus on American life in its entirety. Most research by American sociologists is conducted within the boundaries of the United States, courses in American society are offered at graduate and undergraduate levels of study, and works by Robin Williams and Don Martindale have attracted attention to American society for a number of years. Nevertheless, American society is not a major field of specialization., Instead, sociology concerns itself with a wide range of topics of narrower interest, as indicated by the titles of the chapters and their subdivisions in this volume. While specializing in these fields, sociology takes into account the findings of other social sciences. In an average sociological text, close to one-half of the references may be to works which belong to another social science or are interdisciplinary.

This poses a bibliographic problem. Lists of readings, bibliographies, library catalogs, and the library collections themselves contain considerable proportions of nonsociological material in sections devoted to sociology. By a broad and popular definition of the field, sociology is equated with general social science, while by a narrow definition it represents the scholarly work of sociologists. However, even the narrow definition is not without ambiguities when it is used to determine whether a work should be properly classified as sociological. Some scholars work in two disciplines and achieve prominence in both; some may contribute to the periodical literature of several disciplines while concentrating their major effort in one of them. The majority of sociologists in the United States are members of the American Sociological Association, but some are not. Fields of original training and current research interests may differ.

The problem of classification of works within the discipline is complicated by the fact that sociology not only grew rapidly in the last quarter of a century, but also branched out into many new avenues of research in that period. In the years from 1945 to 1970, the membership of the American Sociological Association grew tenfold from about 1,200 to 12,903. This growth was reflected in the relative increase in the number of books and articles published in the 1960s and in the continuing high volume of production in the 1970s, in comparison with earlier decades. The sum total of sociological works published in the United States is substantial: it is estimated that sociological publications, whether in the form of books or scholarly articles, amount to at least 10,000 in each category.

This bibliography focuses on books relevant to the study of American society, but recognizes that periodical literature is an equally important source of knowledge of American life. Cumulative indexes to the scholarly journals provide access to a large number of articles published over a period of decades. Such indexes have been published by the AMERICAN SOCIOLOGICAL REVIEW, which is the official journal of the American Sociological Association; by the AMERICAN JOURNAL OF SOCIOLOGY, published by the University of Chicago Press; and by SOCIAL FORCES, published by the University of North Carolina Press. INDEX TO THE AMERICAN SOCIOLOGICAL REVIEW, VOLUMES 1-25 (1936-1960), published in 1961, was followed by an INDEX TO VOLUMES 26-30 (1961-1965), published in 1965, and by the most recent INDEX TO VOLUMES 31-35 (1966-1970). CUMULATIVE INDEX TO THE AMERICAN JOURNAL OF SOCIOLOGY, VOLUMES 1-70 (1895-1965) was published in 1966 and followed in 1971 by a SUPPLEMENTARY INDEX TO THE CUMULATIVE INDEX, AMERICAN JOURNAL OF SOCIOLOGY, VOLUMES 71-75 (1965-1970). In 1974 a CUMULATIVE INDEX, VOLUMES 1-50 (1922-1972) was published by SOCIAL FORCES.

These bibliographic achievements by three leading journals organize and make available for research a substantial amount of sociological material. The editor of the CUMULATIVE INDEX TO SOCIAL FORCES states in the introduction: "Here is a record of 50 years' work in sociology and cognate fields. The legacy of SOCIAL FORCES is sizeable and rich: almost 2,200 authors of 3,200 articles, making for 8,000 entries in the subject index, classified under 667 categories. There are also 5,500 book reviews and 138 essays." No such complete enumeration is offered by the editors of the other indexes, except that the editor of the CUMULATIVE INDEX TO THE AMERICAN JOURNAL OF SOCIOLOGY notes that "...the Subject Index contains nearly 16,000 entries, an average of about four per article." This would indicate that close to 4,000 articles are listed in that volume; 239 articles are specifically mentioned in the SUPPLEMENTARY INDEX for 1965-70. The editor of the INDEX TO THE AMERICAN SOCIOLOGICAL REVIEW, VOLUMES 1-25 mentions in the preface that, since the compilation of the index for the first twenty volumes, published in 1956, "...about 700 additional entries have been made in the Subject Index (now less inclusive than formerly), about 630 in the Author Index, and almost 2,000 in the Book Review Index." No enumerations are given in the two other indexes to AMERICAN SOCIOLOGICAL REVIEW. An estimate, based on a count of items in random samples of pages in all the indexes of the three journals, indicates a total listing of almost 10,000 articles and about 18,000 book reviews.

Each index volume contains a subject, author, and book review index. The CUMULATIVE AND SUPPLEMENTARY INDEXES TO THE AMERICAN JOURNAL OF SOCIOLOGY supply, in addition, brief annotations for almost all articles in the author index. The significance of this type of index is briefly commented upon by the editor of the CUMULATIVE INDEX TO SOCIAL FORCES: "...a tool for research, for building bibliographies, for studies in the sociology of sociology, and for teaching--developing syllabi, easy spotting of articles pertinent to students' interests, and appraisals of books possibly germane to courses and students' papers."

Besides cumulative indexes to particular journals, abstracting and indexing services and bibliographies provide the most effective means of searching in a wide range of periodicals for articles on specific topics. The major resources of this kind are mentioned in this chapter, with bibliographical details after the text, while supplementary publications are listed in the following chapter on reference works.

SOCIOLOGICAL ABSTRACTS, published since November 1952 and international in scope, abstracts articles from most American sociological journals and many foreign ones. Currently, abstracts of about 6,000 articles and papers and of more than 500 books are published each year under fifty-eight headings. Author and subject indexes are cumulated annually in the final issue of the volume. Supplementary issues (forty-seven of them by mid-1974) abstract papers presented at annual meetings of the American Sociological Association, Eastern Sociological Society, Midwestern Sociological Society, the International Sociological Association, which cosponsor the journal, and at meetings of other regional associations. A DECENNIAL INDEX 1953-1962 lists over 20,000 authors and more than 14,000 abstracts. Computer searches of the abstracts from 1965 are now possible.

SOCIAL SCIENCES AND HUMANITIES INDEX, known from 1907 to 1965 as the INTERNATIONAL INDEX TO PERIODICALS, provides through December 1973 a subject and author index for about 200 English language periodicals, which include the AMERICAN SOCIOLOGICAL REVIEW, the AMERICAN JOURNAL OF SOCIOLOGY, JOURNAL OF MARRIAGE AND THE FAMILY, SOCIAL FORCES, and SOCIAL PROBLEMS. With the issue of June 1974 SOCIAL SCIENCES INDEX became a separate publication, indexing articles and book reviews in 263 social science periodicals, 185 of which were not previously indexed in SOCIAL SCIENCES AND HUMANITIES INDEX; coverage of sociological journals has been considerably increased.

INTERNATIONAL BIBLIOGRAPHY OF SOCIOLOGY was published annually from 1952 to 1961 by UNESCO (United Nations Educational, Scientific and Cultural Organization) in Paris, and since 1962 by Aldine in Chicago. Each volume, compiled by the International Committee for Social Sciences Documentation, in cooperation with UNESCO, includes 3,000 to 5,000 entries for books, articles, reports, and book reviews, arranged under broad subject headings with author and topical indexes.

READERS' GUIDE TO PERIODICAL LITERATURE has been published since 1900. It indexes about 160 American periodicals such as TIME, NEWSWEEK, U.S. NEWS AND WORLD REPORT, and SATURDAY REVIEW/WORLD, as well as some more specialized journals which include SCIENTIFIC AMERICAN, RAMPARTS, and SOCIETY (formerly TRANS-ACTION).

ARTICLES IN AMERICAN STUDIES, 1954-1968; A CUMULATION OF THE ANNUAL BIBLIOGRAPHIES FROM AMERICAN QUARTERLY, is an annotated bibliography of interdisciplinary periodical articles dealing with "...the characteristics, relationships and ramifications of various aspects of American Civilization." For the period 1956 to 1967 it includes a category of selected articles in sociology and anthropology; sociology was treated as a separate category for articles published in 1968.

BOOK REVIEW DIGEST, published since 1905, indexes selected book reviews from about seventy-five English language periodicals and provides short excerpts from these reviews. It does not cover social science journals systematically, and the reviews of scholarly books tend to be those of interest to the layman.

BOOK REVIEW INDEX, published since 1965, cites reviews from about 225 North American and British journals and newspapers and seeks an inclusive record of about 65,000 reviews a year of some 35,000 new books.

The resources discussed in this chapter are listed in the bibliography which follows, along with selected monographs from a series published under the sponsorship of the American Sociological Association. The Arnold and Caroline Rose Monograph series is of special interest to graduate students, since some of the titles are based on doctoral dissertations and others report grant-supported research.

BIBLIOGRAPHY

A. CUMULATIVE INDEXES TO SOCIOLOGICAL JOURNALS

1. AMERICAN JOURNAL OF SOCIOLOGY. CUMULATIVE INDEX TO THE
    AMERICAN JOURNAL OF SOCIOLOGY, VOLUMES 1-70, 1895-1965.
    Chicago: University of Chicago Press, 1966. 259 p.

2. _____. SUPPLEMENTARY INDEX TO THE CUMULATIVE INDEX,
    VOLUMES 71-75, 1965-1970. Chicago: University of Chicago Press,
    1971. 43 p.

3. AMERICAN SOCIOLOGICAL REVIEW. INDEX TO THE AMERICAN
    SOCIOLOGICAL REVIEW, VOLUMES 1-25, 1936-1960. New York:
    American Sociological Association, 1961. 312 p.

4. _____. INDEX TO THE AMERICAN SOCIOLOGICAL REVIEW, VOL-
    UMES 26-30, 1961-1965. Washington, D.C.: American Sociological
    Association, 1965. 92 p.

5. _____. INDEX TO THE AMERICAN SOCIOLOGICAL REVIEW, VOL-
    UMES 31-35, 1966-1970. Washington, D.C.: American Sociological
    Association, n.d. 75 p.

6. SOCIAL FORCES. CUMULATIVE INDEX, VOLUMES 1-50, 1922-1972.
    Chapel Hill: University of North Carolina Press, 1974. 194 p.

B. MAJOR ABSTRACTS, INDEXES, AND BIBLIOGRAPHIES

7. BOOK REVIEW DIGEST. New York: Wilson, 1905--. Monthly, except
    February and July, with annual cumulation.

8. BOOK REVIEW INDEX. Detroit: Gale Research Co., 1965--. Bi-
    monthly, with annual cumulation.

9. Cohen, Hennig, ed. ARTICLES IN AMERICAN STUDIES 1954-1968;
    A CUMULATION OF THE ANNUAL BIBLIOGRAPHIES FROM AMERICAN
    QUARTERLY. 2 vols. Ann Arbor, Mich.: Pierian Press, 1972. 898 p.

    For AMERICAN QUARTERLY, see item 159.

10. INTERNATIONAL BIBLIOGRAPHY OF SOCIOLOGY. Paris: UNESCO,

1952-61; Chicago: Aldine, 1962--. Annual.

11. READERS' GUIDE TO PERIODICAL LITERATURE. New York: Wilson, 1900--. Semimonthly, September-June; monthly, July and August; quarterly and annual cumulations.

12. SOCIAL SCIENCES AND HUMANITIES INDEX. New York: Wilson, 1907--. Quarterly.

   From 1907 to 1965 known as INTERNATIONAL INDEX TO PERIODICALS. From June 1974 divided into two separate quarterly publications: HUMANITIES INDEX and SOCIAL SCIENCES INDEX.

13. SOCIOLOGICAL ABSTRACTS. Sociological Abstracts, Inc., P.O. Box 22206, San Diego, Calif. 92122. 1952--. Five issues per year, with a separate cumulative index.

C. ARNOLD AND CAROLINE ROSE MONOGRAPH SERIES

14. Gasson, Ruth M., et al. ATTITUDES AND FACILITATION IN THE ATTAINMENT OF STATUS. Washington, D.C.: American Sociological Association, 1972. 37 p.

15. Gordon, Chad. LOOKING AHEAD: SELF-CONCEPTIONS, RACE AND FAMILY AS DETERMINANTS OF ADOLESCENT ORIENTATION TO ACHIEVEMENT. Washington, D.C.: American Sociological Association, 1972. 120 p.

16. Hauser, Robert Mason. SOCIOECONOMIC BACKGROUND AND EDUCATIONAL PERFORMANCE. Washington, D.C.: American Sociological Association, 1972. x, 166 p.

17. Kerckhoff, Alan C. AMBITION AND ATTAINMENT: A STUDY OF FOUR SAMPLES OF AMERICAN BOYS. Washington, D.C.: American Sociological Association, 1974. vi, 106 p.

18. Klatzky, Sheila R. PATTERNS OF CONTACT WITH RELATIVES. Washington, D.C.: American Sociological Association, 1972. xv, 117 p.

19. Orum, Anthony M. BLACK STUDENTS IN PROTEST: A STUDY OF THE ORIGINS OF THE BLACK STUDENT MOVEMENT. Washington, D.C.: American Sociological Association, 1972. v, 89 p.

20. Rosenberg, Morris, and Simmons, Roberta G. BLACK AND WHITE

SELF-ESTEEM: THE URBAN SCHOOL CHILD. Washington, D.C.: American Sociological Association, 1972. ix, 160 p.

21. Schwartz, Michael, and Stryker, Sheldon. DEVIANCE, SELVES AND OTHERS. Washington, D.C.: American Sociological Association, 1971. v, 128 p.

22. Turk, Herman. INTERORGANIZATIONAL ACTIVATION IN URBAN COMMUNITIES: DEDUCTIONS FROM THE CONCEPT OF SYSTEM. Washington, D.C.: American Sociological Association, 1973. x, 67 p.

Chapter 2

REFERENCE WORKS

Chapter 2
REFERENCE WORKS

A. GUIDES TO BIBLIOGRAPHY

23. Bart, Pauline, and Frankel, Linda. THE STUDENT SOCIOLOGIST'S HANDBOOK. Cambridge, Mass.: Schenkman, distributed by General Learning Press, Morristown, N.J., 1971. 226 p.

    A practical guide to research and resource materials, governmental and nongovernmental sources of data. Provides overviews of government publications and of the periodical literature.

24. Clarke, Jack Alden. RESEARCH MATERIALS IN THE SOCIAL SCIENCES. 2nd ed. Madison: University of Wisconsin Press, 1967. 56 p.

    An annotated guide designed primarily for graduate students in the social sciences.

25. Freides, Thelma. LITERATURE AND BIBLIOGRAPHY OF THE SOCIAL SCIENCES. New York: Bowker, 1974. xviii, 284 p.

    This textbook describes the organization of scholarly communication in the social sciences, and serves as a guide to the bibliography of sociology, anthropology, economics, psychology, and related fields.

26. Hoselitz, Berthold Frank. A READER'S GUIDE TO THE SOCIAL SCIENCES. Rev. ed. New York: Free Press, 1970. xiv, 423 p.

    The section on sociology (pp. 1-40), written by Peter M. Blau and Joan W. Moore, covers the development of sociology and contemporary sociological literature in selected areas.

27. Schmeckebier, Laurence F., and Eastin, Roy B. GOVERNMENT PUBLICATIONS AND THEIR USE. 2nd rev. ed. Washington, D.C.: Brookings, 1969. 502 p.

A survey of U.S. government publications and a guide to
their location and use.

28. White, Carl M., et al. SOURCES OF INFORMATION IN THE SO-
CIAL SCIENCES: A GUIDE TO THE LITERATURE. 2nd ed. Chicago:
American Library Association, 1973. xviii, 702 p.

The major guide to the literature of sociology, psychology,
anthropology, economics, political science, geography, history, and education. In the sociology section (pp. 243-306),
a discussion of topics on which sociologists are writing is
followed by annotated lists of about 440 reference items.

29. Winchell, Constance M. GUIDE TO REFERENCE BOOKS. 8th ed.
Chicago: American Library Association, 1967. 741 p.

Updated at two-year intervals by supplements, this is the
standard guide to general works of reference.

B. ENCYCLOPEDIAS AND DICTIONARIES

30. ENCYCLOPEDIA OF SOCIOLOGY. Edited by Peter J. O'Connell.
Guilford, Conn.: Dushkin Publishing Co., 1973. 336 p.

More than 1,300 short articles, with photographs, tables,
graphs, charts, and brief biographical sketches of past and
present contributors to the development of sociological thought.
Contains a bibliography (pp. 317-28).

31. ENCYCLOPEDIA OF THE SOCIAL SCIENCES. Edited by E.R.A. Seligman and Alvin Johnson. 15 vols. New York: Macmillan, 1930-35.

Prepared under the auspices of ten learned societies with the
assistance of scholars throughout the world. Emphasizes the
historical development of social thought and of the social
sciences and includes numerous biographical articles.

32. Gould, Julius, and Kolb, William, eds. A DICTIONARY OF THE
SOCIAL SCIENCES. New York: Free Press, 1964. xvi, 761 p.

A UNESCO-sponsored collection of essays which define key
concepts in sociology, social psychology, economics, political
science, and anthropology.

33. Hoult, Thomas Ford. DICTIONARY OF MODERN SOCIOLOGY.
Totowa, N.J.: Littlefield, Adams, 1969. xviii, 408 p.

Defines sociological concepts in terms of their current usage
and illustrates many of them by quotations from sociological
literature. Entries are also classified according to specialty

(pp. 355-75), and a bibliography (pp. 376-408) lists works and authors cited.

34.   INTERNATIONAL ENCYCLOPEDIA OF THE SOCIAL SCIENCES.   Edited by David L. Sills.   17 vols.   New York: Macmillan, 1968.

Articles up to 5,000 words in length on important concepts, theories, and methods in the social sciences, and on about 600 prominent social scientists with bibliographies of classic and contemporary works.

35.   Mitchell, Geoffrey Duncan.   A DICTIONARY OF SOCIOLOGY. Chicago: Aldine, 1968.   224 p.

Although prepared in Great Britain, this dictionary refers often to American sociologists and links their work to European scholarship.   Provides a short description of each term, followed by reference to its uses, both historical and contemporary.

36.   Theodorson, George A., and Theodorson, Achilles G.   A MODERN DICTIONARY OF SOCIOLOGY.   New York: Crowell, 1969.   xviii, 469 p.

Defines important concepts in sociology and related terms from psychology, cultural anthropology, philosophy, and statistics. Frequently provides the original source of the term.

C. ABSTRACTS IN SPECIAL FIELDS

37.   ABSTRACTS FOR SOCIAL WORKERS.   National Association of Social Workers, 2 Park Avenue, New York, N.Y.   10016.   1965--.   Quarterly.

Abstracts of articles from about 200 journals in social work and related fields, as well as selected books and reports. Contains author and subject indexes which cumulate annually.

38.   ABSTRACTS IN ANTHROPOLOGY.   Greenwood Periodicals, Inc., 51 Riverside Avenue, Westport, Conn.   06880.   1970--.   Quarterly.

Abstracts of articles from over forty journals and of papers presented at meetings of learned societies; classified as ethnology, linguistics, archaeology, and physical anthropology, with author and subject indexes.

39.   ABSTRACTS OF FOLKLORE STUDIES.   Austin: University of Texas Press, 1963--.   Quarterly.

Published for the American Folklore Society. Abstracts from one hundred journals in folklore studies, ethnomusicology, and related areas; arranged by journal title in alphabetical order with a name and subject index. A section of bibliographical notes surveys literature not published in journals.

40. ABSTRACTS ON CRIMINOLOGY AND PENOLOGY (formerly, EXCERPTA CRIMINOLOGICA). Kluwer, Polstraat 10, Deventer, Netherlands. 1961--. Bimonthly with annual cumulation.

Lists about 2,500 abstracts annually, many of them from U.S. and British journals, covering crime and delinquency, the control and treatment of offenders, criminal procedures, and the administration of justice.

41. AMERICA: HISTORY AND LIFE; A GUIDE TO PERIODICAL LITERATURE. American Bibliographical Center/Clio Press, 2040 Alameda Padre Serra, Santa Barbara, Calif. 93103. 1964--. Quarterly.

Article abstracts and citations from about 1,700 American and foreign periodicals; beginning with volume eleven, 1974, includes an index to book reviews. Covers all aspects of the nation's history and life from the earliest times to the present.

42. CRIME AND DELINQUENCY ABSTRACTS. Chevy Chase, Md.: National Institute of Mental Health, 1963-72. Bimonthly, with annual cumulated indexes.

This journal was published originally by the National Council on Crime and Delinquency in two sections entitled CURRENT PROJECTS IN THE PREVENTION, CONTROL AND TREATMENT OF CRIME AND DELINQUENCY and INTERNATIONAL BIBLIOGRAPHY IN CRIME AND DELINQUENCY. The publication, sponsored by the Clearinghouse on Mental Health Information, provided abstracts of articles, books, and research projects.

43. CRIME AND DELINQUENCY LITERATURE. National Council on Crime and Delinquency, 411 Hackensack Avenue, Hackensack, N.J. 07601. 1968--. Quarterly.

Each issue contains a review of recent research and developments in a specific subject area, as well as abstracts of current literature arranged under such headings as the law and the courts; crime and the offender; and law enforcement and the police. Innovative programs are noted and a question and answer section is also featured. Computer searches of the bibliographic information can be made.

44. LANGUAGE AND LANGUAGE BEHAVIOR ABSTRACTS. Sociological

Abstracts, Inc., P.O. Box 22206, San Diego, Calif. 92122. 1967--.
Quarterly.

Published through 1973 at the University of Michigan, each
volume contains about 1,300 abstracts from 1,000 publications
in thirty-two languages and twenty-five disciplines, arranged
in a classified scheme which includes sections on sociolinguis-
tics and sociology. A cumulative index to the first five volumes was published in 1973. From 1972 the bibliographic
information is available for computer searching.

45.   POVERTY AND HUMAN RESOURCES ABSTRACTS.   Beverly Hills, Calif.:
Sage Publications, 1966--. Bimonthly.

Published with the cooperation of the Institute of Labor and
Industrial Relations, University of Michigan--Wayne State
University. There are about 1,000 abstracts of periodicals,
books, pamphlets, and reports in each volume, on such
topics as legal rights and assistance for the poor, manpower
and labor force participation, education, income, and social
mobility.

46.   PSYCHOLOGICAL ABSTRACTS. American Psychological Association,
1200 Seventeenth Street NW, Washington, D.C. 20036. 1927--.
Monthly, with semiannual cumulated indexes.

Particularly useful for the period prior to the establishment of
SOCIOLOGICAL ABSTRACTS. In current issues a number of
sociological journals are selectively abstracted, with social
psychology as one of the major divisions of the classification
scheme. Cumulative author and subject indexes have been
separately published by G.K. Hall, Boston, Massachusetts,
since 1960. Computer searches are possible through the
PASAR (PSYCHOLOGICAL ABSTRACTS Search and Retrieval)
information retrieval system.

47.   RESEARCH IN EDUCATION. Washington, D.C.: Government Printing
Office, 1966--. Monthly.

Published by the National Institute of Education of the U.S.
Department of Health, Education and Welfare as the abstracting journal of its Educational Resources Information Center
and prepared by its sixteen constituent clearinghouses. It
covers all Office of Education project reports and other education related report literature. A title change, to RE-
SOURCES IN EDUCATION, is expected with the January
1975 issue. Most of the material abstracted is available in
microfiche format and ordering information is provided. Computer searches of the bibliographic data base for RESEARCH
IN EDUCATION and its companion publication, CURRENT
INDEX TO JOURNALS IN EDUCATION (see item 57), may
be requested.

48. SAGE URBAN STUDIES ABSTRACTS. Beverly Hills, Calif.: Sage
    Publications, 1973--. Quarterly.

    About 250 abstracts per issue of articles, books, pamphlets,
    government publications, significant speeches, and legislative
    research studies on urban affairs.

49. SOCIAL SCIENCE ABSTRACTS; A COMPREHENSIVE ABSTRACTING
    AND INDEXING JOURNAL OF THE WORLD'S PERIODICAL LITERA-
    TURE IN THE SOCIAL SCIENCES. 5 vols. New York: Social Sci-
    ence Abstracts, 1929-33.

    A classified arrangement of 70,464 abstracts of articles from
    more than 4,000 journals; author and subject indexes appear
    in volume five.

    SOCIOLOGICAL ABSTRACTS. See item 13.

50. WOMEN STUDIES ABSTRACTS. P.O. Box 1, Rush, N.Y. 14543.
    1970--. Quarterly.

    Abstracts articles about women from a wide range of periodi-
    cals; indexes reviews of books about women; and cites articles
    of related interest.

D. INDEXES AND INDEXING SERVICES

51. Abramson, Harold J., and Sofios, Nicholas, eds. INDEX TO
    SOCIOLOGY READERS 1960-1965. 2 vols. Metuchen, N.J.:
    Scarecrow Press, 1973. 1125 p.

    Indexes by author and subject the contents of 227 readers
    (40 percent of whose contributors were sociologists) and
    provides full citations to the original journal articles.

52. ABS GUIDE TO RECENT PUBLICATIONS IN THE SOCIAL AND
    BEHAVIORAL SCIENCES. New York: American Behavioral Scientist,
    1965. xxi, 781 p.

    A cumulated list of 6,664 works first annotated in the
    AMERICAN BEHAVIORAL SCIENTIST (see item 157);
    updated since 1966 by annual volumes which cumulate
    and extend the entries in the "New Studies" section of
    the journal.

53. ALTERNATIVE PRESS INDEX: AN INDEX TO ALTERNATIVE AND
    UNDERGROUND PUBLICATIONS. Alternative Press Center, Bag
    Service 2500, Postal Station E, Toronto, Ontario, Canada. 1969--.
    Quarterly.

A subject index to about 130 liberal and radical publications; issues have appeared slowly and irregularly.

AMERICAN STATISTICS INDEX. See item 84.

BOOK REVIEW DIGEST. See item 7.

BOOK REVIEW INDEX. See item 8.

54. Chicorel, Marietta, ed. CHICOREL INDEX TO ABSTRACTING AND INDEXING SERVICES: SERIALS IN HUMANITIES AND THE SOCIAL SCIENCES. 2 vols. New York: Chicorel Library Publishing Co., 1974. 920 p.

   A list of about 30,000 American and foreign periodicals; the title of each journal is followed by the names of the abstracting and indexing services which include it.

CIS INDEX TO PUBLICATIONS OF THE UNITED STATES CONGRESS. See item 85.

55. Council of Planning Librarians. EXCHANGE BIBLIOGRAPHIES. Council of Planning Librarians, P.O. Box 229, Monticello, Ill. 61856. 1957--.

   Each bibliography provides up-to-date references on a topic of special interest to those involved in planning and related fields.

56. CURRENT CONTENTS: SOCIAL AND BEHAVIORAL SCIENCES. Institute for Scientific Information, 325 Chestnut Street, Philadelphia, Pa. 19106. 1969--. Weekly.

   One of a series of current awareness services, this publication reports the tables of contents of more than 1,000 American and foreign journals as they are published. Addresses of first authors are given, along with information about a reprint ordering service, computer searches of the data base, and the compilation of subject bibliographies.

57. CURRENT INDEX TO JOURNALS IN EDUCATION. CCM Information Corporation, 866 Third Avenue, New York, N.Y. 10022. 1969--. Monthly.

   Indexes and briefly annotates articles in over 700 English language journals in education and related fields. A companion to RESEARCH IN EDUCATION (see item 47), bibliographic information in the two publications is available for computerized retrieval.

58. EDUCATION INDEX. New York: Wilson, 1929/30--. Monthly.

A cumulative author and subject index to over 200 education journals, yearbooks, proceedings, and bulletins.

GOVERNMENT REPORTS INDEX. See item 108.

59. INDEX MEDICUS. Washington, D.C.: Government Printing Office, 1960--. Distributed for the National Library of Medicine. Monthly.

Indexes the world's biomedical periodical literature by author and subject; a separate annual edition is published as CUMU-LATED INDEX MEDICUS. Provides access to articles on the sociological aspects of health and illness appearing in medical, public health, and psychiatric journals, as well as sociological and psychological journals. Computer-produced by MEDLARS (the Medical Literature Analysis and Retrieval System of the National Library of Medicine) the data base can be searched by computer.

60. INDEX TO CURRENT URBAN DOCUMENTS. Westport, Conn.: Green-wood Press, 1972--. Quarterly, with annual cumulation.

A geographic and subject index to official documents issued by 197 of the largest U.S. and Canadian cities, and twenty-six counties of one million or more inhabitants, as determined by the 1970 census.

61. INDEX TO PERIODICAL ARTICLES BY AND ABOUT NEGROES. Boston: G.K. Hall, 1950--. Annual.

Indexes about twenty journals, mostly by subject and author. Current titles include THE BLACK SCHOLAR, FREEDOMWAYS, the JOURNAL OF BLACK STUDIES, and other journals fre-quently not indexed elsewhere. Cumulated volumes are avail-able for 1950-59 and for 1960-70.

MONTHLY CATALOG OF UNITED STATES GOVERNMENT PUBLICA-TIONS. See item 93.

62. MONTHLY CHECKLIST OF STATE PUBLICATIONS. Washington, D.C.: Government Printing Office, 1910--. Distributed for the Library of Congress. Monthly.

A record of documents issued by the states and various inter-state and state organizations received by the Library of Con-gress. Indexed annually.

63. NEW YORK TIMES INDEX. New York Times, Times Square, New

York, N.Y. 10036. 1851--. Semimonthly, with separate annual cumulation.

A subject and name index, with summaries of major articles and editorials. Entries are arranged chronologically within the subject divisions and provide date, page, and column information for each item.

64. POPULATION INDEX. Office of Population Research, Princeton University, Princeton, N.J. 08540. 1935--. Quarterly.

An annotated, classified, international bibliography of books, periodical articles, and government publications on all aspects of population studies. Each issue contains an author and geographic index. These indexes cumulate annually, and for the period 1935-68 have been published in nine volumes as the POPULATION INDEX BIBLIOGRAPHY (Boston: G.K. Hall, 1971). There is no subject index.

65. PUBLIC AFFAIRS INFORMATION SERVICE. BULLETIN. Public Affairs Information Service, Inc., 11 Fortieth Street, New York, N.Y. 10018. 1915--. Weekly, except for the last two weeks each quarter, with quarterly and annual cumulations.

A subject index to books, periodicals, pamphlets, government publications, and other materials dealing with social and economic questions. A companion publication, PAIS FOR-EIGN LANGUAGE INDEX has been issued since 1972 by PAIS, Inc.

READERS' GUIDE TO PERIODICAL LITERATURE. See item 11.

SOCIAL SCIENCES AND HUMANITIES INDEX. See item 12.

66. SOCIAL SCIENCES CITATION INDEX. Institute for Scientific Information, 325 Chestnut Street, Philadelphia, Pa. 19106. 1973--. Quarterly, with annual cumulations.

Has three main parts: a citation index, arranged by author, which provjdes for each name a chronological listing of publications cited, and for each publication, the names of those who have cited it within a given period; a source index, which gives bibliographic details of the citations; and a Permuterm index which allows for a subject approach through coordinated key words in titles. Lists of institutions with which authors are affiliated, and of source journals, are included. Bibliographic data can be retrieved by computer.

SOCIAL SCIENCES INDEX. See item 12.

67. WALL STREET JOURNAL INDEX. Dow Jones Books, P.O. Box 60, Princeton, N.J. 08540. 1958--. Monthly.

> Indexes the Eastern (New York) edition; entries appear in two sections, corporate news and general news.

E. PUBLISHING INFORMATION ABOUT BOOKS

68. ALTERNATIVES IN PRINT. Office of Educational Services, Ohio State University Libraries, Columbus, Ohio 43210. 1971--. Annual.

> An index and listing of "...some movement publications reflecting today's radical social change activities."

69. AMERICAN BOOK PUBLISHING RECORD. New York: Bowker, 1960--. Monthly.

> A subject list, arranged by Dewey Decimal classification, which provides full cataloging details for books published in America the previous month with an author index. Based on information provided in Bowker's WEEKLY RECORD.

70. BIBLIOGRAPHIC SURVEY; THE NEGRO IN PRINT. Negro Bibliographic and Research Center, 117 R Street, Washington, D.C. 20022. 1965-72. Bimonthly.

> An annotated list of books, periodicals, and paperbacks published between 1965 and 1972.

71. BLACK BOOKS BULLETIN. Institute of Positive Education, 7848 South Ellis Avenue, Chicago, Ill. 60619. 1971--. Quarterly.

> Lists books by Black writers and surveys the publishing of material on Black America.

72. BOOKS IN PRINT: AUTHORS; TITLES; SUBJECTS. New York: Bowker, 1948--. Annual.

> A multivolume set which is the standard guide to American books currently in print. It serves as an index to U.S. publishers' catalogs, which are published by Bowker in the PUBLISHERS' TRADE LIST ANNUAL. A companion volume, PAPERBOUND BOOKS IN PRINT, provides additional coverage of paperback publishing.

73. CUMULATIVE BOOK INDEX. New York: Wilson, 1928--. Bimonthly.

> Lists books in English by author and title and also under broad subject headings, as they are published. The annual or bi-

ennial cumulations of the CUMULATIVE BOOK INDEX and the annual volumes of the AMERICAN BOOK PUBLISHING RECORD provide comprehensive overviews of American publishing, with the exception of publications of the U.S. government.

74. DIRECTORY OF PUBLISHED PROCEEDINGS: SERIES SSH – SOCIAL SCIENCES/HUMANITIES. Interdok Corporation, P.O. Box 326, Harrison, N.Y. 10528. 1968--. Quarterly, with annual index.

Lists in chronological sequence, according to the date of the original meeting, the published proceedings of conferences, seminars, symposia, and congresses in the social sciences and humanities.

75. FORTHCOMING BOOKS: AUTHORS; TITLES; SUBJECTS. New York: Bowker, 1966--. Bimonthly.

Lists books whose publication is expected within the next five months, as well as those published since the last edition of BOOKS IN PRINT (see item 72). More detailed announcements of American publishers' forthcoming works are given in Bowker's PUBLISHERS WEEKLY.

F. PERIODICAL AND NEWSPAPER DIRECTORIES AND GUIDES

Part 1: Directories

76. AYER'S DIRECTORY OF NEWSPAPERS AND PERIODICALS. Philadelphia: N.W. Ayer and Son, 1880--. Annual.

A state-by-state, city-by-city listing of newspapers and journals, which includes classified lists of ethnic, religious, and fraternal publications.

77. IRREGULAR SERIALS AND ANNUALS: AN INTERNATIONAL DIRECTORY. 3rd ed. New York: Bowker, 1974. xl, 989 p.

A companion volume to ULRICH'S INTERNATIONAL PERIODICALS DIRECTORY (see item 80), it lists by subject about 25,000 titles.

78. LISTE MONDIALE DES PERIODIQUES SPECIALISES DANS LES SCIENCES SOCIALES [World list of social science periodicals]. 3rd ed., rev. and enl. Paris: UNESCO, 1966. 448 p.

Scholarly periodicals in the social sciences current in 1963 are listed by title, institution, and subject in this volume,

which is updated by an annual section of the INTERNATION-
AL SOCIAL SCIENCE JOURNAL.

79. STANDARD PERIODICAL DIRECTORY. New York: Oxbridge, 1964--.
Annual.

A classified listing, with title and subject index, of current
American magazines. Most titles are briefly annotated.

80. ULRICH'S INTERNATIONAL PERIODICALS DIRECTORY: A CLASSIFIED
GUIDE TO CURRENT PERIODICALS, FOREIGN AND DOMESTIC,
1973-74. 15th ed. New York: Bowker, 1974. xl, 2706 p.

Publication details and order information for about 55,000
current periodicals. Arranged in broad subject categories
with title index; in most cases, it cites the abstracts or indexing services which cover the listed periodical.

Part 2: Guides

81. Goldwater, Walter. RADICAL PERIODICALS IN AMERICA, 1890-
1970. Rev. ed. New Haven: Yale University Press, 1966. 51 p.

An annotated list of 321 radical periodicals with information
on the groups which issued them.

82. Katz, William A., and Gargal, Berry. MAGAZINES FOR LIBRARIES:
FOR THE GENERAL READER, AND SCHOOL, JUNIOR COLLEGE,
COLLEGE AND PUBLIC LIBRARIES. 2nd ed. New York: Bowker,
1972. 822 p.

Classified annotated list of over 4,500 titles. The sociology
section includes about fifty journals. Communications and
media, the counterculture, folklore, occupations and employment, and urban studies are other areas with substantial listings. A supplement will appear in 1975.

83. Miller, Robert H., et al. FROM RADICAL LEFT TO EXTREME RIGHT:
A BIBLIOGRAPHY OF CURRENT PERIODICALS OF PROTEST AND
CONTROVERSY. 2nd ed. 2 vols. Ann Arbor, Mich.: Campus
Publishers, 1970. 1000 p.

Full bibliographic information with annotations for more than
400 titles.

G. U.S. GOVERNMENT PUBLICATIONS

84. AMERICAN STATISTICS INDEX. Washington, D.C.: Congressional
     Information Service, 1973--. Monthly.

     A subject index to federal statistics of the United States.

85. CIS INDEX TO PUBLICATIONS OF THE UNITED STATES CONGRESS.
     Washington, D.C.: Congressional Information Service, 1970--. Monthly.

     Abstracts, indexes, and lists hearings, reports, committee prints,
     and other congressional papers. Detailed index includes sub-
     jects of documents and hearings, subjects discussed by individ-
     ual witnesses, names of committees and subcommittees, and
     names of corporate or individual authors or witnesses and their
     affiliations.

86. United States Bureau of Labor Statistics. PUBLICATIONS OF THE
     BUREAU OF LABOR STATISTICS 1886-1971. Bureau of Labor Statistics,
     Bulletin no. 1749. Washington, D.C.: Government Printing Office,
     1972. 184 p.

     This catalog is updated by semiannual publications lists.

87. United States Bureau of the Census. CATALOG. Washington, D.C.:
     Government Printing Office, 1946--. Quarterly, with monthly supple-
     ments cumulated annually.

     Since 1966 appears in two sections: Part one - PUBLICA-
     TIONS; Part two - DATA FILES AND SPECIAL TABULA-
     TIONS. Part one lists, for example, the separate reports of
     the censuses of population and housing, and the current popu-
     lation reports series P20, P23, P25, and P60. Publications
     before 1946 are listed in the CATALOG OF UNITED STATES
     CENSUS PUBLICATIONS 1790-1945.

88. _____. GUIDE TO CENSUS BUREAU DATA FILES AND SPECIAL
     TABULATIONS. Washington, D.C.: Government Printing Office, 1969.
     162 p.

     Describes the data files and selected special tabulations origi-
     nating during the period from 1958 to 1968 and available in
     1969.

89. _____. GUIDE TO PUBLICATIONS AND PROGRAMS: SUBJECTS
     AND AREAS, 1973. Washington, D.C.: Government Printing Office,
     1973. 227 p.

     A comprehensive review of statistical programs of the Census
     Bureau and of the reports issued by the Bureau from 1968 to
     1972; reports for 1960 through 1967 were listed in a similar
     GUIDE published in 1968.

90. United States Department of Commerce. UNITED STATES DEPARTMENT OF COMMERCE PUBLICATIONS - CATALOG AND INDEX. Washington, D.C.: Government Printing Office, 1954--. Annual.

   Updates the U.S. Department of Commerce CATALOG published in 1952 which covered the period from the first decennial census in 1790 through October 1950, and its 1950-52 supplement published in 1953.

91. United States Department of Health, Education, and Welfare. CATALOG OF PUBLICATIONS. United States Department of Health, Education, and Welfare, Washington, D.C. 20201. 1971--. Quarterly, with annual cumulation.

   Lists by title and by subject H.E.W. publications of the current fiscal year, i.e., Publications of Office of Secretary, Food and Drug Administration, Health Services and Mental Health Administration, National Institutes of Health, Office of Education, Social and Rehabilitation Service, and Social Security Administration. Prior to 1971, some of these administrative units issued separate publications lists.

92. United States Manpower Administration. INDEX TO PUBLICATIONS OF THE MANPOWER ADMINISTRATION. United States Department of Labor, Manpower Administration, Washington, D.C. 20210. 1969--. Annual, cumulative.

   A subject index to publications of the Manpower Administration, to the chapters and major subdivisions of the MANPOWER REPORTS OF THE PRESIDENT, and to all articles in MANPOWER magazine.

93. United States Superintendent of Documents. MONTHLY CATALOG OF UNITED STATES GOVERNMENT PUBLICATIONS. Washington, D.C.: Government Printing Office, 1895--. Monthly.

   Announces publications issued by all branches of the U.S. government and its departments and agencies. Arrangement is by issuing agency in a numbered sequence to which the author, title, and subject indexes refer. Indexes cumulate annually, and author indexes have been published separately in decennial cumulations.

H. LIBRARY CATALOGS AND UNION LISTS

94. Harvard University Library. SOCIOLOGY. Widener Library Shelflist, no. 45 and no. 46. 2 vols. Cambridge, Mass.: Harvard University Library, distributed by Harvard University Press, 1973. Vol. 1, 688 p.; vol. 2, 616 p.

Contains 49,000 titles (25,913 in English) of books, periodicals, and other serials, and pamphlets on sociological history and theory, social groups and institutions, social problems and reforms, and social psychology. The first volume has two parts: a classified list and a chronological one. The second volume is an author and title index to the first. Much general social science material is included, but many titles dealing with sociological aspects of American life are classified elsewhere.

95. A LONDON BIBLIOGRAPHY OF THE SOCIAL SCIENCES. 4 vols. and supplements. London: London School of Economics and Political Science, 1931-1932--.

This is a catalog of the holdings of certain London libraries and special collections in the social sciences, with emphasis on sociology, economics, and political science. The original four-volume set has been updated by supplements (London: Mansell Information Publishing Ltd.); the seventh supplement (1973), which covers the period 1969-72, brings the volumes to twenty-eight. Arrangement is by subject, which may be subdivided by topic or country; names of countries are also included in the main list of subjects. Substantial lists of sociological writings about the United States are to be found here.

96. NEW SERIAL TITLES. Washington, D.C.: Library of Congress; New York: Bowker, 1961--. Eight times a year.

Continues the UNION LIST OF SERIALS (see item 97), listing serials which began publishing on January 1, 1950, or later, and giving their library locations. Cumulations have been published by Bowker as NEW SERIAL TITLES 1950-70 (4 vols., 1973) and NEW SERIAL TITLES 1971-73 (1974).

97. UNION LIST OF SERIALS IN LIBRARIES OF THE UNITED STATES AND CANADA. 3rd ed. 5 vols. New York: Wilson, 1965.

An alphabetical listing by title of 156,499 journals and other serials which had commenced publication by 1949; shows their locations in 956 libraries in the United States and Canada.

98. United States Library of Congress. LIBRARY OF CONGRESS: BOOKS: SUBJECTS. Washington, D.C.: 1950--. Monthly.

A subject arrangement of the entries which appear in the NATIONAL UNION CATALOG: BOOKS: AUTHORS (see item 99). Quinquennial cumulations have been published by Rowman and Littlefield, Totowa, New Jersey.

99. _____. NATIONAL UNION CATALOG: BOOKS: AUTHORS.
Washington, D.C.: 1948--. Monthly.

Lists, under individual or corporate author, the holdings of
the Library of Congress and some of the large research collections in the United States. Cumulative lists, representing
Library of Congress printed cards and titles reported by other
American libraries, have been published for the period prior
to 1956 (London: Mansell Information Publishing Ltd., 1968--),
1956 through 1967 (Totowa, N.J.: Rowman and Littlefield,
1970--), and 1968-72 (Ann Arbor, Mich.: J.W. Edwards,
1973--). The scope is international, but major emphasis is on
English language, especially American, materials.

100. _____. NEWSPAPERS IN MICROFORM: UNITED STATES 1948-72.
Washington, D.C.: 1973. xxiii, 1056 p.

The seventh in a continuing cumulative series, this publication
lists 34,289 titles of U.S. newspapers that have been reduced
to microform since 1948, and provides references to their
locations in the United States and its territories and posses-
sions.

I. DATA FILES AND STATISTICS SOURCES

101. Council of Social Science Data Archives. SOCIAL SCIENCE DATA
ARCHIVES IN THE UNITED STATES. New York: 1967. 45 p.

The Council of Social Science Data Archives at the University
of Pittsburgh acted as a clearinghouse for information in this
area; this publication lists the social science data archives
available in 1967.

102. National Technical Information Service. DIRECTORY OF COMPUTER-
IZED DATA FILES AND RELATED SOFTWARE AVAILABLE FROM FEDERAL
AGENCIES, 1974. Springfield, Va.: 1974. (NTIS-SR-74-01.)

The first edition of a projected annual guide to machine-read-
able federal data files, data bases, and related software.
Describes what is currently available, and how and where to
obtain specific files held by sixty agencies, including the
Environmental Protection Agency, National Science Foundation,
NASA, and the Departments of Agriculture, Labor, Commerce,
and Defense.

103. Sessions, Vivian, ed. DIRECTORY OF DATA BASES IN THE SOCIAL
AND BEHAVIORAL SCIENCES. New York: Science Associates/Inter-
national, 1974. xvi, 300 p.

Major emphasis is on substantive data bases, but bibliographic data bases are also included.

104. Wasserman, Paul, and Paskar, Joanne, eds. STATISTICS SOURCES: A SUBJECT GUIDE TO DATA ON INDUSTRIAL, BUSINESS, SOCIAL, EDUCATIONAL, FINANCIAL AND OTHER TOPICS FOR THE UNITED STATES AND INTERNATIONALLY. 4th ed. Detroit: Gale Research Co., 1974. 950 p.

An annotated guide to selected statistical sources, such as census volumes, special Bureau of the Census reports, annuals, yearbooks, and other printed materials issued by trade associations, professional societies, commercial concerns, colleges and universities, and government agencies.

J. THESES, DISSERTATIONS, AND RESEARCH IN PROGRESS

105. B/R/S MONTHLY INDEX. Behavioral Research Survey Center, 1 Park Avenue, New York, N.Y. 10016. 1969--. Monthly.

Lists behavioral research studies for which government contracts have been awarded; based on information supplied by the U.S. Department of Commerce in COMMERCE BUSINESS DAILY.

106. CURRENT SOCIOLOGICAL RESEARCH. New York: American Sociological Association, 1953-63.

An annual compilation derived from questionnaires sent to members of the Association.

107. DISSERTATION ABSTRACTS INTERNATIONAL. Ann Arbor, Mich.: University Microfilm, 1938--. Monthly.

Issued from 1938 to 1951 as MICROFILM ABSTRACTS and from 1951 to 1969 as DISSERTATION ABSTRACTS; a retrospective index by author and subject for the period 1938-72 was published in 1973. Abstracts of dissertations submitted by cooperating institutions are arranged by author within broad subject areas; information for the ordering of microfilm or photocopies is included. Indexed by author and by subject using key words taken from the titles of the dissertations. Computer searches are possible through the DATRIX (Direct Access to Reference Information: a Xerox Service) system.

108. GOVERNMENT RESEARCH AND DEVELOPMENT REPORTS. Springfield, Va.: National Technical Information Service, 1946 . Monthly.

Issued earlier as U.S. GOVERNMENT RESEARCH REPORTS and

as GOVERNMENT REPORTS ANNOUNCEMENTS, these are abstracts of research reports released by more than 200 government agencies. Abstracts are arranged in twenty-two subject fields; field five includes the behavioral and social sciences. Since 1965 the reports have been indexed by GOVERNMENT REPORTS INDEX, which lists corporate and personal authors, contract numbers, accession/report numbers, and subjects. Computer searches of the data base can be arranged.

109. Lunday, G. Albert. SOCIOLOGY DISSERTATIONS IN AMERICAN UNIVERSITIES, 1893-1966. Commerce: East Texas State University, 1969. 277 p.

Lists under twenty-six topical headings and indexes by author the 3,993 doctoral dissertations in sociology accepted by American universities between 1893 and 1966.

From 1916 to 1966, the AMERICAN JOURNAL OF SOCIOLOGY listed annually doctoral dissertations in progress and the doctoral degrees in sociology conferred in the previous year by U.S. and Canadian universities. A list of the 1969/70 and 1970/71 recipients of the Ph.D. in sociology and the titles of their dissertations is given in the August 1972 issue of THE AMERICAN SOCIOLOGIST (pp. 9-23). The 1971/72 and 1972/73 lists appear in the GUIDE TO GRADUATE DEPARTMENTS OF SOCIOLOGY, published in 1974 by the American Sociological Association, Washington, D.C.

110. MASTERS ABSTRACTS: ABSTRACTS OF SELECTED MASTERS THESES ON MICROFILM. Ann Arbor, Mich.: University Microfilm, 1962--. Quarterly.

Masters' theses from cooperating institutions are listed in a broad subject arrangement with author and subject indexes. Ordering information for microfilm or photocopy is included.

From 1916 to 1961, the AMERICAN JOURNAL OF SOCIOLOGY published an annual list of M.A. degrees in sociology conferred in the previous year by U.S. and Canadian universities.

111. SCIENCE AND TECHNOLOGY RESEARCH IN PROGRESS, 1972-1973. 12 vols. in 15. Orange, N.J.: Academic Media, in cooperation with the Smithsonian Science Information Exchange, 1973.

Each of the twelve volumes covers a major discipline in the physical, life, and social sciences and lists titles of research projects in progress in 1972-73. These projects are listed with the Smithsonian Science Information Exchange, and computer searches of the bibliographic data may be arranged.

Of special interest to sociologists are volumes eleven and twelve. Volume eleven, BEHAVIORAL SCIENCES (xiv, 521 p.),

includes over 9,500 research projects in aging, education and
training, industrial and engineering psychology, and related
fields. Volume twelve, SOCIAL SCIENCES (xiv, 564 p.),
lists more than 9,800 research projects in sociology, criminology, law, race and ethnic relations, manpower, poverty,
urban research, and other social and economic areas.

K. DIRECTORIES

112. AMERICAN MEN AND WOMEN OF SCIENCE. Volumes 7 and 8: THE
SOCIAL AND BEHAVIORAL SCIENCES. 12th ed. New York and
London: Jaques Cattell Press/Bowker, 1973.

Biographical information on Americans and Canadians in sociology, anthropology, economics, geography, political science,
psychology, statistics, and environmental and urban affairs,
alphabetically arranged by name with a geographical listing.
A separate 350-page SOCIAL AND BEHAVIORAL SCIENCES
DISCIPLINE INDEX was published in 1974.

113. American Sociological Association. DIRECTORY OF MEMBERS. Washington, D.C.: 1950--.

Usually published at three-year intervals. The 1973 edition
lists 14,544 members alphabetically by name, geographically
by location of their employment, and also according to areas
of competence.

114. _____. GUIDE TO GRADUATE DEPARTMENTS OF SOCIOLOGY.
Washington, D.C.: 1969--. Annual.

The GUIDE was first published in 1965 and updated through
1968 by information published in THE AMERICAN SOCIOLO-
GIST (see item 124). The 1974 volume provides information
on the course offerings and faculty of 215 graduate sociology
programs in U.S., Canadian, and two foreign universities.
Recent Ph.D. graduates are listed and the titles of their dissertations are given.

115. ENCYCLOPEDIA OF ASSOCIATIONS. 9th ed. 3 vols. Detroit:
Gale Research Co., 1975.

Volume one is a classified directory of voluntary organizations,
arranged by their area of major concern, with a name, key-
word title, and subject index; volume two provides a geographic listing; volume three is the quarterly publication, NEW
ASSOCIATIONS AND PROJECTS, which updates the set.

116. FOUNDATION DIRECTORY. 4th ed. New York: Columbia University Press, 1971. 642 p. (For the Foundation Center.)

   Information about 5,454 charitable, educational, and cultural foundations is listed here, and kept up-to-date by the FOUNDATION CENTER INFORMATION QUARTERLY (1972--), which also announces specialized grants, new services and publications of the Center, and bibliographies.

117. FOUNDATION GRANTS INDEX. Compiled by the Foundation Center. New York: Columbia University Press, 1971--. Annual.

   A cumulative record of grants made by foundations, charitable trusts, and corporations, indexed by field of interest and compiled from information which first appeared in FOUNDATION NEWS (1960--), a bimonthly publication of the Center.

118. RESEARCH CENTERS DIRECTORY. 5th ed. Detroit: Gale Research Co., 1975. xi, 1039.

   Lists more than 6000 nonprofit permanent research centers and their supporting units, both university-sponsored and independent. Updated three times a year by NEW RESEARCH CENTERS.

119. United States Library of Congress. National Referral Center. A DIRECTORY OF INFORMATION RESOURCES IN THE UNITED STATES FEDERAL GOVERNMENT. Washington, D.C.: Government Printing Office, 1974. 416 p.

   Lists most federal agencies and departments, and indicates their areas of interest, publications, and information services; includes a supplement of government sponsored information analysis centers.

120. _____. A DIRECTORY OF INFORMATION RESOURCES IN THE UNITED STATES: SOCIAL SCIENCES. Rev. ed. Washington, D.C.: Government Printing Office, 1973. 700 p.

   Includes professional societies, university research bureaus and institutes, federal and state agencies, as well as technical libraries and information and documents centers.

121. WORLD INDEX OF SOCIAL SCIENCE INSTITUTIONS. Paris: UNESCO, 1970.

   A loose-leaf directory of centers of research, advanced training and documentation, and professional associations; additional entries are provided by the INTERNATIONAL SOCIAL SCIENCE JOURNAL, also published by UNESCO.

Chapter 3

PERIODICAL LITERATURE

JOURNALS IN SPECIAL FIELDS

Chapter 3

PERIODICAL LITERATURE

This chapter lists periodicals in sociology and related fields. Additional titles of American and international journals can be found in the publications described in chapters one and two, especially in the indexes and abstracts listed there. For most of the periodicals, the annotations mention the pertinent indexing and abstracting services. These services cover the periodicals from various dates and with varying degrees of comprehensiveness.

The following abbreviations have been used in this chapter:

ABSTRACTS FOR SOCIAL WORKERS: AbSocWk

ABSTRACTS ON CRIMINOLOGY AND PENOLOGY: AbCrim

AMERICA: HISTORY AND LIFE: AmerH

INDEX MEDICUS: IMed

PSYCHOLOGICAL ABSTRACTS: PsychAb

PUBLIC AFFAIRS INFORMATION SERVICE. BULLETIN: PAIS

READERS' GUIDE TO PERIODICAL LITERATURE: RG

SOCIAL SCIENCES AND HUMANITIES INDEX: SSHI

SOCIAL SCIENCES INDEX: SSI

SOCIOLOGICAL ABSTRACTS: SocAb

A. SOCIOLOGICAL JOURNALS

122. AMERICAN JOURNAL OF SOCIOLOGY. University of Chicago Press, 5801 Ellis Avenue, Chicago, Ill. 60637. 1895--. Bimonthly.

Founded in 1895 at the University of Chicago, the AMERICAN JOURNAL OF SOCIOLOGY is the oldest American journal in the field of sociology and, along with the AMERICAN SOCIOLOGICAL REVIEW (see item 123), one of the most influential today. Dedicated to contemporary sociological practice and theory, "...the JOURNAL presents a broad spectrum of views on a wide variety of current problems: social change, community and group structure, institutions and social organizations, personality, population, methodology, and social theory." Regular features include "Commentary and Debate" and a book review section. Up to 1966 the Journal listed annually masters' theses and newly begun dissertations and completed Ph.D.'s in sociology. Special issues have included: STATUS AND ACHIEVEMENT IN THE UNITED STATES: 1969, in volume 75 (Issue 4, part 2) January 1970; VARIETIES OF POLITICAL EXPRESSION IN SOCIOLOGY, in volume 78 (Issue 1) July 1972; and CHANGING WOMEN IN A CHANGING SOCIETY, in volume 78 (Issue 4) January 1973. Cumulative indexes cover the period from 1895 to 1970 (see items 1 and 2). It is also indexed in SocAb, PsychAb, SSHI, and SSI.

123. AMERICAN SOCIOLOGICAL REVIEW. American Sociological Association, 1722 N Street NW, Washington, D.C. 20036. 1936--. Bimonthly.

The official journal of the American Sociological Association has the largest circulation among the professional journals. It includes articles in all fields of sociology, many based on empirical research and statistical data analysis; other articles deal with new trends and developments in theory and research. It contained a book review section from 1936 to 1971; from 1972 this has been published separately as CONTEMPORARY SOCIOLOGY (see item 126). A section on the profession featured from 1958 through 1964 was expanded and published separately from 1965 in THE AMERICAN SOCIOLOGIST (see item 124).

Cumulative indexes covering the period from 1936 to 1970 have been published (see items 3, 4, and 5). It is also indexed in SocAb, PsychAb, SSHI, and SSI.

124. THE AMERICAN SOCIOLOGIST. American Sociological Association, 1722 N Street NW, Washington, D.C. 20036. 1965--. Quarterly.

Articles about the profession of sociology, its functions, its internal affairs, and its relation to the nonsociological community. In 1971 four issues appeared under the name SOCIOLOG in a briefly adopted tabloid format.

From 1965 to 1972 THE AMERICAN SOCIOLOGIST also included news and announcements, official reports and proceedings, and the employment bulletin. From 1972 these matters formed the basis of a separate publication, ASA FOOTNOTES (see item 125).

125. ASA FOOTNOTES. American Sociological Association, 1722 N Street

NW, Washington, D.C. 20036. 1972--. Nine times a year; tabloid.

Publishes the official reports and proceedings of the Association; some articles on the profession; news and announcements of awards, grants, and meetings; obituaries; and an employment bulletin.

126. CONTEMPORARY SOCIOLOGY: A JOURNAL OF REVIEWS. American Sociological Association, 1722 N Street NW, Washington, D.C. 20036. 1972--. Bimonthly.

The book reviewing journal of the American Sociological Association, it covers sociological literature through individual reviews and review symposia. Each issue includes a list of publications received.

A cumulative index which lists about 1,100 reviews from the first three volumes (1972-74) appears in the November 1974 issue of CONTEMPORARY SOCIOLOGY, Vol. 3, pp. 557-86.

127. THE INSURGENT SOCIOLOGIST. Department of Sociology, University of Oregon, Eugene, Oreg. 97403. 1968--. Three or four times a year.

Established by the radical caucus of the American Sociological Association, it is "committed to publishing material critical of the presently prevailing forms of sociology as well as material that contributes to the development of a new sociology dedicated to both the understanding of man and society and to human liberation."

128. JOURNAL OF POLITICAL AND MILITARY SOCIOLOGY. c/o Department of Sociology, Northern Illinois University, De Kalb, Ill. 60115. 1973--. Semiannual.

Articles are concerned with the relationship between political and social structure, with values and issues of social policy. Book reviews and essays cover about ten books in each issue.

129. RURAL SOCIOLOGY. Auburn University, Auburn, Ala. 36830. 1936--. Quarterly.

The official journal of the Rural Sociological Society deals with all aspects of rural life. It has a book review section and a topical list of new publications received, the "Bulletin Index," which includes books, government reports, and agricultural experiment station bulletins. These entries have been cumulated for the period 1936 through 1970 and published separately under the editorship of Alvin L. Bertrand (see item 380). From 1973 the news section, which regularly included listings of recent theses and dissertations in rural sociology, became a separate bimonthly publication, NEWSLINE. Indexed in SocAb, SSI, and PAIS.

130. SOCIAL FORCES. University of North Carolina Press, Box 510, Chapel Hill, N.C. 27514. 1922--. Quarterly.

Publishes articles in theoretical and applied sociology, especially on the family, population, community, stratification, deviance, occupational sociology, and social psychology; many articles are followed by substantial bibliographies. Since 1972 the journal has been associated with the Southern Sociological Society. From volume fifty-one, 1972/73, it has included annually a classified inventory of propositions embodied in its articles as an aid to teaching and research. A cumulative index to the first fifty volumes was published in 1974 (see item 6). Indexed in SocAb, PsychAb, PAIS, SSHI, and SSI.

131. SOCIAL PROBLEMS: OFFICIAL JOURNAL OF THE SOCIETY FOR THE STUDY OF SOCIAL PROBLEMS. Social Problems Executive Office, P.O. Box 533, Notre Dame, Ind. 46556. 1953--. Five times a year.

Articles reflect the interests of the various divisions of the society: community research and development; crime and juvenile delinquency; drinking and drugs; intergroup relations; international tensions; the family; psychiatric sociology; social problems theory; sociology and social welfare; youth and aging; poverty and human resources; educational problems; and environmental problems. Occasional book review essays; each issue lists publications received. Indexed in PAIS, PsychAb, SSHI, SSI, and SocAb.

132. SOCIOLOGICAL INQUIRY. Ontario Institute for Studies in Education, University of Toronto, 252 Bloor Street West, Toronto 5, Ontario, Canada. 1930--. Quarterly.

Journal of the National Sociology Honor Society (a quarterly publication of the united chapters of Alpha Kappa Delta). Most of the recent articles have been concerned with theory and methodology. Indexed in AbSocWk and SocAb.

133. SOCIOLOGISTS FOR WOMEN IN SOCIETY. NEWSLETTER. c/o Professor Paule Verdet, Department of Sociology, Boston University, 96 Cummington Street, Boston, Mass. 02215. 1971--. Quarterly.

Provides news of activities related to employment, research, and publications undertaken by women in sociology and related fields; lists job opportunities.

134. SOCIOLOGY AND SOCIAL RESEARCH: AN INTERNATIONAL JOURNAL. University of Southern California, Los Angeles, Calif. 90007.

1916--. Quarterly.

Founded by Emory S. Bogardus; articles often deal with attitudes and their measurement. Book reviews are included in
each issue. Indexed in PAIS, PsychAb, SSHI, SSI, and SocAb.

135. TEACHING SOCIOLOGY. Sage Publications, 275 South Beverly Drive,
Beverly Hills, Calif. 90212. 1973--. Semiannual.

Aims "...to contribute to the recognition of the teaching
function as an important part of the academic profession."
Articles are concerned with innovations in course organization,
the use of new technology in teaching, and student evalu-
ations of teaching. Reviews of books and related materials by
students or teachers who have used them are planned for future
issues.

B. REGIONAL JOURNALS OF SOCIOLOGY

136. FREE INQUIRY. Department of Sociology, Oklahoma State University
of Agriculture and Applied Science, Stillwater, Okla. 74074. 1972--.
Semiannual.

The journal of the Oklahoma Sociological Society.

137. HUMBOLDT JOURNAL OF SOCIAL SCIENCES. Humboldt State University, 211 Administration Building, Arcata, Calif. 95521. 1973--.
Semiannual.

A newly-established journal, "...reflecting original research
interests of sociologists on the West coast."

138. PACIFIC SOCIOLOGICAL REVIEW. Sage Publications, 275 South
Beverly Drive, Beverly Hills, Calif. 90212. 1958--. Quarterly.

Official publication of the Pacific Sociological Association.
Some articles are selected from papers presented at the annual
meetings of the association. Includes theoretical and methodological articles and studies on topics such as latchkey children
and the meaning of work among the hard-core unemployed.
Occasional special issues are devoted to a single topic. Indexed in AbSocWk and SocAb.

139. SOCIOLOGICAL FOCUS. Department of Sociology, University of
Akron, Akron, Ohio. 44325. 1968--. Quarterly.

Journal of the North Central Sociological Association. Indexed
in SocAb.

140. SOCIOLOGICAL QUARTERLY. The Sociological Quarterly, 1004 Elm Street, Columbia, Mo. 65201. 1960--. Quarterly.

Journal of the Midwest Sociological Society; publishes articles on historical topics and on research studies, e.g., correlates of fashion leadership; a self-consistency approach to prisonization. Book reviews appear as "feature review" symposia. Indexed in SocAb, PsychAb, AbSocWk, SSHI, and SSI.

141. SOCIOLOGICAL SYMPOSIUM. Department of Sociology, Virginia Polytechnic Institute and State University, Blacksburg, Va. 24061. 1968--. Semiannual.

"Supports and promotes the multi-perspective of behavioral science." Each issue is devoted to one topic, such as deviant occupations, current research on violence, or youth and politics. Indexed in SocAb and AbSocWk.

142. SOUTHERN SOCIOLOGIST. Department of Sociology, Virginia Polytechnic Institute and State University, Blacksburg, Va. 24061. 1968--. Quarterly.

Publication of the Southern Sociological Society.

143. SUMMATION. Department of Sociology, Michigan State University, East Lansing, Mich. 48823. 1968--. Semiannual.

Each issue is devoted to one or two subjects, e.g., peace research, and includes book reviews. Indexed in SocAb.

144. WISCONSIN SOCIOLOGIST. Wisconsin State University, Eau Claire, Wis. 54701. 1960--. Quarterly.

Journal of the Wisconsin Sociological Association. Indexed in SocAb.

C. STUDENT-EDITED JOURNALS

145. BERKELEY JOURNAL OF SOCIOLOGY: A CRITICAL REVIEW. 410 Barrows Hall, University of California, Berkeley, Calif. 94720. 1955--. Annual.

Published by the Graduate Sociology Club of the Department of Sociology, University of California, Berkeley. The first four volumes were entitled BERKELEY PUBLICATIONS IN SOCIETY AND INSTITUTIONS. "A publication offering critical review essays on recent literature in sociology and related disciplines...challenges the social sciences to confront the crises of the world with intellectual curiosity, historical awareness, and theoretical competence. The JOURNAL is dedicated to the vision of social science as a humane area of study whose aim is to discover the conditions of social life that foster peace, justice, economic and political liberty, and the full development of the human potential."

146. CATALYST. Sociology Club, Box G Norton Union, State University of New York at Buffalo, Buffalo, N.Y. 14214. 1965--. Semiannual.

Indexed in SocAb.

147. THE COMMONWEALTH SOCIOLOGIST. Department of Sociology, 206 Liberal Arts Building, Pennsylvania State University, University Park, Pa. 16802. 1974--. Semiannual.

Published by graduate students in the Pennsylvania State University departments of sociology and rural sociology.

148. THE CORNELL JOURNAL OF SOCIAL RELATIONS. Sociology Department, Uris Hall, Cornell University, Ithaca, N.Y. 14850. 1968--. Semiannual.

Edited by graduate students in and sponsored by the departments of anthropology, psychology, and sociology of the College of Arts and Sciences, the department of human development and family studies of the College of Human Ecology, the department of rural sociology of the College of Agriculture, and the School of Industrial and Labor Relations. Recent articles are concerned with coeducation and college women, ethnomethodology, and self-concept of low-income women. Indexed in SocAb and PsychAb.

149. ET AL. Box 77264, Los Angeles, Calif. 90007. 1967--. Three times a year.

"ET AL has been created as a medium for the informal exchange of ideas in the social sciences. Each issue highlights a specific topic and provides a medium for the expression of new ideas and the examination of current and future trends in the social sciences."

150. HAWAII PONO JOURNAL. Wist Hall 200, 1776 University Avenue, University of Hawaii, Honolulu, Hawaii. 96822. 1971--. Quarterly.

151. HEURISTICS; THE JOURNAL OF INNOVATIVE SOCIOLOGY. Department of Sociology, Northern Illinois University, De Kalb, Ill. 60115. 1969--. Semiannual.

152. THE HUMAN FACTOR: A JOURNAL OF RADICAL SOCIOLOGY.

The Human Factor, The Bureau of Applied Social Research, 605 West 115th Street, Room 203, New York, N.Y. 10025. 1960--. Three times a year.

> Journal of the Graduate Sociology Student Union, Columbia University. Special issues may be devoted to a single theme such as the liberation of American women; selected issues in Marxism.

153. KANSAS JOURNAL OF SOCIOLOGY. Department of Sociology, University of Kansas, Lawrence, Kans. 66405. 1964--. Semiannual.

> Published by the graduate students of the department, the journal "...endeavors to further scholarly inquiry into social phenomena." Articles by recent graduates and established scholars on code switching in Hawaiian creole, church participation and the older adult, and Black English and the American value system. Some book reviews are included. Indexed in SocAb.

154. REVIEW OF SOCIAL THEORY. Department of Sociology and Rural Sociology, University of Missouri, Columbia, Mo. 65201. 1972--. Semiannual.

> A student-edited journal, devoted to issues in social science with theoretical implications across disciplinary lines; issues in theory construction and theoretical methodology; and issues in the philosophy of social science. Indexed in SocAb.

155. SOUTHEASTERN REVIEW: A JOURNAL OF SOCIOLOGY AND ANTHROPOLOGY. Department of Sociology and Anthropology, University of Virginia, Charlottesville, Va. 22903. 1973--. Semiannual.

D. INTERDISCIPLINARY JOURNALS

156. AMERICAN ACADEMY OF POLITICAL AND SOCIAL SCIENCE: ANNALS. American Academy of Political and Social Science, 3927 Chestnut Street, Philadelphia, Pa. 19104. 1889--. Bimonthly.

> Each issue usually appears as a symposium of articles on a single topic. These symposia are sometimes republished, occasionally with additional material. About one-third of each issue is devoted to book reviews, arranged in a classification scheme which uses sociology as one of its divisions. Indexed in AmerH, SocAb, PAIS, RG, and SSI.

157. AMERICAN BEHAVIORAL SCIENTIST. Sage Publications, 275 South Beverly Drive, Beverly Hills, Calif. 90212. 1957--. Bimonthly.

Founded by Alfred de Grazia, this journal is concerned with areas where several disciplines overlap and where social science research has policy implications for social change. The "New Studies" section is an annotated listing of new books, pamphlets, and articles on behavioral science topics; it forms the basis of an annual supplement to the separately published 1957-65 cumulation (see item 52). Some issues of the journal have been published as individual volumes in the Sage Contemporary Social Science Issues series. Indexed in SSHI, SSI, and SocAb.

158. AMERICAN JOURNAL OF ECONOMICS AND SOCIOLOGY. American Journal of Economics and Sociology, Inc., 50 East Sixty-ninth Street, New York, N.Y. 10021. 1941--. Quarterly.

Published "...in the interest of constructive synthesis in the social sciences," it is indexed in SocAb, SSHI, and SSI.

159. AMERICAN QUARTERLY. Box 1, Logan Hall, University of Philadelphia, Philadelphia, Pa. 19104. 1949--. Quarterly.

The official journal of the American Studies Association; its aim is "...to aid in giving a sense of direction to studies in the culture of the United States, past and present. Editors and contributors therefore concern themselves not only with the areas of American life which they know best but with the relation of those areas to the entire American scene and to world society." From 1955 to 1972 annual supplements contained a selected, annotated interdisciplinary bibliography of current articles on American studies; a cumulation of the bibliographies for 1954-68 has been separately published under the editorship of Hennig Cohen (see item 9). From 1973 book reviews in each issue have replaced the annual bibliographical supplement. Indexed in SSHI and in the HUMANITIES INDEX.

160. BEHAVIOR TODAY. Ziff-Davis Publishing Co., Subscription Department, P.O. Box 2993, Boulder, Colo. 80302. 1969--. Weekly except July.

A newsletter directed to those working in the fields of psychology, sociology, anthropology, social work, guidance, and political science. It includes brief reports of recent research and its funding; notices of meetings and workshops; and classified advertisements, including a monthly listing of employment opportunities. Computerized bibliographic information searches are described; information on funds released for behavioral science research projects is provided by the Smithsonian Science Information Exchange.

161. DAEDALUS, JOURNAL OF THE AMERICAN ACADEMY OF ARTS AND SCIENCES. American Academy of Arts and Sciences, 165 Allandale Street, Jamaica Plain Station, Boston, Mass. 02130. 1846--. Quar-

terly.

Issues are symposia on a central theme, such as post-traditional societies, the search for knowledge, language as a human problem, and the no-growth society. A number of issues have appeared in expanded form as separately published books, e.g., THE WOMAN IN AMERICA, edited by Robert Jay Lifton (Boston: Houghton Mifflin, 1965) and THE NEGRO AMERI-CAN, edited by Talcott Parsons and Kenneth B. Clark (Boston: Houghton Mifflin, 1966). Indexed in SocAb, SSHI, and in HUMANITIES INDEX.

162. HUMAN BEHAVIOR, THE NEWSMAGAZINE OF THE SOCIAL SCIENCES. Manson Western Corporation, Subscription Department, P.O. Box 2810, Boulder, Colo. 80302. 1972--. Monthly.

Briefly presents new social science information under such headings as therapy, politics, public welfare, addictions, feminism, folkways, and social behavior; includes bibliographic citations. Amitai Etzioni contributes a public affairs column, relating social science research to national policies.

163. JOURNAL OF CONFLICT RESOLUTION: RESEARCH ON WAR AND PEACE BETWEEN AND WITHIN NATIONS. Sage Publications, 275 South Beverly Drive, Beverly Hills, Calif. 90212. 1957--. Quarterly.

Published until September 1972 by the Center for Research on Conflict Resolution at the University of Michigan, the journal is an interdisciplinary forum for the publication of research and theory on human conflict, both international and inter-group. Indexed in SSHI, SSI, and SocAb.

164. JOURNAL OF INTERGROUP RELATIONS. National Association of Human Rights Workers, 1112 Nineteenth Avenue South, Nashville, Tenn. 37212. 1959-66. New series, 1970--. Quarterly.

Articles on topics of interest to practitioners and theoreticians in the human rights cause written by sociologists, psychologists, social workers, and administrators. Indexed in AmerH.

165. JOURNAL OF SOCIAL ISSUES. Society for the Psychological Study of Social Issues, Box 1248, Ann Arbor, Mich. 48106. 1945--. Quarterly.

The official publication of the Society, which is a division of the American Psychological Association; presents research on the psychological aspects of important social issues. Articles are most often devoted to a single theme, e.g., pornography--attitudes, use, and effects; or Asian-Americans--a success story. Indexed in SSHI, SSI, PsychAb, and SocAb.

166. JOURNAL OF THE COMMUNITY DEVELOPMENT SOCIETY. Community Development Society, 720 Clark Hall, Columbia, Mo. 65201. 1970--. Semiannual.

> Publishes articles on community development theory, practice, and research by authors who are sociologists, agricultural economists, and administrators, on such topics as nonmetropolitan poverty and community institutions, and a study of the Finger Lakes region in upstate New York.

167. THE PUBLIC INTEREST. National Affairs, Inc., 10 East Fifty-third Street, New York, N.Y. 10022. Subscription address is Box 542, Chelsea P.O., New York, N.Y. 10011. 1965--. Quarterly.

> The four or five articles in each issue are sometimes grouped around a single theme, e.g., prison reform or the Great Society. The current reading section briefly notes selected periodical articles. Indexed in RG and SSI.

168. SCIENTIFIC AMERICAN. 415 Madison Avenue, New York, N.Y. 10007. 1845--. Monthly.

> Articles and reviews of books on the physical, life, and behavioral sciences are written for laymen by experts; offprints are available separately or combined in anthologies. A cumulative index for the period 1948-71 was published by W.H. Freeman Co., San Francisco, California, in 1972. Indexed in RG.

169. SOCIAL POLICY. Social Policy Corporation, Suite 500, 184 Fifth Avenue, New York, N.Y. 10010. 1970--. Bimonthly.

> Publishes polemical articles concerning political aspects of the organization and delivery of human services. Covers such topics as community control, welfare rights, education, and health care; contains book reviews, film reviews, and news about community action groups. Indexed in SSI.

170. SOCIAL RESEARCH; AN INTERNATIONAL QUARTERLY OF THE SOCIAL SCIENCES. New School for Social Research, 66 West Twelfth Street, New York, N.Y. 10011. 1934--. Quarterly.

> Articles by economists, philosophers, political scientists, sociologists, and psychologists are often grouped around one theme. Contributors to the April 1974 issue on religion included Talcott Parsons, Andrew M. Greeley, Martin E. Marty, Gabriel Vahanian, and Louis Schneider. Indexed in SocAb, PAIS, SSHI, and SSI.

171. SOCIAL SCIENCE. Social Science Publishing Co., Winfield, Kans.

67156. 1925--. Quarterly.

The official journal of Pi Gammu Mu, the National Social
Science Honor Society; often includes articles and book
reviews by sociologists.

172. SOCIAL SCIENCE QUARTERLY (formerly SOUTHWEST SOCIAL SCIENCE
QUARTERLY). Southwestern Social Science Association, College of
Business, Louisiana State University, Baton Rouge, La. 70808. 1920--.
Quarterly.

Whole issues may be devoted to a particular topic, e.g., the
Chicano experience in the United States; a substantial section
is devoted to book reviews. Indexed in SocAb, PAIS, AmerH,
and SSI.

173. SOCIETY (formerly TRANS-ACTION, SOCIAL SCIENCE AND MODERN
SOCIETY). Box A, Rutgers - The State University, New Brunswick,
N.J. 08903. 1963--. Monthly.

Each issue of this widely-circulated periodical contains five
or six articles with biographical notes on their authors, a
photo-essay, a book and film review, news of current research,
and a brief list of new social science books. A number of
the articles which first appeared in TRANS-ACTION or in
SOCIETY have been published by Transaction Books in a series
of anthologies on such topics as American bureaucracy, the
Black experience, and law and order. Indexed in SocAb and
RG.

E. CRIME AND DELINQUENCY

174. CRIME AND DELINQUENCY. National Council on Crime and Delinquency, 411 Hackensack Avenue, Hackensack, N.J. 07601. 1955--.
Quarterly.

Each issue contains eight or nine articles and about the same
number of book reviews. There is a news and notes section.
Contributors include sociologists, psychologists, and lawyers.
Indexed in SSI and AbCrim.

175. CRIMINOLOGY; AN INTERDISCIPLINARY JOURNAL. Sage Publications,
275 South Beverly Drive, Beverly Hills, Calif. 90212. 1963--.
Quarterly.

The official publication of the American Society of Criminology,
it is "...devoted to crime and deviant behavior as found in
sociology, psychiatry, law, and social work, as well as newer
disciplines such as urban design, systems analysis, and decision
theory as applied to crime and criminal justice." Major

emphasis is on empirical research and scientific methodology. Dorothy C. Tompkins contributes a regular feature "Across the Desk" which includes notes on publications in the field. Indexed in PAIS, SocAb, SSI, AbSocWk, and AbCrim.

176. FEDERAL PROBATION: A JOURNAL OF CORRECTIONAL PHILOSOPHY AND PRACTICE. Supreme Court Building, Washington, D.C. 20544. 1937--. Quarterly.

Edited by the Probation Division of the Administrative Office of the U.S. Courts, Washington, D.C., and published in cooperation with the Bureau of Prisons, U.S. Department of Justice, it includes articles, book reviews, lists of reports and books received; reviews significant articles in professional periodicals and in legal journals. The new careers column features successful cases of probation. Indexed in SSI and AbCrim.

177. ISSUES IN CRIMINOLOGY: A SOCIAL SCIENCE JOURNAL IN CRIMINOLOGY AND CORRECTIONS. School of Criminology, 101 Haviland Hall, University of California, Berkeley, Calif. 94720. 1965--. Semiannual.

Published by graduate students of the School of Criminology of the University of California at Berkeley. Each issue contains four or five articles and three or four book reviews. Indexed in SSI and AbCrim.

178. JOURNAL OF CRIMINAL LAW AND CRIMINOLOGY. Williams and Wilkins, 428 East Preston Street, Baltimore, Md. 21202. 1910--. Quarterly.

Published by the Northwestern University School of Law and formerly known as the JOURNAL OF CRIMINAL LAW, CRIMINOLOGY AND POLICE SCIENCE. From 1973 articles appear in two sections--criminal law and criminology. Police science is now dealt with in the JOURNAL OF POLICE SCIENCE AND ADMINISTRATION (see item 179). From 1970 there is an annual review of Supreme Court decisions and from 1974, a section of brief research notes. Eight or nine book reviews or review essays appear in each issue. Indexed in AbCrim, PAIS, and PsychAb.

179. JOURNAL OF POLICE SCIENCE AND ADMINISTRATION. International Association of Chiefs of Police (IACP), 11 Firstfield Road, Gaithersburg, Md. 20760. 1973--. Quarterly.

A joint publication of the Northwestern University School of Law and IACP, each issue includes articles, book reviews, and technical abstracts. Indexed in SSI and AbCrim.

180. JOURNAL OF RESEARCH IN CRIME AND DELINQUENCY. National Council on Crime and Delinquency, 411 Hackensack Avenue, Hackensack, N.J. 07601. 1963--. Semiannual.

Each issue contains nine or ten articles by sociologists, criminologists, and psychologists who report on original research in crime and delinquency or provide a critical analysis of related theories and concepts. Indexed in SSI and AbCrim.

F. DEMOGRAPHY

181. DEMOGRAPHY. Population Association of America, P.O. Box 14182, Benjamin Franklin Station, Washington, D.C. 20044. 1964--. Quarterly.

Each issue contains about twelve articles, comments on articles, and a book review symposium. Indexed in SSI.

182. INTERNATIONAL MIGRATION. Intergovernmental Committee for European Migration (ICEM), 9, rue du Valais, Geneva, Switzerland. 1962--. Quarterly.

The quarterly review of ICEM and the Research Group for European Migration Problems, this publication is concerned with "...the role of migratory movements in the contemporary world." Recent issues include articles by American sociologists on indices of integration into the American community; Cuban architects and engineers in the United States; and the exchange of population between the United States and Canada in the 1960s.

183. INTERNATIONAL MIGRATION REVIEW. Center for Migration Studies, 209 Flagg Place, Staten Island, N.Y. 10304. 1964--. Quarterly.

Issues contain five or six articles on such topics as the Greek Orthodox church in the United States and assimilation; ethnicity and religiosity among college students; and bureaucracy and immigrant adjustment. There are about twenty book reviews in each issue and a list of books received. The "Review of Reviews" section provides abstracts of articles, reports, books, and meetings, coded geographically and according to such topics as migration policy, ethnicity, and refugees. Indexed in SocAb and AmerH.

184. MILBANK MEMORIAL FUND QUARTERLY/HEALTH AND SOCIETY. Prodist, Room 502, 156 Fifth Avenue, New York, N.Y. 10010. 1923--. Quarterly.

Demography has been the major concern of this journal, but

recent issues reflect increasing concern with various aspects of health care policy. Indexed in SocAb.

185. POPULATION BULLETIN. Population Reference Bureau, 1758 Massachusetts Avenue NW, Washington, D.C. 20036. 1945--. Bimonthly.

Each thirty or forty page issue is devoted to a single topic and is prepared by the staff of the Bureau, a private, non-profit educational organization founded in 1929 "...to gather, interpret and publish information about population trends and their economic, environmental and social effects." Indexed in SSI.

POPULATION INDEX. See item 64.

186. POPULATION STUDIES: A JOURNAL OF DEMOGRAPHY. Population Investigation Committee, London School of Economics, Houghton Street, Aldwych, London WC 2A 2AE, England. 1947--. Three times a year.

International in scope, but issues often include two or three articles by American specialists on current or historical American demographic topics. About ten book reviews appear in each issue.

187. SOCIAL BIOLOGY (formerly EUGENICS QUARTERLY). University of Chicago Press, 5801 Ellis Avenue, Chicago, Ill. 60637. 1954--. Quarterly.

Published by the Society for the Study of Social Biology "...to further knowledge of the biological and sociocultural forces affecting human populations." Articles deal with major demographic issues and such topics as comparative studies of fertility, intellectual performance, race and socioeconomic status, and social indicators. Each issue contains five or six book reviews and abstracts of periodical articles on genetics. Indexed in IMed, PsychAb, SocAb, and SSI.

188. TEACHING NOTES ON POPULATION. Foreign Area Materials Center, State Education Department, University of the State of New York, 60 East Forty-second Street, New York, N.Y. 10017. 1973--. Irregular.

A newsletter, published as a cooperative venture by the Council for Intercultural Studies and Programs and Lawrence University, Appleton, Wisconsin. It contains articles on new teaching strategies, reviews of instructional resources in population studies, and a section of news and notes.

G. EDUCATION

189. EDUCATION AND URBAN SOCIETY. Sage Publications, 275 South
Beverly Drive, Beverly Hills, Calif. 90212. 1968--. Quarterly.

"A multidisciplinary forum for social scientific research on
education as a social institution within urban environments."
Issues may focus on a central theme, such as organization
development in city school systems. Book reviews are included.
Indexed in SSI.

190. HARVARD EDUCATIONAL REVIEW. Graduate School of Education,
Longfellow Hall, Harvard University, 13 Appian Way, Cambridge,
Mass. 02138. 1931--. Quarterly.

Emphasizes theoretical topics with three or four articles on
opinion and research and about ten book reviews in each
issue. Indexed in EDUCATION INDEX and CURRENT INDEX
TO JOURNALS IN EDUCATION.

191. JOURNAL OF HIGHER EDUCATION. Ohio State University Press,
2070 Neil Avenue, Columbus, Ohio. 43210. 1930--. Monthly,
October - June.

A publication of the American Association for Higher Education,
each issue contains four or five articles and a book review
section. Indexed in EDUCATION INDEX and CURRENT IN-
DEX TO JOURNALS IN EDUCATION.

192. JOURNAL OF NEGRO EDUCATION. Howard University Press, Howard
University, P.O. Box 863, Administration Building, Washington, D.C.
20001. 1932--. Quarterly.

Founded by Charles H. Thompson and published under the
auspices of the Bureau of Educational Research, it collects,
appraises, and disseminates facts about Negro education, and
stimulates further research. Besides articles, each issue contains book and media reviews. A cumulative index to the
first thirty-one volumes has been published. Indexed in EDU-
CATION INDEX, PsychAb, SocAb, CURRENT INDEX TO
JOURNALS IN EDUCATION, and INDEX TO PERIODICAL
ARTICLES BY AND ABOUT NEGROES.

193. NEGRO EDUCATIONAL REVIEW. Box 2895, West Bay Annex, Jackson-
ville, Fla. 32203. 1950--. Quarterly.

Founded by the National Teachers' Research Association and
directed to Negro college and university teachers. From 1974
the journal aims to be "...a forum for the discussion of Afro-
American issues." Articles may be written by educators,

economists, and sociologists; book reviews are included. In
1973 the journal resumed the listing of masters' theses undertaken in selected colleges and universities which had been an
annual feature of the 1951-61 volumes. Indexed in EDUCA-
TION INDEX and INDEX TO PERIODICAL ARTICLES BY AND
ABOUT NEGROES.

194. REVIEW OF EDUCATIONAL RESEARCH. American Educational Research
Association, 1126 Sixteenth Street NW, Washington, D.C. 20036.
1931--. Quarterly.

Publishes "...critical integrative reviews of research literature
bearing on education"; recent topics included integrating
faculty and student life cycles; desegregation and minority
group performance; and student political attitudes. Indexed
in PsychAb, EDUCATION INDEX, and CURRENT INDEX TO
JOURNALS IN EDUCATION.

195. SOCIOLOGY OF EDUCATION. American Sociological Association,
1722 N Street NW, Washington, D.C. 20036. 1927--. Quarterly.

"This journal provides a forum for studies of education by
scholars in all the social sciences from all parts of the world."
Issues occasionally concentrate on one theme, such as new
research on the academic professions. Indexed in SocAb, SSI,
EDUCATION INDEX, and CURRENT INDEX TO JOURNALS IN
EDUCATION.

196. TEACHERS COLLEGE RECORD. Teachers College, Columbia University,
525 West 120th Street, New York, N.Y. 10027. 1900--. Monthly.

"A forum for articulate discussion by those engaged in the
teaching activity," it includes articles on the philosophy and
methods of education and a book review section. Indexed
in PsychAb, EDUCATION INDEX, and CURRENT INDEX TO
JOURNALS IN EDUCATION.

197. URBAN EDUCATION. Sage Publications, 275 South Beverly Drive,
Beverly Hills, Calif. 90212. 1967--. Quarterly.

"Exists to improve the quality of education in the city by
making the results of relevant empirical and scholarly inquiry
more available."

H. ETHNIC RELATIONS

198. AZTLAN: CHICANO JOURNAL OF THE SOCIAL SCIENCES AND THE
ARTS. Aztlan Publications, University of California at Los Angeles,

Campbell Hall 3121, 405 Hilgard Avenue, Los Angeles, Calif. 90024. 1970--. Semiannual.

Articles, mostly in English but some in Spanish, cover social, political, historical, literary, and educational aspects of Chicano culture. Indexed in SSI.

199. BLACK SCHOLAR: A JOURNAL OF BLACK STUDIES AND RESEARCH. Box 908, Sausalito, Calif. 95965. 1969--. Monthly.

Issues are sometimes devoted to a single theme, such as the Black soldier, the Black woman, or Black studies; book reviews and literary contributions are included. Indexed in SocAb, SSI, and INDEX TO PERIODICAL ARTICLES BY AND ABOUT NEGROES.

200. ETHNICITY: AN INTERDISCIPLINARY JOURNAL OF THE STUDY OF ETHNIC RELATIONS. Academic Press, 111 Fifth Avenue, New York, N.Y. 10003. 1974--. Quarterly.

A new journal devoted to the empirical and theoretical study of ethnic diversity and integration. Published by the Center for the Study of American Pluralism at the University of Chicago, it will be concerned with "...understanding both the persistence of ethnic consciousness and the interaction of ethnic groups within a society."

201. JOURNAL OF AFRO-AMERICAN ISSUES. Educational Community Counselors and Associates, 1629 K Street NW, Suite 520, Washington, D.C. 20006. 1972--. Quarterly.

"Devoted to scientific and theoretical determination and expli- cation of issues affecting Blacks in America." There are oc- casional special issues, such as one concerned with Blacks and the U.S. criminal justice system.

202. JOURNAL OF ETHNIC STUDIES. College of Ethnic Studies, Western Washington State College, Bellingham, Wash. 96225. 1973--. Quarterly.

An interdisciplinary journal devoted to the study of major nonwhite and white ethnic groups in North America.

203. JOURNAL OF HUMAN RELATIONS. Central State University, Wilber- force, Ohio 45384. 1952--. Quarterly.

An interdisciplinary approach to human relations is provided in this journal, committed to "...intelligent libertarian revolution, which seeks to discriminate between the reactionary violence of blind revolt and methods of conscious, nonviolent, revolu- tionary change." Indexed in PsychAb, PAIS, and INDEX TO

PERIODICAL ARTICLES BY AND ABOUT NEGROES.

204. JOURNAL OF SOCIAL AND BEHAVIORAL SCIENCES. Box 3003, Duke
University Medical Center, Durham, N.C. 27710. 1926--. Quarterly.

The official publication of the Association of Social and Behavioral Scientists, the journal probes new directions in theory
and research. Recent issues were concerned with such topics
as the Black family and Black education. Book reviews are
included.

205. PHYLON: THE ATLANTA UNIVERSITY REVIEW OF RACE AND CUL-
TURE. Atlanta University, 223 Chestnut Street, Atlanta, Ga. 30314.
1940--. Quarterly.

Founded by W.E.B. Du Bois, the articles in this journal are
concerned with historical, sociological, and demographic topics. Book reviews appear in a section entitled "Literature of
Race and Culture." Indexed in SocAb, SSHI, SSI, and IN-
DEX TO PERIODICAL ARTICLES BY AND ABOUT NEGROES.

I. FAMILY AND LIFE CYCLE

206. FAMILY PROCESS. Nathan W. Ackerman Family Institute, 149 East
Seventy-eighth Street, New York, N.Y. 10021. 1962--. Quarterly.

A multidisciplinary journal of family study, research, and
treatment. Indexed in SocAb, PsychAb, and AbSocWk.

207. INDUSTRIAL GERONTOLOGY: STUDIES OF PROBLEMS OF WORK
AND AGE. The National Council on the Aging, 1828 L Street NW,
Washington, D.C. 20036. 1969--. New series, 1974--. Quarterly.

"A compendium of current papers on middle-aged and older
workers." Articles relate to the transition from employment
to retirement and to retirement itself. The new series includes
a book review section.

208. JOURNAL OF GERONTOLOGY. Gerontological Society, 1 Dupont
Circle, No. 520, Washington, D.C. 20036. 1946--. Quarterly.

Articles report research in the natural and social sciences on
the problems of aging and are arranged in three sections:
biological and medical sciences; psychology and the social
sciences; and social gerontology. A feature of each issue is
the list of current publications in gerontology and geriatrics
prepared by Nathan W. Shock which updates earlier gerontological bibliographies (see item 1669).

A cumulated author index to this section appears in the last issue of each volume. From 1971 the JOURNAL has listed doctoral dissertations on aging accepted in American institutions of higher education; the July 1974 list included dissertations on aging accepted for higher degrees in Great Britain and Ireland from 1956 to 1972. There is also a book review section. Indexed in IMed, PsychAb, PAIS, and SSI.

209. JOURNAL OF MARRIAGE AND THE FAMILY (formerly MARRIAGE AND FAMILY LIVING). National Council on Family Relations, 1219 University Avenue SE, Minneapolis, Minn. 55414. 1939--. Quarterly.

Articles deal with theoretical issues and research on all aspects of marriage and family life. There is a book review section and an international department for articles from abroad. A cumulative index to the twenty-four volumes of MARRIAGE AND FAMILY LIVING covers the period from 1939 to 1962 and an index to Volumes 25 through 31 of JOURNAL OF MARRIAGE AND THE FAMILY, for the period from 1963 to 1969, has also been published. Indexed in SocAb, SSHI, and SSI.

210. YOUTH AND SOCIETY: A QUARTERLY JOURNAL. Sage Publications, 275 South Beverly Drive, Beverly Hills, Calif. 90212. 1969--. Quarterly.

"An interdisciplinary and international journal concerned with broad social and political implications of youth culture and development." Each issue has five or six articles on such matters as political socialization, the impact of youth culture on society, and patterns of acquisition of adult roles. The focus is on middle adolescence through young adulthood, and many of the articles deal with youth in the United States.

J. HEALTH RESEARCH

211. AMERICAN JOURNAL OF PUBLIC HEALTH. American Public Health Association, 1015 Eighteenth Street NW, Washington, D.C. 20036. 1911--. Monthly.

The official journal of the American Public Health Association (APHA), it features articles, book reviews, news of the profession, and an employment bulletin. The title has varied slightly over the years. Indexed in SocAb, PAIS, and IMed.

212. COMMUNITY MENTAL HEALTH JOURNAL. Behavioral Publications, 2852 Broadway, New York, N.Y. 10025. 1965--. Quarterly.

"Devoted to emergent approaches in mental health research,

theory, and practice as they relate to community, broadly
defined." Book and film reviews and a list of publications
received are also included. Indexed in IMed, PsychAb, and
SocAb.

213. INTERNATIONAL JOURNAL OF THE ADDICTIONS. Marcel Dekker
Journals, P.O. Box 11305, Church Street Station, New York, N.Y.
10248. 1966--. Bimonthly.

An interdisciplinary journal concerned with all types of drug
abuse.

214. JOURNAL OF HEALTH AND SOCIAL BEHAVIOR. American Sociological Association, 1722 N Street NW, Washington, D.C. 20036.
1960--. Quarterly.

Articles examine, from the sociological viewpoint, problems
relating to physical and mental health and deal with such
topics as alcoholism, college student marijuana use and societal
alienation, and organizational factors and health status. A
cumulative index to the first ten volumes has been published.
Indexed in IMed, SocAb, PsychAb, and SSI.

215. JOURNAL OF SEX RESEARCH: THE PUBLICATION OF THE SOCIETY
FOR THE SCIENTIFIC STUDY OF SEX, INC. The Society for the
Scientific Study of Sex, Inc., 1364 Lexington Avenue, New York,
N.Y. 10028. 1965--. Quarterly.

"Serves the interdisciplinary exchange of knowledge in the
field of sex." Each issue contains eight or nine articles on
such topics as premarital sex experience, family stability, and
human rights in relation to induced abortion.

216. QUARTERLY JOURNAL OF STUDIES ON ALCOHOL. Center of Alcohol Studies, Rutgers - The State University, New Brunswick, N.J.
09803. 1940--. Quarterly.

An international journal concerned with all aspects of research
on alcohol, it has been published since 1968 in two parts:
articles appear in part A; abstracts of journal articles and
monographs are provided in part B by the Documentation Division of the Center. This bibliographic information is reissued
in various formats and updates the INTERNATIONAL BIBLIOG-
RAPHY OF STUDIES ON ALCOHOL (see item 1471). A title
change, to JOURNAL OF STUDIES ON ALCOHOL, was made
in January 1975. From this date the journal will be published monthly, with the former part A appearing in odd-
numbered months, and the former part B in even-numbered
months. Indexed in IMed, PsychAb, SocAb, and SSI.

K. METHODOLOGY AND QUANTITATIVE RESEARCH

217. JOURNAL OF THE AMERICAN STATISTICAL ASSOCIATION. 806 Fifteenth Street NW, Washington, D.C. 20005. 1888--. Quarterly.

    Includes articles on social, business, and economic statistics; demographic studies; and biometrics. Indexed in PsychAb.

218. QUALITY AND QUANTITY: EUROPEAN-AMERICAN JOURNAL OF METHODOLOGY. Elsevier Scientific Publishing Co., P.O. Box 211, Amsterdam, The Netherlands. 1967--. Quarterly.

    A journal which "...systematically correlates disciplines such as mathematics and statistics with those of the social sciences, particularly sociology, economics and social psychology." Papers on causal analysis, models of classification, and methods for constructing typologies have appeared in recent issues.

219. REVIEW OF PUBLIC DATA USE. Clearinghouse and Laboratory for Census Data, Suite 900, 1601 North Kent Street, Arlington, Va. 22209. 1973--. Quarterly.

    Articles describe the use of federal data in research projects.

220. ROPER PUBLIC OPINION RESEARCH CENTER. NEWSLETTER. Roper Public Opinion Research Center, Williams College, Williamstown, Mass. 01267. 1967--. Semiannual.

    Describes survey data available through the Center and its International Survey Library Association Program.

221. SOCIAL INDICATORS NEWSLETTER. Social Science Research Council, Center for Social Indicators, 1755 Massachusetts Avenue NW, Washington, D.C. 20036. 1973--. Quarterly.

    Publishes news of surveys and archives and of future conferences; briefly reviews books and reports from the United States and abroad.

222. SOCIAL SCIENCE RESEARCH: A QUARTERLY JOURNAL OF SOCIAL SCIENCE METHODOLOGY AND QUANTITATIVE RESEARCH. Academic Press, 111 Fifth Avenue, New York, N.Y. 10003. 1972--. Quarterly.

    Papers deal with substantive issues in all social sciences and with social science methodology.

223. SOCIOLOGICAL METHODS AND RESEARCH: A QUARTERLY JOURNAL. Sage Publications, 275 South Beverly Drive, Beverly Hills, Calif.

90212. 1972--. Quarterly.

"Devoted to sociology as a cumulative empirical science...."
Articles are not purely statistical but are tied to empirical
applications.

224. SS DATA: NEWSLETTER OF SOCIAL SCIENCE ARCHIVAL ACQUISI-
TIONS. Laboratory for Political Research, 321 A Schaeffer Hall,
University of Iowa, Iowa City, Iowa. 52240. 1971--. Quarterly.

Abstracts, arranged under such headings as sociology, political
science, history, education, public opinion surveys, and instructional data sets, provide information on the acquisitions
of social science data archives. A directory of participating
archives is included in each issue and selected individual
archives are described.

225. STATISTICAL REPORTER. Government Printing Office, Washington,
D.C. 20402. 1946--. Monthly.

Prepared by the Statistical Policy Division of the Office of
Manpower and Budget; provides information on current developments in federal statistics.

L. POPULAR CULTURE AND MASS MEDIA

226. JOURNALISM QUARTERLY. School of Journalism, 431 Murphy Hall,
University of Minnesota, Minneapolis, Minn. 55455. 1924--. Quarterly.

Devoted to research in journalism and mass communication,
this is the subscription journal of the Kappa Tau Alpha Society,
published by the Association for Education in Journalism. Each
issue also includes a classified section of book reviews, an
annotated list of books and bibliographies, news of latest
developments in the theory and methodology of communication,
and summaries of major doctoral and masters' theses. Indexed
in PAIS and SSI.

227. JOURNAL OF AMERICAN FOLKLORE. University of Texas Press, P.O.
Box 7819, Austin, Tex. 78712. 1888--. Quarterly.

The official publication of the American Folklore Society, it
covers all aspects of American folk literature, art, music, and
dance. There are book reviews, notes and queries, and an
annual folklore bibliography. Indexed in ABSTRACTS OF FOLK-
LORE STUDIES, SSHI, and HUMANITIES INDEX.

228. JOURNAL OF COMMUNICATION. The Annenberg School of Communications, University of Pennsylvania, 3620 Walnut Street C5, Philadelphia, Pa. 19174. 1951--. Quarterly.

Published in cooperation with the International Communication Association, the journal is devoted to research and theory in communication and is directed to those "...who are interested in, and challenged by, the processes, problems and potential of human interaction." Special sections cover book reviews, notices of work in progress, and news of meetings, organizations, and publications.

229. JOURNAL OF LEISURE RESEARCH. National Recreation and Park Association, 1700 Pennsylvania Avenue NW, Washington, D.C. 20006. 1969--. Quarterly.

Provides an interdisciplinary approach to the problems of leisure and their solution; includes research notes, a book review, and lists of books received. Indexed in SSI.

230. JOURNAL OF POPULAR CULTURE. University Hall, Bowling Green University, Bowling Green, Ohio. 43402. 1967--. Quarterly.

Official publication of the Popular Culture Association, the Popular Literature Section (Comparative Literature II) of the Modern Language Association of America, and of the Popular Culture Section of the Midwest Modern Language Association. Articles deal with all aspects of popular culture, including folklore. Issues also include book reviews and a section of short articles on films. Indexed in the HUMANITIES INDEX.

M. PUBLIC OPINION

231. CURRENT OPINION. Roper Public Opinion Research Center, Williams College, Williamstown, Mass. 01267. 1973--. Monthly.

"A digest of the public's views on contemporary issues," it publishes brief reports on the results of polls conducted throughout the United States.

232. GALLUP OPINION INDEX. 53 Bank Street, Princeton, N.J. 08540. 1965--. Monthly.

Reports on the findings of surveys conducted by the Gallup polls. A cumulation of such reports for the period 1935 through 1971 has been published (see item 1272).

233. PUBLIC OPINION QUARTERLY. Columbia University Press, 136

South Broadway, Irvington-on-Hudson, N.Y. 10533. 1937--. Quarterly.

In this official journal of the American Association for Public Opinion Research, articles are selected "...to illuminate problems of communication and public opinion." There are sections for book reviews, current poll results, ongoing research, news, and notes. The Advisory Committee on Communication of Columbia University provides editorial sponsorship. Indexed in SocAb, PsychAb, PAIS, SSHI, and SSI.

ROPER PUBLIC OPINION RESEARCH CENTER. NEWSLETTER.

See item 220.

N. RELIGION

234. ADRIS NEWSLETTER. Association for the Development of Religious Information Systems, Department of Sociology and Anthropology, Marquette University, Milwaukee, Wis. 53233. 1971--. Monthly.

235. JOURNAL FOR THE SCIENTIFIC STUDY OF RELIGION. Society for the Scientific Study of Religion, University of Connecticut, Box U68A, Storrs, Conn. 06268. 1961--. Quarterly.

Articles are concerned with "...theories, research findings, and methodological problems encountered in the study of religion." Issues also contain research notes, book reviews, news and notes, and, from 1972, a review of public opinion polls. Indexed in SocAb and HUMANITIES INDEX.

236. RELIGIOUS EDUCATION. Religious Education Association, 545 West 111th Street, New York, N.Y. 10025. 1906--. Bimonthly.

"A platform for free discussion of religious issues and their bearing on education," this journal publishes articles concerned with the teaching of religion, especially in higher education. Symposia on various aspects of religion and society are featured, along with book reviews and selected abstracts of doctoral dissertations.

237. REVIEW OF RELIGIOUS RESEARCH. P.O. Box 228, Cathedral Station, New York, N.Y. 10025. 1959--. Three times a year.

The official publication of the Religious Research Association. Indexed in SocAb.

238. SOCIOLOGICAL ANALYSIS: A JOURNAL IN THE SOCIOLOGY OF

RELIGION. The Association for the Sociology of Religion, Loyola University, Los Angeles, Calif. 90045. 1940--. Quarterly.

Formerly published as the AMERICAN CATHOLIC SOCIOLOGI-CAL REVIEW, it contains theoretical and empirical articles on religion and values, often accompanied by extensive bibliographies. The official journal of the Association for the Sociology of Religion, it is indexed in SocAb.

O. SOCIAL PSYCHOLOGY

239. JOURNAL OF APPLIED BEHAVIORAL SCIENCE. National Institute for Applied Behavioral Science, P.O. Box 9155, Rosslyn Station, Arlington, Va. 22209. 1965--. Bimonthly.

The goals of the journal are "...to develop or test theoretical and conceptual approaches to planned change that have both predictive and explanatory power and clear implications for future action." Articles are concerned with such topics as social intervention, organizational behavior and change, group dynamics, and encounter groups.

240. JOURNAL OF APPLIED SOCIAL PSYCHOLOGY. V.H. Winston and Sons, 1511 K Street NW, Washington, D.C. 20005. 1971--. Quarterly.

Devoted to applications of experimental behavioral science research to problems of society. Articles report laboratory and field research in three areas: problems of society; problems of human development, learning, and education; and problems of political, social, and industrial organizations.

241. JOURNAL OF PERSONALITY AND SOCIAL PSYCHOLOGY. American Psychological Association, 1200 Seventeenth Street NW, Washington, D.C. 20036. 1965--. Monthly.

Formed, in part, from a division of the JOURNAL OF ABNOR-MAL AND SOCIAL PSYCHOLOGY (1906--), this journal publishes articles on psychodynamic processes in normal populations, social motivation, the socialization process, attitudes, social interaction, and the psychological aspects of social structure. Indexed in PsychAb and SSI.

242. JOURNAL OF SOCIAL PSYCHOLOGY. Journal Press, 2 Commercial Street, Provincetown, Mass. 02657. 1929--. Bimonthly, 3 volumes each year.

Founded by John Dewey and Carl Murchison, the journal is "...devoted to studies of persons in group settings, and of culture and personality." It includes a section of reports in summary form, for which supplementary tabular data are available on microfiche; crosscultural notes; and a list of books currently received. Indexed in PsychAb and SSI.

243. SOCIOMETRY: A JOURNAL OF RESEARCH IN SOCIAL PSYCHOLOGY. American Sociological Association, 1722 N Street NW, Washington, D.C. 20036. 1937--. Quarterly.

Founded by J.L. Moreno, the journal "...is concerned with the entire range of interests and problems in social psychology, ...the investigation of the processes and products of social interaction, and the development of significant empirical and theoretical generalizations therefrom." Indexed in SocAb, PsychAb, PAIS, and SSI.

P. URBAN STUDIES

244. URBAN AFFAIRS QUARTERLY. Sage Publications, 275 South Beverly Drive, Beverly Hills, Calif. 90212. 1965--. Quarterly.

This journal seeks to facilitate "...the interchange of ideas and concerns between those engaged in basic or applied research and those responsible for making and implementing policy and programs." Articles present research and analysis with implications for public policy and the quality of urban life. Occasional research notes and book reviews are included, and the March issue each year contains a Directory of Urban Research Centers in the United States and abroad. Indexed in SocAb, AbSocWk, PAIS, and SSI.

245. URBAN AND SOCIAL CHANGE REVIEW. McGuin Hall, Boston College, Chestnut Hill, Mass. 02167. 1967--. Semiannual.

First published as the REVIEW of the Institute of Human Sciences of Boston College, it seeks to make the scientific community aware of the kinds of information needed by human services decision makers and to inform the latter of research relevant to action programs and concrete social problems. An information clearinghouse is a regular feature.

246. URBAN LIFE AND CULTURE. Sage Publications, 275 South Beverly Drive, Beverly Hills, Calif. 90212. 1972--. Quarterly.

"Publishes works of urban ethnography. Employing participant-observation and intensive qualitative interviewing studies... strives to convey the inner life and texture of the diverse social enclaves and personal circumstances of urban societies." Book reviews appear as part of the section "New Ethnographies," which contains brief annotations on relevant fiction and non-fiction. Indexed in SocAb and SSI.

Q. WORK AND MANAGEMENT

247. ADMINISTRATIVE SCIENCE QUARTERLY. Malott Hall, Cornell University, Ithaca, N.Y. 14850. 1956--. Quarterly.

"Dedicated to advancing the understanding of administration through empirical investigation"; about a quarter of each issue is devoted to book reviews and a list of publications received. Indexed in PsychAb, SocAb, and PAIS.

248. INDUSTRIAL AND LABOR RELATIONS REVIEW. New York School of Industrial and Labor Relations, Cornell University, Ithaca, N.Y. 14850. 1947--. Quarterly.

An interdisciplinary journal with about six articles in each issue on topics in personnel administration, industrial sociology, labor history, industrial psychology, and related fields. Book reviews are arranged in a classified order. Indexed in PAIS and SocAb.

249. JOURNAL OF HUMAN RESOURCES: EDUCATION, MANPOWER, AND WELFARE POLICIES. University of Wisconsin Press, Box 1379, Madison, Wis. 53701. 1966--. Quarterly.

Published under the auspices of the Industrial Relations Research Institute and the Institute for Research on Poverty of the University of Wisconsin, it "...provides a forum for analysis of the role of education and training in enhancing production skills, employment opportunities, and income, as well as of manpower, health, and welfare policies as they relate to the labor market and to economic and social development." There are usually five or six articles, some short communications, a book review, and list of publications received. Indexed in SocAb and SSI.

250. SOCIOLOGY OF WORK AND OCCUPATIONS; AN INTERNATIONAL JOURNAL. Sage Publications, 275 South Beverly Drive, Beverly Hills, Calif. 90212. 1974--. Quarterly.

To be published with the support of the Department of Psychiatry, University of Illinois Medical Center, and the Department of Sociology, University of Illinois at Chicago Circle, the journal will provide "...an interdisciplinary forum for sociological research and theory in the area of work, occupations and leisure."

Chapter 4

AMERICAN SOCIETY

Chapter 4

AMERICAN SOCIETY

A. REFERENCE WORKS AND BIBLIOGRAPHIES

251. Gendell, Murray, and Zetterberg, Hans L., eds. A SOCIOLOGICAL ALMANAC FOR THE UNITED STATES. 2nd ed. New York: Scribner, 1964. xv, 94 p.

252. Smigel, Erwin O. HANDBOOK ON THE STUDY OF SOCIAL PROBLEMS. Chicago: Rand McNally, 1971. xvii, 734 p.

   Twenty-nine contributors bring a variety of orientations to the study of crime, education, industrial problems, physical and mental illness, race, and religion. Substantial bibliography.

253. United States Bureau of the Census. COUNTY AND CITY DATA BOOK, 1972. A Statistical Abstract Supplement. Washington, D.C.: Government Printing Office, 1973. 1076 p.

   Statistical information from census and other sources for standard metropolitan statistical areas, urbanized areas, counties, cities, and unincorporated areas.

254. _____. HISTORICAL STATISTICS OF THE UNITED STATES, COLONIAL TIMES TO 1957. Washington, D.C.: Government Printing Office, 1960. 789 p.

255. _____. HISTORICAL STATISTICS OF THE UNITED STATES. CONTINUATION TO 1962 AND REVISIONS. Washington, D.C.: Government Printing Office, 1968. 154 p.

256. _____. STATISTICAL ABSTRACT OF THE UNITED STATES, Washington, D.C.: Government Printing Office, 1878--. Annual.

   A summary of social, political, and economic statistics which also serves as a guide to sources of national statistical information.

257. United States Office of Management and Budget. SOCIAL INDICATORS 1973. Washington, D.C.: Government Printing Office, 1974. 258 p.

Statistical time series selected and organized to describe social conditions and social trends in the areas of health, public safety, education, employment, income, housing, leisure and recreation, and population. A second edition of the report is planned for 1976.

258. Wilcox, Leslie D., et al. SOCIAL INDICATORS AND SOCIETAL MONITORING: AN ANNOTATED BIBLIOGRAPHY. Amsterdam, London, and New York: Elsevier Scientific Publishing Co., distributed by Jossey-Bass, San Francisco, Calif., 1972. xv, 464 p.

B. SOCIAL STRUCTURE

259. Barnes, Harry Elmer, and Ruedi, Oreen M. THE AMERICAN WAY OF LIFE; AN INTRODUCTION TO THE STUDY OF CONTEMPORARY SOCIETY. 2nd ed. New York: Prentice-Hall, 1950. 931 p.

260. Bennis, Warren G., and Slater, Philip E. THE TEMPORARY SOCIETY. New York: Harper, 1968. x, 147 p.

Five essays which discuss changes in key institutions: organizational life, family, interpersonal relationships, and authority.

261. Eitzen, D. Stanley. SOCIAL STRUCTURE AND SOCIAL PROBLEMS IN AMERICA. Boston: Allyn & Bacon, 1974. x, 438 p.

Analyzes culture, norms, values, stratification and inequality, social institutions, change, and power in American society. Discusses such issues as Black power, women's liberation, and distribution of wealth. Bibliographic notes follow each chapter.

262. Kleinberg, Benjamin S. AMERICAN SOCIETY IN THE POSTINDUSTRIAL AGE: TECHNOCRACY, POWER AND THE END OF IDEOLOGY. Columbus: Charles E. Merrill, 1973. vi, 279 p.

Description of the crisis in American public life in which differentiation of occupations and subcultural life styles clash with the integration and centralization of economic and political institutions.

263. Martindale, Don Albert. AMERICAN SOCIAL STRUCTURE; HISTORI-
CAL ANTECEDENTS AND CONTEMPORARY ANALYSIS. New York:
Appleton-Century-Crofts, 1960. xiv, 521 p.

Analysis of social structure through regional, rural, urban,
ethnic, and status communities, each introduced by an historical overview.

264. _____. AMERICAN SOCIETY. Princeton, N.J.: Van Nostrand,
1960. 570 p.

The United States as a mass society is analyzed through changes
occurring in the modern community and through the reorganization of social and cultural institutions. Bibliography.

265. _____. INSTITUTIONS, ORGANIZATIONS, AND MASS SOCIETY.
Boston: Houghton Mifflin, 1966. xvi, 576 p.

Criticism of functionalism in organization theory from the viewpoint of social behaviorism; analysis of large-scale economic
organizations, social control, socialization, and personality
in the United States.

266. Reynolds, Larry T., and Henslin, James M., eds. AMERICAN SOCIETY:
A CRITICAL ANALYSIS. New York: David McKay, 1973. xiv, 337 p.

A collection of original essays which discuss American society from
the viewpoint of institutions: economics, political, military,
scientific, religious, medical, educational, familial, and legal.

267. Williams, Robin M., Jr. AMERICAN SOCIETY; A SOCIOLOGICAL
INTERPRETATION. 3rd ed. New York: Knopf, 1970. xvii, 639,
xi p.

A comprehensive and detailed analysis of the social structure
of the United States, extensively revised since the second
edition in 1960 and first edition in 1951. Discusses in fifteen
chapters all the major institutions, institutional variation, and
values in American life, social organization, and problems of
integration. Annotated readings follow each chapter.

C. PERSONALITY AND ATTITUDES

268. Elder, Glen H., Jr. CHILDREN OF THE GREAT DEPRESSION: SO-
CIAL STRUCTURE AND PERSONALITY. Chicago: University of Chicago
Press, 1974. 384 p.

A longitudinal study of 167 individuals born in 1920 and 1921,
from their school years in Oakland, California, in the 1930s
through the 1960s.

269. Gerth, Hans, and Mills, C. Wright. CHARACTER AND SOCIAL STRUCTURE: THE PSYCHOLOGY OF SOCIAL INSTITUTIONS. New York: Harcourt, Brace, 1953. 490 p.

   Study of character and personality is related to the transformation of political, economic, military, religious, and kinship institutions.

270. Klapp, Orrin E. HEROES, VILLAINS, AND FOOLS; THE CHANGING AMERICAN CHARACTER. Englewood Cliffs, N.J.: Prentice-Hall, 1962. x, 176 p.

   Analysis of popular American social types which reveal values of the larger society. Concludes that American ideals are becoming debased.

271. _____. SYMBOLIC LEADERS: PUBLIC DRAMAS AND PUBLIC MEN. Chicago: Aldine, 1964. 272 p.

   Distinguishes symbolic from organizational leaders in discussing the public roles of different social types.

272. Lemon, Richard. THE TROUBLED AMERICAN. New York: Simon & Schuster, 1970. 256 p.

   Author analyzes 1969 Gallup poll interviews of 2,165 white adult "middle Americans" (60 percent of the U.S. population earning $5,000 - $15,000), and their attitudes toward American society in general and the Negro in particular.

273. Lipset, Seymour Martin, and Lowenthal, Leo, eds. CULTURE AND SOCIAL CHARACTER; THE WORK OF DAVID RIESMAN REVIEWED. Glencoe, Ill.: Free Press, 1961. xiv, 466 p.

   Twenty-six contributors present criticism and appraisal of THE LONELY CROWD (see item 276).

274. Riesman, David. ABUNDANCE FOR WHAT? AND OTHER ESSAYS. Garden City, N.Y.: Doubleday, 1965. 579 p.

   Thirty essays on culture and social character, including discussions of youth, suburbia, sociability, and careers.

275. _____. FACES IN THE CROWD; INDIVIDUAL STUDIES IN CHARACTER AND POLITICS. Yale University Studies in National Policy, no. 4. New Haven: Yale University Press, 1952. 751 p.

   Twenty case studies, based on interviews obtained while the scheme of character types in THE LONELY CROWD (see item 276) was being developed.

276. _____. THE LONELY CROWD; A STUDY OF THE CHANGING
AMERICAN CHARACTER. Yale University Studies in National Policy,
no. 3. New Haven: Yale University Press, 1950. xvii, 386 p.

> The classic study of the emerging "other-directed" American,
> one in a three-fold typology of character which also includes
> the tradition-directed and inner-directed.

D. VALUES

277. Henry, Jules. CULTURE AGAINST MAN. New York: Random House,
1963. xiv, 495 p.

> Discussion of two major themes which shape the reality of
> American life--a preoccupation with wealth and an obsessive
> fear of annihilation by a foreign power.

278. Hofstadter, Richard. ANTI-INTELLECTUALISM IN AMERICAN LIFE.
New York: Knopf, 1963. xiii, 434 p.

> Discusses the influence of evangelical religion upon the cul-
> tural establishment of the eighteenth century and other more
> recent currents of anti-intellectualism. Bibliography.

279. Lipset, Seymour Martin. THE FIRST NEW NATION; THE UNITED
STATES IN HISTORICAL AND COMPARATIVE PERSPECTIVE. New
York: Basic Books, 1963. xv, 366 p.

> A study of the American value system in relation to character,
> religion, and trade unionism and a comparative analysis of
> democratic values in several societies.

280. Means, Richard L. THE ETHICAL IMPERATIVE; THE CRISIS IN AMERI-
CAN VALUES. Garden City, N.Y.: Doubleday, 1969. 277 p.

> Examination of orientations toward intellectualism, bureaucracy,
> the military-industrial complex, inequality, and violence.

281. Slater, Philip E. THE PURSUIT OF LONELINESS; AMERICAN CULTURE
AT THE BREAKING POINT. Boston: Beacon Press, 1970. xiii, 154 p.

> Discusses excessive stress on individualism, lack of social con-
> cern in American culture, and the frustrating consequences of
> these values; unfulfilled desires for community, for dependence,
> and for engagement. The dominance and pathology of techni-
> cal culture is challenged by the rising counterculture.

E. SOCIAL CHANGE

282. Bell, Daniel. THE COMING OF POST-INDUSTRIAL SOCIETY: A
VENTURE IN SOCIAL FORECASTING. New York: Basic Books, 1973.
507 p.

A social forecast anticipating a shift from manufacturing to
service economy, and a central position of science and knowledge used for social control and the direction of innovation
and change.

283. _____. TOWARD THE YEAR 2000; WORK IN PROGRESS. Boston:
Houghton Mifflin, 1968. ix, 400 p.

Twenty-three authors discuss specific problems, such as those
of educational and religious institutions, youth, and communities. All but one of the essays appeared in the summer 1967
issue of DAEDALUS (see item 161).

284. Bensman, Joseph, and Vidich, Arthur J. THE NEW AMERICAN SOCI-
ETY: THE REVOLUTION OF THE MIDDLE CLASS. Chicago: Quadrangle, 1971. xiv, 306 p.

Study of institutional cliques and life styles of different social
classes in American society since the Great Depression and
World War II.

285. Davis, Chester A. AMERICAN SOCIETY IN TRANSITION. New York:
Appleton-Century-Crofts, 1970. xiii, 285 p.

Discusses social change in American institutions (capitalism and
the welfare state, family, education, religion) and their present functions in the mass society. Bibliography.

286. Handlin, Oscar. THE AMERICAN PEOPLE IN THE TWENTIETH CENTU-
RY. 2nd rev. ed. Library of Congress Series in American Civilization.
Boston: Beacon Press, 1966. vi, 248 p.

Historical discussion of the impact on American society of early
twentieth-century immigration and world wars.

287. Mack, Raymond W. TRANSFORMING AMERICA; PATTERNS OF SO-
CIAL CHANGE. New York: Random House, 1967. xix, 199 p.

A survey of problems arising out of changes in American population, education, and political and economic institutions.
Bibliography.

288. Taviss, Irene, ed. THE COMPUTER IMPACT. Englewood Cliffs, N.J.:
Prentice-Hall, 1970. xi, 297 p.

Twenty-nine selections from books, conference proceedings, and periodicals.

289. _____. OUR TOOL-MAKING SOCIETY. Englewood Cliffs, N.J.: Prentice-Hall, 1972. xi, 145 p.

Examination of the effects of technological change on values, social and political problems, and life styles.

290. Toffler, Alvin. FUTURE SHOCK. New York: Random House, 1970. 505 p.

Rapid cultural change to which the human organism cannot adapt leads to the disruption of normal decision-making processes. Impermanence, novelty, and "overchoice" is coped with by "ad-hocracy," a chaotic diffusion of decision making at all organizational levels.

F. SOCIAL INDICATORS

291. Bauer, Raymond A., ed. SOCIAL INDICATORS. Cambridge, Mass.: The M.I.T. Press, 1966. xxii, 357 p.

Analysis of social indicators, statistics, statistical series, and other forms of evidence; assessment of their reliability, predictive value, and classification.

292. Campbell, Angus, and Converse, Philip E., eds. THE HUMAN MEANING OF SOCIAL CHANGE. New York: Russell Sage Foundation, 1972. 547 p.

A collection of twelve essays to supplement INDICATORS OF SOCIAL CHANGE: CONCEPTS AND MEASUREMENTS, edited by E.B. Sheldon and W.E. Moore (see item 296). Analyzes attitudes, expectations, aspirations, and values. Discusses such topics as use of time, meaning of work and leisure, consumer attitudes, alienation, and engagement.

293. Gross, Bertram M., ed. SOCIAL INTELLIGENCE FOR AMERICA'S FUTURE: EXPLORATIONS IN SOCIETAL PROBLEMS. Boston: Allyn & Bacon, 1969. xxv, 541 p.

Twenty essays, originally published in 1967 as two successive issues of the ANNALS of the American Academy of Political and Social Science, discuss social indicators in the political system, cultural context, the area of social problems, and environment.

294. _____. THE STATE OF THE NATION: SOCIAL SYSTEMS ACCOUNT-

ING. London: Tavistock; New York: Barnes and Noble, 1966.
ix, 166 p.

Development and use of social indicators.

295. Land, Kenneth C., and Spilerman, Seymour, eds. SOCIAL INDICATOR
MODELS. New York: Russell Sage Foundation, 1974. 411 p.

Discusses mathematical models, analysis of changes in social
indicators and social policy, and interrelationships between
social indicators. Based on a Conference on Social Indicator
Models sponsored by the Russell Sage Foundation in 1972.

296. Sheldon, Eleanor B., and Moore, Wilbert E., eds. INDICATORS OF
SOCIAL CHANGE: CONCEPTS AND MEASUREMENTS. New York:
Russell Sage Foundation, 1968. x, 822 p.

Sixteen contributors examine in fourteen chapters changes in
American society and analyze major structural components.
Bibliography.

297. United States Department of Health, Education and Welfare. TOWARD
A SOCIAL REPORT. Ann Arbor: University of Michigan Press, 1970.
101 p.

Analysis of factors related to social well-being is discussed in
separate chapters on health and illness, social mobility, physical environment, income and property, public order and safety,
learning, science and art, participation, and alienation.

G. ANTHOLOGIES

298. Arnold, David O., ed. THE SOCIOLOGY OF SUBCULTURES. Berkeley:
Glendessary Press, 1970. 171 p.

Four sections cover early and recent formulations, subculture
boundaries, and theory. Only American subcultures such as
lower-class culture, out-groups, and counterculture are considered.

299. Atchley, Robert C., ed. UNDERSTANDING AMERICAN SOCIETY.
Belmont, Calif.: Wadsworth, 1971. viii, 525 p.

Collection of readings which analyze change in major American
institutions; discussion of economy, government, the military,
education, religion, science, health, and crime.

300. Baltzell, E[dward] Digby, ed. THE SEARCH FOR COMMUNITY IN
MODERN AMERICA. New York: Harper & Row, Publishers, 1968.
162 p.

Essays about the institutionalization of new social and legal relationships in the context of neighborliness in the urban and bureaucratic social order.

301. Berger, Bennett M. LOOKING FOR AMERICA; ESSAYS ON YOUTH, SUBURBIA, AND OTHER AMERICAN OBSESSIONS. Englewood Cliffs, N.J.: Prentice-Hall, 1971. 331 p.

Collected essays on youth culture, the myth of suburbia, the problems of leisure, and the acceptance of sociology by the academic community. Bibliography.

302. Ehrensaft, Philip, and Etzioni, Amitai. ANATOMIES OF AMERICA: SOCIOLOGICAL PERSPECTIVE. London: Macmillan, 1969. xii, 499 p.

Anthology of fifty-three selections on major aspects of American life.

303. Feldman, Saul D., and Thielbar, Gerald W. LIFE STYLES: DIVERSITY IN AMERICAN SOCIETY. Boston: Little, Brown and Co., 1972. 383 p.

Collection of readings on the determination of life styles by age, sex, time, region, religion, income, social class, ethnicity, and deviance.

304. Horowitz, Irving Louis, ed. THE TROUBLED CONSCIENCE: AMERICAN SOCIAL ISSUES. Palo Alto, Calif.: James E. Freel and Associates, 1971. xiii, 395 p.

Selected articles from THE CENTER MAGAZINE on reform and revolution, youth values, Black aspirations, and the white establishment.

305. Mankoff, Milton. THE POVERTY OF PROGRESS: THE POLITICAL ECONOMY OF AMERICAN SOCIAL PROBLEMS. New York: Holt, Rinehart and Winston, 1972. xiii, 524 p.

Readings on the American political economy--the structure of capitalism, private use of public power, militarism, racism, the knowledge industry, and problems of maintaining the social order. Bibliography (pp. 506-12).

306. Rainwater, Lee, ed. SOCIAL PROBLEMS AND PUBLIC POLICY: INEQUALITY AND JUSTICE: A SURVEY OF INEQUALITIES OF CLASS, STATUS, SEX, AND POWER. Chicago: Aldine, 1974. 456 p.

More than forty selections on social issues of American society, including many research reports.

307. Rosen, Bernard C., et al., eds. ACHIEVEMENT IN AMERICAN SOCI-ETY. Cambridge, Mass.: Schenkman, 1969. x, 653 p.

Essays, papers, and research reports on the impact of social environment (family, peer group, ethnicity, social class) upon achievement in education and occupation, and the relationship between achievement and social mobility.

308. Shostak, Arthur B., ed. PUTTING SOCIOLOGY TO WORK. New York: David McKay, 1974. 283 p.

Twenty-four case studies in the application of sociology to modern social problems, most written specially for this volume. Annotated bibliography (pp. 271-80).

309. Zeitlin, Maurice, ed. AMERICAN SOCIETY, INC.; STUDIES OF THE SOCIAL STRUCTURE AND THE POLITICAL ECONOMY OF THE UNITED STATES. Chicago: Markham, 1970. xvi, 527 p.

Demonstrates the concentration of wealth and power in America and the consequences of poverty and conflict.

H. SOCIAL PROBLEMS

310. Becker, Howard S., ed. SOCIAL PROBLEMS: A MODERN APPROACH. New York: Wiley, 1966. vii, 770 p.

Fourteen selections which cover such topics as poverty, housing and urban renewal, adolescents and the aged, delinquency, crime and mental illness, race relations, population, and war.

311. Bryant, Clifton D., ed. SOCIAL PROBLEMS TODAY: DILEMMAS AND DISSENSUS. Philadelphia: Lippincott, 1971. 546 p.

Selections discuss conflicts, inequities, institutional ineffectiveness, and destructive disorders in American society. Bibliography.

312. Dentler, Robert A. MAJOR SOCIAL PROBLEMS. 2nd ed. Chicago: Rand McNally, 1972. ix, 564 p.

A revision of his earlier text, MAJOR AMERICAN SOCIAL PROBLEMS (1967). Discusses in eleven chapters generic social problems of war and violence; poverty and racism; population; urban and rural environmental problems; and deviant behavior.

313. Freeman, Howard E., and Jones, Wyatt C. SOCIAL PROBLEMS: CAUSES AND CONTROLS. New York: Random House, 1970. xiv, 560 p.

This text discusses identification of social problems and their relationship to social order, pervasive problems (poverty, discrimination, deterioration of urban life, and corruption), and specific problems related to life cycles.

314. Horton, Paul B., and Leslie, Gerald R. THE SOCIOLOGY OF SOCIAL PROBLEMS. 5th ed. New York: Appleton-Century-Crofts, 1974. xi, 784 p.

Discusses both traditional problems such as race relations and crime, and contemporary issues such as civil liberties and militarism.

315. _____, eds. STUDIES IN THE SOCIOLOGY OF SOCIAL PROBLEMS. New York: Appleton-Century-Crofts, 1971. ix, 581 p.

Seventy-eight selections in eighteen chapters of sociology and social commentary.

316. Johnson, Elmer H. SOCIAL PROBLEMS OF URBAN MAN. Homewood, Ill.: Dorsey Press, 1973. xiv, 585 p.

A text of twenty-one chapters, each covering a specific social problem.

317. Lindenfeld, Frank, ed. RADICAL PERSPECTIVES ON SOCIAL PROBLEMS: READINGS IN CRITICAL SOCIOLOGY. 2nd ed. New York: Macmillan, 1973. xi, 468 p.

Selections from a critical social viewpoint discuss problems common to industrial societies, ideologies, and agencies of change.

318. McDonagh, Edward C., and Simpson, Jon E., eds. SOCIAL PROBLEMS: PERSISTENT CHALLENGES. 2nd ed. New York: Holt, Rinehart and Winston, 1969. viii, 667 p.

Fifty-three selections cover urbanism; mass culture; economic, political, educational, and familial problems; race relations; and personality problems.

319. Merton, Robert K., and Nisbet, Robert [A.], eds. CONTEMPORARY SOCIAL PROBLEMS: AN INTRODUCTION TO THE SOCIOLOGY OF DEVIANT BEHAVIOR AND SOCIAL DISORGANIZATION. 3rd ed. New York: Harcourt Brace Jovanovich, 1971. xiii, 754 p.

The third revised edition of a text originally published in 1961. Fifteen chapters cover deviant behavior such as crime, mental disorders, and suicide, as well as social disorganization in such areas as race relations, family, and work. Study of social problems is related to sociological theory.

320. Perrucci, Robert, and Pilisuk, Marc. THE TRIPLE REVOLUTION: SOCIAL PROBLEMS IN DEPTH. Boston: Little, Brown and Co., 1968. 689 p.

   Collection of papers on technological militarism and the impact of its ideology upon American society; cybernation, depersonalization, and decision control; and movements for human rights.

321. Rosenberg, Bernard, et al. MASS SOCIETY IN CRISIS: SOCIAL PROBLEMS AND SOCIAL PATHOLOGY. 2nd ed. New York: Macmillan, 1971. xiv, 526 p.

   Forty-seven papers on extreme situations (total institutions, mass terror, genocide) and different approaches to the solution of social problems. Deviance, discrimination, and alienation are discussed along with preventive strategies and social planning.

322. Scarpitti, Frank R. SOCIAL PROBLEMS. New York: Holt, Rinehart and Winston, 1974. 656 p.

   This text analyzes major problems of American society including health care, mental disorders, drugs and alcohol, communications, the corporate state, work, and environment.

323. Shostak, Arthur B. MODERN SOCIAL REFORMS: SOLVING TODAY'S SOCIAL PROBLEMS. New York: Macmillan, 1974. x, 411 p.

   New approaches to social problems; a text with thirteen selected readings and annotated bibliography (pp. 397-403).

324. Skolnick, Jerome [H.], and Currie, Elliot. CRISIS IN AMERICAN INSTITUTIONS. 2nd ed. Boston: Little, Brown and Co., 1973. x, 526 p.

   Analysis of systemic problems (inequality, racism, sexism, corporate power, militarism) and problems arising out of institutional crises in schools and higher education, health care and welfare, and in police operations and criminal law.

325. Turner, Jonathan H. AMERICAN SOCIETY: PROBLEMS OF STRUCTURE. New York: Harper & Row, Publishers, 1972. xix, 299 p.

   Social problems are viewed as a result of structural forces in American society. Bibliography (pp. 271-89).

326. Winter, J. Alan, et al. VITAL PROBLEMS FOR AMERICAN SOCIETY: MEANINGS AND MEANS. New York: Random House, 1968. xiii, 527 p.

   Thirty-five selections discuss such topics as population growth, church-state and civilian-military relationships, draft, extremism, youth culture, and urban planning, and attempt to determine the key values and goals of American society.

Chapter 5

POPULATION

Chapter 5

POPULATION

A. REFERENCE WORKS

327. Bogue, Donald J. PRINCIPLES OF DEMOGRAPHY. New York: Wiley, 1969. xiii, 917 p.

    This volume covers the whole field of population study; bibliographies accompany each chapter.

328. Hauser, Philip M., and Duncan, Otis Dudley, eds. THE STUDY OF POPULATIONS: AN INVENTORY AND APPRAISAL. Chicago: University of Chicago Press, 1959. xvi, 864 p.

    An encyclopedic summary of the field of demography. Part 1 discusses demography as a science. Part 2 is comparative. Part 3 (twelve chapters) covers population composition, distribution, fertility, mortality, growth, and migration.

B. CENSUS MONOGRAPHS

329. Bancroft, Gertrude. THE AMERICAN LABOR FORCE: ITS GROWTH AND CHANGING COMPOSITION. New York: Wiley, 1958. xiv, 256 p. (For the Social Science Research Council in cooperation with the U.S. Department of Commerce, Bureau of the Census.)

    Brings up to date John D. Durand's THE LABOR FORCE IN THE UNITED STATES 1890-1960 (New York: Social Science Research Council, 1948). Devotes attention to the increasing participation of white women in the labor force.

330. Bernert, Eleanor. AMERICA'S CHILDREN. New York: Wiley, 1958. xiv, 185 p. (For the Social Science Research Council in cooperation with the U.S. Department of Commerce, Bureau of the Census.)

    The variables of age, sex, region, residence, and race are interrelated to analyze childhood dependency, family arrange-

ments, school enrollment and progress, and labor force participation.

331. Duncan, Otis Dudley, and Reiss, Albert J., Jr. SOCIAL CHARACTER-
ISTICS OF URBAN AND RURAL COMMUNITIES, 1950. New York:
Wiley, 1956. xviii, 421 p. (For the Social Science Research Council,
in cooperation with the U.S. Department of Commerce, Bureau of the
Census.)

Fundamental characteristics of communities--size, spatial organization, growth, decline, and functional specialization--which
are related to variations in socioeconomic level, distribution,
and movement of population.

332. Folger, John K., and Nam, Charles B. EDUCATION OF THE AMERI-
CAN POPULATION. A 1960 Census Monograph. Washington, D.C.:
Government Printing Office, 1967. ix, 290 p.

Analysis of the relation of school enrollment and educational
attainment to other social and economic characteristics of the
population. Three major aspects are considered: enrollment
of students, characteristics of teachers, and educational attainment of the adult population.

333. Glick, Paul C. AMERICAN FAMILIES. New York: Wiley, 1957.
xiv, 240 p. (For the Social Science Research Council, in cooperation
with the U.S. Department of Commerce, Bureau of the Census.)

Covers such topics as family composition and life cycle, socioeconomic changes, marriages and remarriages, separation, divorce and widowhood, and future family formation.

334. Grabill, Wilson H., et al. THE FERTILITY OF AMERICAN WOMEN.
New York: Wiley, 1958. xvi, 448 p. (For the Social Science Re-
search Council, in cooperation with the U.S. Department of Commerce,
Bureau of the Census.)

Trends in fertility from the colonial period; the relationship of
fertility to place and type of residence, nativity, occupation,
and educational attainment.

335. Hathaway, Dale E., et al. PEOPLE OF RURAL AMERICA. A 1960
Census Monograph. Washington, D.C.: Government Printing Office,
1968. ix, 289 p. (Prepared in cooperation with the Social Science
Research Council.)

Ten chapters on number and distribution of rural population,
age and sex composition, differential fertility, educational
status, employment income, and earnings. Develops the hypothesis that proximity to large metropolitan centers plays a crucial

role in determining the characteristics of rural areas; rural areas are seen as interdependent with metropolitan centers.

336. Hutchinson, E. P. IMMIGRANTS AND THEIR CHILDREN, 1850–1950. New York: Wiley, 1956. xiv, 391 p. (For the Social Science Research Council, in cooperation with the U.S. Department of Commerce, Bureau of the Census.)

Analyzes a century of census information on the foreign-born population of the United States. Discusses geographic and occupational distribution of the foreign-born at different decades.

337. Miller, Herman P. INCOME DISTRIBUTION IN THE UNITED STATES. A 1960 Census Monograph. Washington, D.C.: Government Printing Office, 1966. viii, 306 p.

Analysis of changes in the distribution of income, based on information collected in three decennial censuses. Finds reduction of inequality in distribution of income between 1940 and 1950, but little change during the next decade.

338. Price, Daniel O. CHANGING CHARACTERISTICS OF THE NEGRO POPULATION. A 1960 Census Monograph. Washington, D.C.: Government Printing Office, 1969. viii, 259 p. (Prepared in cooperation with the Social Science Research Council.)

Changes in the demographic characteristics and economic status of the Negro population in America since 1870, with special emphasis on the period from 1940 to 1960 when a major redistribution of the Negro population occurred.

339. Sheldon, Henry D., and Tibbitts, Clark. THE OLDER POPULATION OF THE U.S. Census Monograph Series. New York: Wiley, 1958. xiii, 223 p. (For the Social Science Research Council, in cooperation with the U.S. Department of Commerce, Bureau of the Census.)

Analysis of changing age structure and the relationship of age to occupation, marital status, housing, and income.

340. Shryock, Henry S., Jr. POPULATION MOBILITY WITHIN THE UNITED STATES. Chicago: Community and Family Study Center, University of Chicago, 1964. x, 470 p.

Internal migration using 1940 and 1950 census data. Historic and geographic variations in spatial mobility. Regional migration, urban and rural types of residence, factors of race, sex, and age. Bibliography.

341. Taeuber, Conrad, and Taeuber, Irene B. THE CHANGING POPULATION

OF THE UNITED STATES. Census Monograph Series. New York: Wiley, 1958. xi, 357 p. (For the Social Science Research Council, in cooperation with the U.S. Department of Commerce, Bureau of the Census.)

> Changes in the U.S. population over 160 years. Part I: numerical growth and spatial distribution, immigration, and internal migration. Part II: population characteristics such as marital status, families, education, economic activities, and income. Part III: fertility and mortality. Part IV: discusses interrelations between natural increase, immigration, and spatial distribution.

342. Taeuber, Irene B., and Taeuber, Conrad. PEOPLE OF THE UNITED STATES IN THE 20TH CENTURY. A 1960 Census Monograph. Washington, D.C.: U.S. Department of Commerce, Bureau of the Census, 1971. xxxvii, 1046 p. (Prepared in cooperation with the Social Science Research Council.)

> Final report in the 1960 Census Monograph Series. Wealth of demographic data on age, fertility, mortality, marital status, migration, and trends in urbanization, economic activity, education, and family life.

C. U.S. POPULATION

343. Bogue, Donald J. THE POPULATION OF THE UNITED STATES. Glencoe, Ill.: Free Press, 1959. xix, 873 p.

> Interprets population changes in the 1950s on the basis of census surveys and estimates.

344. Day, Lincoln H., and Day, Alice Taylor. TOO MANY AMERICANS. Boston: Houghton Mifflin Co., 1964. ix, 298 p.

> Argues in favor of stationary population and ready access for all to birth control information.

345. Farley, Reynolds. GROWTH OF THE BLACK POPULATION: A STUDY OF DEMOGRAPHIC TRENDS. Chicago: Markham, 1970. 286 p.

> Demographic history from the colonial period to the present.

346. Kuznets, Simon, and Thomas, Dorothy S. POPULATION REDISTRIBUTION AND ECONOMIC GROWTH, UNITED STATES, 1870-1950. 3 vols. Philadelphia: American Philosophical Library, 1957-64. Vol. 1, 759 p.; vol. 2, 289 p.; vol. 3, 368 p.

> Reference tables on migration, labor force, manufacturing, and income. Analysis of trends in labor forces, redistribution

of manufacturing, tendencies in regional growth, and changing structure of economic activity.

347. Price, Daniel O., ed. THE 99TH HOUR: THE POPULATION CRISIS IN THE UNITED STATES. Chapel Hill: University of North Carolina Press, 1967. 130 p.

Lectures at a 1965–66 seminar on population policy at the University of North Carolina centering on the issue of future population size.

348. Stockwell, Edward G. POPULATION AND PEOPLE. Chicago: Quadrangle, 1968. xii, 307 p.

A comprehensive study of significant population trends in the United States--mortality, fertility, migration and mobility, and population composition and growth. Discussion of social change and social problems.

D. STATES AND METROPOLITAN AREAS

349. Bogue, Donald J. COMPONENTS OF POPULATION CHANGE, 1940–50: ESTIMATES OF NET MIGRATION AND NATURAL INCREASE FOR EACH STANDARD METROPOLITAN AREA AND STATE ECONOMIC AREA. Chicago: University of Chicago Press, 1957. v, 145 p.

Gives birth and death statistics for the decade from 1940 to 1950, and analyzes population growth in terms of reproductive change and migration in standard metropolitan statistical areas and in state economic areas.

350. _____. THE STRUCTURE OF THE METROPOLITAN COMMUNITY: A STUDY OF DOMINANCE AND SUBDOMINANCE. Ann Arbor: University of Michigan School of Graduate Studies, 1949. x, 210 p.

Analysis of census material shows that population density, community size, and activities are dependent upon distance from the nearest metropolitan center.

351. Davis, Kingsley, and Styles, Frederick G., eds. CALIFORNIA'S TWENTY MILLION; RESEARCH CONTRIBUTIONS TO POPULATION POLICY. Population Monograph Series, no. 10. Berkeley: Institute of International Studies, University of California, 1971. 349 p.

A collection of research papers based on a symposium on California population problems and policies.

352. Ford, Thomas R. HEALTH AND DEMOGRAPHY IN KENTUCKY.

Lexington: University of Kentucky Press, 1964. xxiii, 150 p.

Examines the nature and distribution of Kentucky's health resources and the relationship of social, economic, and demographic factors to health. Includes data from the 1960 U.S. census.

353. Schnore, Leo F. THE URBAN SCENE: HUMAN ECOLOGY AND DEMOGRAPHY. New York: Free Press of Glencoe, 1965. x, 374 p.

A collection of twenty articles on metropolitan growth and decentralization, suburban communities, racial composition of metropolitan populations, and urban transportation systems.

354. Smith, T. Lynn, and Hitt, Homer L. THE PEOPLE OF LOUISIANA. Baton Rouge: Louisiana State University Press, 1952. xviii, 272 p.

Brings together results of Louisiana population studies since 1932; census figures go back to 1810.

355. Thompson, Warren S. GROWTH AND CHANGES IN CALIFORNIA'S POPULATION. Los Angeles: Haynes Foundation, 1955. xxx, 377 p.

Population history of California covers 100 years and eleven censuses. Urban characteristics of the state, dependence of growth on migration, and high levels of income and education.

356. Zopf, Paul E., Jr. NORTH CAROLINA: A DEMOGRAPHIC PROFILE. Chapel Hill, N.C.: Carolina Population Center, 1965. xvii, 441 p.

E. FERTILITY AND MORTALITY

357. Coale, Ansley J., and Zelnik, Melvin. NEW ESTIMATES OF FERTILITY AND POPULATION IN THE U.S.; A STUDY OF ANNUAL WHITE BIRTHS FROM 1855 TO 1960 AND OF COMPLETENESS OF ENUMERATION IN THE CENSUSES FROM 1880 TO 1960. Princeton, N.J.: Princeton University Press, 1963. xvi, 186 p.

Estimates of annual births through computations and adjustments; comparison of trends in fertility in selected European countries and the United States.

358. DeJong, Gordon F. APPALACHIAN FERTILITY DECLINE: A DEMO-GRAPHIC AND SOCIOLOGICAL ANALYSIS. Lexington: University of Kentucky Press, 1968. xii, 138 p.

Decline in fertility in Southern Appalachia between 1950 and 1960 is interpreted in terms of out-migration, changes in residence, and changes in attitudes toward fertility.

359. Dodge, David L., and Martin, Walter T. SOCIAL STRESS AND CHRONIC ILLNESS: MORTALITY PATTERNS IN INDUSTRIAL SOCIETY. Notre Dame, Ind.: University of Notre Dame Press, 1970. xxvi, 331 p.

>   The incidence and prevalence of chronic illness in industrial society is related to social stress arising from incompatible role performance and varies inversely with the degree of status integration.

360. Hatt, Paul K. BACKGROUNDS OF HUMAN FERTILITY IN PUERTO RICO: A SOCIOLOGICAL SURVEY. Princeton, N.J.: Princeton University Press, 1952. xxiv, 512 p.

>   Based on a previously constructed sample of about 6000 households, the study analyzes socioeconomic status, rural-urban birth and residence, age difference, and trends in fertility.

361. Kiser, Clyde V., et al. TRENDS AND VARIATIONS IN FERTILITY IN THE UNITED STATES. An American Public Health Association Vital and Health Statistics Monograph. Cambridge, Mass.: Harvard University Press, 1968. xxx, 338 p.

>   Covers such topics as fertility trends and control, marriage patterns, illegitimacy, and the relationship between fertility and economic conditions.

362. Kitagawa, Evelyn M., and Hauser, Philip M. DIFFERENTIAL MORTAL- ITY IN THE UNITED STATES: A STUDY IN SOCIOECONOMIC EPI- DEMIOLOGY. Cambridge, Mass.: Harvard University Press, 1973. xx, 255 p.

>   Uses 1960 census data to examine mortality in relation to education, income, occupation, socioeconomic status, and place of residence.

363. Okun, Bernard. TRENDS IN BIRTH RATES IN THE UNITED STATES SINCE 1870. Baltimore: The Johns Hopkins University Press, 1958. 203 p.

>   Two essays, based on the Kuznets and Thomas study, POPULA- TION REDISTRIBUTION AND ECONOMIC GROWTH, UNITED STATES, 1870-1950 (see item 346), analyze birth ratios for whites and Blacks since 1870. A third essay reviews various approaches to the study of fertility.

364. Ryder, Norman B., and Westoff, Charles F. REPRODUCTION IN THE UNITED STATES, 1965. Princeton, N.J.: Princeton University Press, 1971. 419 p.

365. United States Commission on Population Growth and the American Future. POPULATION AND THE AMERICAN FUTURE; THE REPORT. Washington, D.C.: Government Printing Office, 1972. 362 p.

> The final report of the Commission presents findings on population growth and distribution, the economy, resources, environment, and public policy. Concludes that no substantial benefit will result from further population growth. Based on hearings and numerous research reports which are to be published separately.

366. Westoff, Charles F., and Potvin, Raymond H. COLLEGE WOMEN AND FERTILITY VALUES. Princeton, N.J.: Princeton University Press, 1967. xx, 237 p.

> Based on data collected by questionnaires from 15,000 freshmen at forty-five institutions; higher education does not appear to have a substantial effect upon fertility values.

367. Westoff, Charles F., et al. FAMILY GROWTH IN METROPOLITAN AMERICA. Princeton, N.J.: Princeton University Press, 1961. xxii, 433 p.

> Investigates family size preference and planning success, based on 1957 data from 1,165 white couples living in seven metropolitan areas; attitudes and psychological characteristics are taken into account rather than socioeconomic status.

368. _____. THE THIRD CHILD: A STUDY IN THE PREDICTION OF FERTILITY. Princeton, N.J.: Princeton University Press, 1963. xxiii, 293 p.

> Based on a 1960 survey of 905 respondents, relates number of children to family size preferences, influenced by active religious affiliation. Psychological variables, such as liking children and adjustment to marriage, appear unrelated to the number of children born.

369. _____. TOWARD THE END OF GROWTH; POPULATION IN AMERICA. Englewood Cliffs, N.J.: Prentice-Hall, 1973. ix, 177 p.

> Discusses recent trends in control of fertility and population growth in fourteen chapters.

370. Westoff, Leslie Aldridge, and Westoff, Charles F. FROM NOW TO ZERO: FERTILITY, CONTRACEPTION AND ABORTION IN AMERICA. Boston: Little, Brown and Co., 1971. xxi, 358 p.

> Different types of fertility control currently practiced by American couples. Bibliography.

371. Whelpton, Pascal K., et al. FERTILITY AND FAMILY PLANNING IN THE UNITED STATES. Princeton, N.J.: Princeton University Press, 1966. xxxiv, 443 p.

> Analysis of a sample of married white women eighteen to forty-four years old indicates general acceptance of planned parenthood.

F. MIGRATION

372. Bernard, William S., et al., eds. AMERICAN IMMIGRATION POLICY, A REAPPRAISAL. New York: Harper, 1950. xx, 341 p.

> A study sponsored by the National Committee on Immigration Policy which considers the effects of the quota system and National Origins Act.

373. Bogue, Donald J., et al. SUBREGIONAL MIGRATION IN THE UNITED STATES, 1935-40. Volume I: STREAMS OF MIGRATION BETWEEN REGIONS: A PILOT STUDY OF MIGRATION FLOWS BETWEEN ENVIRONMENTS. Oxford, Ohio: Scripps Foundation, Miami University, 1957. vi, 333 p.

374. _____. SUBREGIONAL MIGRATION IN THE UNITED STATES, 1935-40. Volume II: DIFFERENTIAL MIGRATION IN THE CORN AND COTTON BELTS. Oxford, Ohio: Scripps Foundation, Miami University, 1953. vi, 248 p.

> Both volumes compare significant characteristics of intrastate migrants to urban places with those of nonmigrants at the points of origin and destination.

375. Brody, Eugene B., ed. BEHAVIOR IN NEW ENVIRONMENTS: ADAPTATION OF MIGRANT POPULATIONS. Beverly Hills: Sage Publications, 1970. 479 p.

> Nineteen papers, originally presented at a 1968 conference on Migration and Behavioral Deviance in Puerto Rico, deal with such topics as rural migration from Appalachia and Kentucky and adaptation of Puerto Rican, Mexican-American, and Black migrants.

G. ECOLOGY

376. Burch, William R., Jr., et al. SOCIAL BEHAVIOR, NATURAL RESOURCES, AND THE ENVIRONMENT. New York: Harper & Row, Publishers, 1972. x, 374 p.

Fifteen selections by sociologists explore the relationship between the social order and natural resources.

377. Campbell, Rex R., and Wade, Jerry L., eds. SOCIETY AND EN-VIRONMENT: THE COMING COLLISION. Boston: Allyn & Bacon, 1972. vii, 376 p.

    Selected readings and original essays introduce the social aspects of the environmental crisis.

378. Klausner, Samuel Z. ON MAN IN HIS ENVIRONMENT. San Francisco: Jossey-Bass, 1971. xiv, 224 p.

    Points to the lack of sociological information on environment. Surveys the work of demographers and human ecologists. Discusses air pollution, noise pollution, outdoor recreation, and environmental research, education, and management.

379. Moos, Rudolf H., and Insel, Paul M., eds. ISSUES IN SOCIAL ECOL-OGY: HUMAN MILIEU. Palo Alto, Calif.: National Press Books, 1974. 616 p.

    Forty-nine essays by fifty-nine contributors (psychologists, sociologists, and authors from other disciplines) discuss man's relationship to his social and physical environment.

Chapter 6

REGIONAL AND RURAL STUDIES

Chapter 6

REGIONAL AND RURAL STUDIES

A. REFERENCE WORKS AND BIBLIOGRAPHIES

380. Bertrand, Alvin L., ed. SEVENTY YEARS OF RURAL SOCIOLOGY IN THE UNITED STATES: ABSTRACTS OF ARTICLES AND BULLETIN BIBLIOGRAPHY. New York: Essay Press, 1972. viii, 428 p.

   Part one consists of abstracts of 1,869 articles on rural soci-ology from American scholarly journals. Part two is a bibli-ography of 4,492 monographs, reports, and bulletins, many of them issued by regional Agricultural Experiment Stations and originally listed in RURAL SOCIOLOGY from 1936 to 1970 (see item 129).

381. Fodell, Beverly. CESAR CHAVEZ AND THE UNITED FARM WORKERS: A SELECTIVE BIBLIOGRAPHY. Detroit: Wayne State University Press, 1974. 103 p.

   Annotated entries emphasize current organizing efforts of the United Farm Workers and include references to general materi-als on California agriculture and Chicano life.

382. Rubano, Judith. CULTURE AND BEHAVIOR IN HAWAII; AN ANNO-TATED BIBLIOGRAPHY. Honolulu: University Press of Hawaii, 1971. xii, 147 p.

383. Sorokin, Pitirim A., et al. A SYSTEMATIC SOURCEBOOK IN RURAL SOCIOLOGY. 3 vols. Minneapolis: University of Minnesota Press, 1930-32.

   Encyclopedic and international in scope.

B. RURAL SOCIOLOGY

384. Beal, George M., et al., eds. SOCIOLOGICAL PERSPECTIVES OF

DOMESTIC DEVELOPMENT. Ames: Iowa State University Press, 1971. 309 p.

Thirteen papers presented at a conference on the problems of planned change, jointly sponsored by the Iowa State University Center for Agricultural and Economic Development and the Rural Sociological Society.

385. Brunner, Edmund de Schweinitz. THE GROWTH OF A SCIENCE; A HALF-CENTURY OF RURAL SOCIOLOGICAL RESEARCH IN THE UNITED STATES. New York: Harper & Row, Publishers, 1957. x, 171 p.

386. Copp, James H., ed. OUR CHANGING RURAL SOCIETY: PERSPECTIVES AND TRENDS. Ames: Iowa State University Press, 1964. x, 354 p.

Ten contributions from the 1961 annual meeting of the Rural Sociological Society at Iowa State University, Ames.

387. Kolb, John H. EMERGING RURAL COMMUNITIES; GROUP RELATIONS IN RURAL SOCIETY: A REVIEW OF WISCONSIN RESEARCH IN ACTION. Madison: University of Wisconsin Press, 1959. ix, 212 p.

Review of rural research and social action programs, mainly undertaken at the University of Wisconsin since 1910.

388. Nelson, Lowry. AMERICAN FARM LIFE. Cambridge, Mass.: Harvard University Press, 1954. xii, 192 p.

An overview of mid-century farm life which stresses the interdependence and similarity of rural and urban populations, centralization of services, and technological advancement.

389. _____. RURAL SOCIOLOGY: ITS ORIGIN AND GROWTH IN THE UNITED STATES. Minneapolis: University of Minnesota Press, 1969. viii, 221 p.

390. Rohrer, Wayne C., and Douglas, Louis H. THE AGRARIAN TRANSITION IN AMERICA: DUALISM AND CHANGE. Indianapolis: Bobbs-Merrill, 1969. 197 p.

The impact of agrarianism on American life over two centuries and its influence on agricultural legislation and governmental policies.

391. Slocum, Walter L. AGRICULTURAL SOCIOLOGY; A STUDY OF SOCIOLOGICAL ASPECTS OF AMERICAN FARM LIFE. New York: Harper & Row, Publishers, 1962. 532 p.

Discussion of rural-urban relations with emphasis on agriculture as an occupation, focusing on the 9 percent of the population living on farms.

392. Smith, T. Lynn, and Zopf, Paul E., Jr. PRINCIPLES OF INDUCTIVE RURAL SOCIOLOGY. Philadelphia: F. A. Davis, 1970. 558 p. Bibliography pp. 501–37.

393. Taylor, Lee, and Jones, Arthur R., Jr. RURAL LIFE AND URBANIZED SOCIETY. New York: Oxford University Press, 1964. xiv, 493 p.

   Interpretation of rural life in America centered around the concept of urbanized social organization.

394. Youmans, E. Grant, ed. OLDER RURAL AMERICANS; A SOCIOLOGICAL PERSPECTIVE. Lexington: University of Kentucky Press, 1967. x, 321 p.

   Description of various aspects of rural life, especially work roles, family, population, economic status, health conditions, and housing.

C. RURAL COMMUNITIES

395. Gallaher, Art, Jr. PLAINVILLE FIFTEEN YEARS LATER. New York: Columbia University Press, 1961. xvi, 301 p.

   Follow-up study of a rural community in Mississippi first studied by "James West" in 1945 in PLAINVILLE, U.S.A. (see item 400).

396. Martindale, Don [Albert], and Hanson, R. G. SMALL TOWN AND THE NATION: THE CONFLICT OF LOCAL AND TRANSLOCAL FORCES. Westport, Conn.: Greenwood, 1969. 211 p.

   Community study of relationship between small midwestern town and mass society. Focus on tensions between intra- and extra-community forces in Benson, Minnesota.

397. Matthews, Elmora M. NEIGHBOR AND KIN; LIFE IN A TENNESSEE RIDGE COMMUNITY. Nashville, Tenn.: Vanderbilt University Press, 1966. xxx, 178 p.

   A descriptive analysis of a rural community of middle Tennessee hill people.

398. Nelson, Lowry. THE MINNESOTA COMMUNITY: COUNTRY AND TOWN IN TRANSITION. Minneapolis: University of Minnesota Press, 1960. 175 p.

Provides a summation of twenty-one years of research in rural sociology, focusing on social change in Minnesota.

399. Vidich, Arthur J., and Bensman, Joseph. SMALL TOWN IN MASS SOCIETY; CLASS, POWER AND RELIGION IN A RURAL COMMUNITY. Rev. ed. Princeton, N.J.: Princeton University Press, 1968. 493 p.

Examines social relationships in an upstate New York community of 3,000, and the impact of the larger society experienced through mass media and remote organizations. Authors explore the conflict between prevailing social myths and social reality.

400. Withers, Carl [James West]. PLAINVILLE, U.S.A. New York: Columbia University Press, 1945. Reprint, 1961. xv, 238 p.

Study of a small rural Ozark community in Missouri through participant observation from 1939 to 1941.

D. APPALACHIA

401. Ford, Thomas R., ed. THE SOUTHERN APPALACHIAN REGION; A SURVEY. Lexington: University of Kentucky Press, 1962. xv, 308 p.

Collection of articles by twenty-one specialists who examine population, migration, and economic problems. A sample of 1466 households and interviews with 379 community leaders reveal continuing individualism and religious fundamentalism.

402. Kaplan, Berton H. BLUE RIDGE: AN APPALACHIAN COMMUNITY IN TRANSITION. Morgantown: West Virginia University, 1971. x, 171 p.

A monograph on the problems of modernization and rapid social change in southern Appalachia. Data collected through open-ended interviews. Bibliography.

403. Photiadis, John D., and Schwarzweller, Harry K., eds. CHANGE IN RURAL APPALACHIA; IMPLICATIONS FOR ACTION PROGRAMS. Philadelphia: University of Pennsylvania Press, 1970. 265 p.

Fifteen selections on the processes of change in contemporary Appalachia.

404. Schwarzweller, Harry K., et al. MOUNTAIN FAMILIES IN TRANSITION; A CASE STUDY OF APPALACHIAN MIGRATION. University Park: Pennsylvania State University Press, 1971. xx, 300 p.

Based on a small-scale social survey in a mining community of eastern Kentucky.

405. Walls, David S., and Stephenson, John B., eds. APPALACHIA IN
THE SIXTIES; DECADE OF REAWAKENING. Lexington: University of
Kentucky Press, 1972. xvi, 261 p.

Twenty-nine articles and essays on federal programs, the economics and politics of the coal industry, the problems con-
fronting migrants, and the life style of the mountaineers.

406. Weller, Jack E. YESTERDAY'S PEOPLE: LIFE IN CONTEMPORARY
APPALACHIA. Lexington: University of Kentucky Press, 1965. xx,
163 p.

Discussion centers on family, community, and the church.

E. THE SOUTH

407. Davis, Allison, et al. DEEP SOUTH; A SOCIAL ANTHROPOLOGICAL
STUDY OF CASTE AND CLASS. Chicago: University of Chicago
Press, 1941. xv, 558 p.

A study of the caste system in the life of Negroes and whites
in a community of more than 10,000 people.

408. Killian, Lewis M. WHITE SOUTHERNERS. New York: Random House,
1970. xiv, 171 p.

Development of the contemporary South, effects of slavery,
civil war, industrialization, and the rise of the southern myth
of persecution. Discussion of conformity to southern values of
marginal white southerners: Catholics, Yankees, and Jews.
Cultural distinctiveness of the South based on regional autonomy.

409. McKinney, John C., and Thompson, Edgar T., eds. THE SOUTH IN
CONTINUITY AND CHANGE. Durham, N.C.: Duke University Press,
1965. xii, 511 p.

Twenty-two essays sponsored by the Southern Sociological
Society and the Center for Southern Studies in the Social
Sciences and Humanities at Duke University.

410. Morland, John K. MILLWAYS OF KENT. Chapel Hill: University
of North Carolina Press, 1958. xxii, 291 p.

Black-white relations in a southern Piedmont community.

411. Odum, Howard W. SOUTHERN REGIONS OF THE UNITED STATES.
Chapel Hill: University of North Carolina Press, 1936. xi, 664 p.

A classic regional study which touches upon geography, population, and culture.

412. _____. THE WAY OF THE SOUTH; TOWARD THE REGIONAL BAL-
ANCE OF AMERICA. New York: Macmillan, 1947. vi, 350 p.

Background, heritage, and development of the South as a
distinct social area.

413. Reed, John Shelton. THE ENDURING SOUTH; SUBCULTURAL PERSIS-
TENCE IN MASS SOCIETY. Lexington, Mass.: D.C. Heath, Lexington Books, 1972. xxi, 135 p.

Analysis of nationwide survey data confirms the popular view
that white southern traits include attachment to locality,
region, and kin; the tendency to condone the private use of
force; and conventional fundamentalist religiosity.

414. Rubin, Morton. PLANTATION COUNTY. Chapel Hill: University
of North Carolina Press, 1951. xxiv, 235 p.

Describes the culture and social structure of a Deep South
county in which plantation agrarianism is changing under the
influence of agricultural technology and government programs,
and through the introduction of industry.

415. Silver, James W. MISSISSIPPI: THE CLOSED SOCIETY. Enl. ed.
New York: Harcourt, Brace & World, 1966. xxix, 375 p.

Discusses race relations in Mississippi, especially following
James Meredith's admission to the University of Mississippi
in 1962.

416. Sindler, Allan P., ed. CHANGE IN THE CONTEMPORARY SOUTH.
Durham, N.C.: Duke University Press, 1963. x, 247 p.

Papers on political and legal change in the post-war South
presented at a Duke University conference in 1962.

417. Thompson, Edgar T., ed. PERSPECTIVES ON THE SOUTH; AGENDA
FOR RESEARCH. Durham, N.C.: Duke University Press, 1967.
xiii, 231 p.

Collection of papers on change in the South presented at a
conference sponsored by the Center for Southern Studies in
the Social Sciences and Humanities at Duke University.

418. Vance, Rupert B., and Demerath, Nicholas J., eds. THE URBAN
SOUTH. Chapel Hill: University of North Carolina Press, 1954.
xii, 307 p.

Eighteen contributors to this symposium illustrate the nature
of urbanization and other changes.

419. Wirt, Frederick M. POLITICS OF SOUTHERN EQUALITY: LAW AND SOCIAL CHANGE IN A MISSISSIPPI COUNTY. Chicago: Aldine, 1970. 335 p.

   Study of the impact of the Civil Rights Acts of 1957 and 1965 on voting, education, and economic opportunity in Panola County.

F. OTHER REGIONS

420. Bourne, Dorothy D., and Bourne, James R. THIRTY YEARS OF CHANGE IN PUERTO RICO; A CASE STUDY OF TEN SELECTED RURAL AREAS. New York: Praeger, 1966. xxvi, 411 p.

   Study of change in ten communities previously surveyed in 1932.

421. Friedland, William H., and Nelkin, Dorothy. MIGRANT AGRICULTURAL WORKERS IN AMERICA'S NORTHEAST. New York: Holt, Rinehart and Winston, 1971. xix, 281 p.

422. Hansen, Niles M. LOCATION PREFERENCES, MIGRATION AND REGIONAL GROWTH: A STUDY OF THE SOUTH AND SOUTHWEST. New York: Praeger, 1973. xv, 186 p.

   Migration patterns of Blacks and whites in southwestern Mississippi, Indians in New Mexico, Mexican-Americans in southern Texas, and Appalachians in eastern Kentucky.

423. Landy, David. TROPICAL CHILDHOOD; CULTURAL TRANSMISSION AND LEARNING IN A RURAL PUERTO RICAN VILLAGE. Chapel Hill: University of North Carolina Press, 1959. xii, 291 p.

   A study of child training which compares Puerto Rican and New England practices.

424. Lind, Andrew W. HAWAII'S PEOPLE. 3rd ed. Honolulu: University of Hawaii Press, 1967. 121 p.

   Hawaiian experience in ethnic and race relations and its reevaluation in the mid-sixties.

425. Padfield, Harland, and Martin, William E. FARMERS, WORKERS AND MACHINES; TECHNOLOGICAL AND SOCIAL CHANGE IN FARM INDUSTRIES OF ARIZONA. Tucson: University of Arizona Press, 1965. xiv, 325 p. Bibliography pp. 316-22.

426. Rushing, William A. CLASS, CULTURE, AND ALIENATION: A

STUDY OF FARMERS AND FARM WORKERS. Lexington, Mass.: D. C. Heath, 1972. xvii, 190 p.

Study of opportunity and deprivation among middle-class farmers and lower-class farm workers in Washington.

427. Steward, Julian H., et al. THE PEOPLE OF PUERTO RICO; A STUDY IN SOCIAL ANTHROPOLOGY. Urbana: University of Illinois Press, 1956. ix, 540 p.

History of Puerto Rican society and culture; field studies of local subcultures; and discussion of theory and methodology.

428. Tumin, Melvin M. SOCIAL CLASS AND SOCIAL CHANGE IN PUERTO RICO. Princeton, N.J.: Princeton University Press, 1961. xxvi, 549 p.

Study of changes in social stratification based on 999 four-hour interviews with a selected sample of heads of households. Education proved to be the most effective variable to determine the class position. The college educated are treated as the upper class which, however, is not the most powerful group.

Chapter 7

URBAN COMMUNITY

Chapter 7

URBAN COMMUNITY

A. REFERENCE WORKS AND BIBLIOGRAPHIES

429. Boyce, Burl N., and Turoff, Sidney. MINORITY GROUPS AND HOUS-
ING: A BIBLIOGRAPHY 1950-1970. Morristown, N.J.: General
Learning Press, 1972. 202 p.

430. Gutman, Robert. URBAN SOCIOLOGY; A BIBLIOGRAPHY. New
Brunswick, N.J.: Urban Studies Center, Rutgers - The State University,
1963. xiii, 44 p.

     Intended to aid doctoral candidates in urban sociology; lists
     books, essays, and articles published primarily from 1945
     through 1962.

431. Meyers, Jon K. BIBLIOGRAPHY OF THE URBAN CRISIS: THE BEHAV-
IORAL, PSYCHOLOGICAL AND SOCIOLOGICAL ASPECTS OF THE
URBAN CRISIS. Public Health Service Publication, no. 1948. Chevy
Chase, Md.: National Institute of Mental Health, 1969. 452 p.

     Lists 2,779 items, most published between 1954 and 1968.

432. Paulus, Virginia, ed. HOUSING: A BIBLIOGRAPHY, 1960-1972.
New York: AMS Press, 1974. 350 p.

433. United States Department of Housing and Urban Development, Library
and Information Division. DICTIONARY CATALOG OF THE UNITED
STATES DEPARTMENT OF HOUSING AND URBAN DEVELOPMENT,
LIBRARY AND INFORMATION DIVISION, WASHINGTON, D.C.
Boston: G. K. Hall, 1973. 19 vols. 14,956 p. First supplement,
1974. 2 vols.

     Much of the material listed was compiled through HUD-spon-
     sored studies. Includes the holdings of the libraries of the
     Federal Housing Administration, Public Housing Administration,
     and the Housing and Home Finance Agency, as well as more

than 12,000 comprehensive planning reports and model cities
reports.

434. Urban Institute. URBAN RESEARCH CENTERS DIRECTORY. Edited
by Grace M. Taher. 2nd ed. Washington, D.C.: 1971. 299 p.

B. COMMUNITY STUDIES

435. Goldstein, Sidney. PATTERNS OF MOBILITY, 1910-1950: THE
NORRISTOWN STUDY. Philadelphia: University of Pennsylvania
Press, 1958. xxii, 254 p.

This monograph uses city directories as a source of data about
age, sex, place of birth, and occupation. Relates high migration rate in and out of the town to the needs of the local
labor market.

436. Goldstein, Sidney, et al. THE NORRISTOWN STUDY: AN EXPERI-
MENT IN INTERDISCIPLINARY RESEARCH TRAINING. Philadelphia:
University of Pennsylvania Press, 1961. xxi, 366 p.

Papers supplementing the 1958 study of Norristown, an industrial town near Philadelphia (see item 435).

437. Hunter, Albert. SYMBOLIC COMMUNITIES: THE PERSISTENCE AND
CHANGE OF CHICAGO'S LOCAL COMMUNITIES. Chicago: University of Chicago Press, 1974. 288 p.

Traces the impact of urban growth on the symbolic-cultural,
the ecological, and the social organizational dimensions of
the Chicago communities first studied in the 1920s by Robert
Park and others.

438. Lantz, Herman R. A COMMUNITY IN SEARCH OF ITSELF; A CASE
HISTORY OF CAIRO, ILLINOIS. Carbondale: Southern Illinois
University Press, 1972. xiii, 235 p.

A case study of Black-white conflict in a declining community.

439. _____. PEOPLE OF COAL TOWN. New York: Columbia University
Press, 1958. Reprint. Carbondale: Southern Illinois University Press,
1971. xvii, 310 p.

Examines the effects of the economy on the lives of the lower
class and ethnic minorities in a southern Illinois mining town.

440. Lynd, Robert S., and Lynd, Helen H. MIDDLETOWN: A STUDY IN
AMERICAN CULTURE. New York: Harcourt, Brace, 1929. xii,
550 p.

Classic study of Muncie, Indiana, chosen as a representative American community.

441. _____. MIDDLETOWN IN TRANSITION; A STUDY IN CULTURAL CONFLICTS. New York: Harcourt, Brace, 1937. xviii, 604 p.

A follow-up study of Middletown after ten years.

442. Poston, Richard Waverly. SMALL TOWN RENAISSANCE; A STORY OF THE MONTANA STUDY. New York: Harper & Brothers, 1950. x, 231 p.

Local community self-study, guided by the University of Montana.

443. Stein, Maurice R. THE ECLIPSE OF COMMUNITY: AN INTERPRETA-TION OF AMERICAN STUDIES. Princeton, N.J.: Princeton University Press, 1960. 354 p.

Reviews major community studies as cases which show the workings of urbanization, industrialization, and bureaucratiza-tion.

444. Vidich, Arthur J., et al., eds. REFLECTIONS ON COMMUNITY STUDIES. New York: Wiley, 1964. xvi, 359 p.

Eleven essays raise questions of ethics, research strategy, and professional politics.

445. Warner, W. Lloyd, ed. YANKEE CITY. Abr. ed. New Haven: Yale University Press, 1963. xii, 432 p.

Abridged edition of the five volume series, prepared by Warner. (See items 446, 743, 860, 953, and 1326.)

446. Warner, W. Lloyd, and Lunt, Paul S. THE SOCIAL LIFE OF A MOD-ERN COMMUNITY. Yankee City Series, vol. 1. New Haven: Yale University Press, 1959. xx, 460 p.

The first study in the classic five volume series on Yankee City (Newburyport, Massachusetts).

C. URBAN GROWTH

447. Berry, Brian J. L., ed. CITY CLASSIFICATION HANDBOOK. New York: Wiley, 1972. 394 p.

Presents new methods for classifying cities and studying their economic, political, and social variations.

448. Caplow, Theodore, et al. THE URBAN AMBIENCE; A STUDY OF SAN JUAN, PUERTO RICO. Totowa, N.J.: Bedminster Press, 1964. 243 p.

Study of urbanization and cultural change in San Juan; six chapters discuss twenty-five neighborhoods.

449. Chapin, Francis Stuart, Jr., and Weiss, Shirley F., eds. URBAN GROWTH DYNAMICS IN A REGIONAL CLUSTER OF CITIES. New York: Wiley, 1962. x, 484 p.

Eighteen previously unpublished papers on urbanization and related problems in the Piedmont industrial crescent in North Carolina.

450. Duncan, Beverly, and Lieberson, Stanley. METROPOLIS AND REGION IN TRANSITION. Beverly Hills: Sage Publications, 1970. 300 p.

Observations on the growth of metropolitan centers and their current economic structure. Bibliography (pp. 291-94).

451. Duncan, Otis Dudley, et al. METROPOLIS AND REGION. Baltimore: The Johns Hopkins University Press, 1960. xviii, 587 p.

Discusses the function and location of modern American metropolises, and the regional relationship of fifty major cities classified as metropolitan centers, regional capitals, or manufacturing centers.

452. _____. SOCIAL CHANGE IN A METROPOLITAN COMMUNITY. New York: Russell Sage Foundation, 1973. 126 p.

Measures social change in the Detroit area since the 1950s by investigating division of responsibility in the family, racial attitudes of whites and Blacks, and participation in religious and social groups.

453. Hadden, Jeffrey K., and Borgatta, Edgar F. AMERICAN CITIES: THEIR SOCIAL CHARACTERISTICS. Chicago: Rand McNally, 1965. vi, 193 p.

A brief sourcebook which uses factor analysis to develop a typology of American cities.

454. Hughes, James W. URBAN INDICATORS, METROPOLITAN EVOLUTION, AND PUBLIC POLICY. Rutgers, N.J.: Transaction Books, 1973. 232 p.

Uses a factor-analysis model to determine residential social patterns of cities and a scheme of urban social indicators.

455. Keller, Suzanne. THE URBAN NEIGHBORHOOD: A SOCIOLOGICAL PERSPECTIVE. New York: Random House, 1968. xv, 201 p.

An examination of characteristics of neighborhoods of interest to urban planners.

456. McKeown, James E., and Tietze, Frederick E., eds. THE CHANGING METROPOLIS. 2nd rev. ed. Boston: Houghton Mifflin, 1971. viii, 200 p.

Discusses the problems, conflicts, and tensions of the contemporary American city.

457. Michelson, William H. MAN AND HIS URBAN ENVIRONMENT: A SOCIOLOGICAL APPROACH. Reading, Mass.: Addison-Wesley, 1970. xiii, 242 p.

Relates life styles, life cycles, social class, and values to urban environment and discusses the issue of environmental determinism. Bibliography (pp. 219-35).

458. Strauss, Anselm L., ed. THE AMERICAN CITY; A SOURCEBOOK OF URBAN IMAGERY. Chicago: Aldine, 1968. xiv, 530 p.

Ninety technical and literary articles on American cities which reflect the responses of journalists, clergymen, planners, politicians, and social scientists; written by American and foreign observers.

459. Vernon, Raymond. METROPOLIS 1985; AN INTERPRETATION OF THE FINDINGS OF THE N.Y. METROPOLITAN REGION STUDY. Cambridge, Mass.: Harvard University Press, 1960. xiii, 252 p.

Final ninth volume of the New York Metropolitan Region Study concludes that the twenty-two-county region is expected to add about 8.6 million residents between 1955 and 1985.

D. URBAN SOCIAL STRUCTURE

460. Beshers, James M. URBAN SOCIAL STRUCTURE. New York: Free Press of Glencoe, 1962. 207 p.

Residential patterns in American cities are explained by race and ethnicity and, in more recent times, by social class.

461. Coleman, Richard P. SOCIAL STATUS IN THE CITY. San Francisco: Jossey-Bass, 1971. viv, 320 p.

Field study of Kansas City in the early 1950s utilizes a multidimensional Index of Urban Status similar to W. L. Warner's Index of Status Characteristics.

462. Greer, Scott A. THE EMERGING CITY; MYTH AND REALITY. New York: Free Press of Glencoe, 1962. 232 p.

Author examines images of the city, stresses ties with larger society, and favors urban decentralization.

463. Laumann, Edward O. BONDS OF PLURALISM: THE FORM AND SUBSTANCE OF URBAN SOCIAL NETWORKS. New York: Wiley, 1973. xi, 326 p.

Discusses ethnic, religious, and socioeconomic factors in social participation in the Detroit metropolitan area.

464. Schnore, Leo. F. CLASS AND RACE IN CITIES AND SUBURBS. Chicago: Markham, 1972. 106 p.

Patterns and results of inter- and intra-metropolitan migration trends; study of race and ethnicity, social class, and type of family as factors in urban migration.

E. GHETTO AND SLUM

465. Clark, Kenneth B. DARK GHETTO; DILEMMAS OF SOCIAL POWER. New York: Harper & Row, Publishers, 1965. xxix, 251 p.

A social psychological interpretation of basic data presented in the 620-page 1964 report of the Harlem Youth Opportunities Unlimited (HARYOU) project.

466. Forman, Robert E. BLACK GHETTOS, WHITE GHETTOS AND SLUMS. Englewood Cliffs, N.J.: Prentice-Hall, 1971. vii, 184 p.

Housing problems and the question of integration or segregation of racial and ethnic groups, especially in the Northeast.

467. Lewis, Oscar. LA VIDA: A PUERTO RICAN FAMILY IN THE CULTURE OF POVERTY - SAN JUAN AND NEW YORK. New York: Random House, 1966. lix, 669 p.

A study, based on taped interviews, of a lower class Puerto Rican family in the industrial system which breeds the culture of poverty.

468. _____. A STUDY OF SLUM CULTURE: BACKGROUNDS FOR LA VIDA. New York: Random House, 1968. xiv, 240 p.

Contains 1960 census data on urban slums in Puerto Rico; answers to questionnaires and interviews in San Juan and New York provide material to illustrate Lewis' theory of a culture of poverty.

469. Liebow, Elliot. TALLY'S CORNER; A STUDY OF NEGRO STREET-CORNER MEN. Boston: Little, Brown and Co., 1967. xvii, 260 p.

Field study in a Washington, D.C., ghetto, done in the early 1960s.

470. McCord, William, et al. LIFE STYLES IN THE BLACK GHETTO. New York: W. W. Norton, 1969. 334 p.

Based on interviews with Blacks in Houston, Los Angeles, Oakland, San Francisco, Detroit, Newark, and Orangeburg.

471. Suttles, Gerald D. THE SOCIAL ORDER OF THE SLUM; ETHNICITY AND TERRITORY IN THE INNER CITY. Chicago: University of Chicago Press, 1968. xxii, 243 p.

A three-year participant observation study of a Chicago slum; describes the search by slum residents for a moral order, when the wider society cannot provide it.

472. Tucker, Sterling. BEYOND THE BURNING: LIFE AND DEATH OF THE GHETTO. New York: Association Press, 1968. 160 p.

An executive director of the Urban League of Washington, D.C., the author proposes the elimination of the ghetto by placing its control in the hands of its residents.

473. Whyte, William Foote. STREET CORNER SOCIETY; THE SOCIAL STRUC-TURE OF AN ITALIAN SLUM. Enl. ed. Chicago: University of Chicago Press, 1955. xxii, 366 p.

A classic study based on three and one-half years of participant observation, first published in 1943.

F. HOUSING AND SEGREGATION

474. Abrams, Charles. FORBIDDEN NEIGHBORS; A STUDY OF PREJUDICE IN HOUSING. New York: Harper & Row, Publishers, 1955. 404 p.

Deals with segregation and discrimination in housing, with major focus on the role of the government in the housing field.

475. Duncan, Beverly, and Hauser, Philip M. HOUSING A METROPOLIS--CHICAGO. Glencoe, Ill.: Free Press, 1960. xxii, 278 p.

Analysis of 1956 statistics of housing differences between
lower and higher income, white and nonwhite, and younger
and older families in Chicago and other urban areas.

476. Duncan, Otis Dudley, and Duncan, Beverly. THE NEGRO POPULATION
OF CHICAGO: A STUDY OF RESIDENTIAL SUCCESSION. Chicago:
University of Chicago Press, 1957. xxiv, 367 p.

Analysis of Negro migration into Chicago especially between
1940 and 1950.

477. Glazer, Nathan, and McEntire, Davis, eds. STUDIES IN HOUSING
AND MINORITY GROUPS. Special Research Report to the Commission
on Race and Housing. Berkeley: University of California Press, 1960.
xvii, 228 p.

Seven studies of housing opportunities for ethnic minorities in
nine cities.

478. Grier, Eunice, and Grier, George. PRIVATELY DEVELOPED INTER-
RACIAL HOUSING: AN ANALYSIS OF EXPERIENCE. Special Research
Report to the Commission on Race and Housing. Berkeley: University
of California Press, 1960. x, 264 p.

A study of 8,000 integrated housing units; problems arose from
local government opposition and financing, rather than from
interracial living.

479. Hawley, Amos H., and Rock, Vincent P., eds. SEGREGATION IN
RESIDENTIAL AREAS: PAPERS ON RACIAL AND SOCIOECONOMIC
FACTORS IN CHOICE OF HOUSING. Washington, D. C.: National
Academy of Sciences, 1973. xi, 235 p.

Papers originally prepared for the Social Science Panel brought
together by the Division of Behavioral Sciences of the National
Research Council. Bibliography.

480. Helper, Rose. RACIAL POLICIES AND PRACTICES OF REAL ESTATE
BROKERS. Minneapolis: University of Minnesota Press, 1969. xiv,
387 p.

A 1958 study and 1964-65 follow-up of practices and ideology
of real estate brokers in Chicago and other cities. Bibliography.

481. Laurenti, Luigi. PROPERTY VALUES AND RACE; STUDIES IN SEVEN
CITIES. Special Research Report to the Commission on Race and Housing. Berkeley: University of California Press, 1960. xix, 256 p.

482. Lieberson, Stanley. ETHNIC PATTERNS IN AMERICAN CITIES. New
York: Free Press of Glencoe, 1963. xv, 230 p.

A study of ethnic segregation in ten American cities for ten
ethnic groups, as revealed by data of 1910, 1920, 1930, and
1950.

483. McEntire, Davis. RESIDENCE AND RACE; FINAL AND COMPREHEN-
SIVE REPORT TO THE COMMISSION ON RACE AND HOUSING.
Berkeley: University of California Press, 1960. xxii, 409 p.

Final volume in a series of studies on minority housing and
segregation. Bibliography includes an annotated list of the
reports made for the Commission.

484. Moore, William F., Jr. THE VERTICAL GHETTO; EVERYDAY LIFE
IN AN URBAN PROJECT. New York: Random House, 1969. xix,
265 p.

Describes day-to-day activities in a public housing project and
discusses characteristics of the tenants.

485. Northwood, Lawrence K., and Barth, Ernest A. T. URBAN DESEGRE-
GATION; NEGRO PIONEERS AND THEIR WHITE NEIGHBORS. Seattle:
Washington University Press, 1965. xv, 131 p.

A study of fifteen black migrations into all-white neighborhoods
in Seattle, with recommendations for social action such as a
fair housing law and nonprofit open house-listing services.

486. Rapkin, Chester, and Grigsby, William G. THE DEMAND FOR HOUS-
ING IN RACIALLY MIXED AREAS; A STUDY OF THE NATURE OF
NEIGHBORHOOD CHANGE. Special Research Report to the Commission
on Race and Housing and the Philadelphia Redevelopment Authority.
Berkeley: University of California Press, 1960. xx, 177 p.

Research in Philadelphia in four areas with varying housing
qualities and in different stages of racial transition.

487. Sutker, Solomon, and Sutker, Sara Smith, eds. RACIAL TRANSITION
IN THE INNER SUBURB: STUDIES OF THE ST. LOUIS AREA. New
York: Praeger, 1974. 192 p.

Describes racial transition in two inner suburbs of St. Louis,
which did not result in either a deterioration of the neighborhood or in the lowering of property values.

488. Taeuber, Karl E., and Taeuber, Alma F. NEGROES IN CITIES; RESI-
DENTIAL SEGREGATION AND NEIGHBORHOOD CHANGE. Population Research and Training Center Monograph. Chicago: Aldine, 1965.
xvii, 284 p.

Analysis of urban residential segregation, with estimates of the
percentage of Negro households that would have to be relocated

to achieve unsegregated housing.

489. Williams, Robin M., Jr., et al. STRANGERS NEXT DOOR: ETHNIC
RELATIONS IN AMERICAN COMMUNITIES. Englewood Cliffs, N.J.:
Prentice-Hall, 1964. xiv, 434 p.

> Data gathered between 1948 and 1956 on the patterns of
> segregation and discrimination in a dozen cities across the
> United States.

G. URBAN PROBLEMS AND RENEWAL

490. Gans, Herbert J. PEOPLE AND PLANS; ESSAYS ON URBAN PROB-
LEMS AND SOLUTIONS. New York: Basic Books, 1968. xvii,
395 p.

> Twenty-nine essays, many concerned with the policy issues
> of social planning.

491. Greer, Scott [A.] URBAN RENEWAL AND AMERICAN CITIES; THE
DILEMMA OF DEMOCRATIC INTERVENTION. Indianapolis: Bobbs-
Merrill, 1966. xiii, 201 p.

> A concise description of the problems and programs associated
> with urban renewal.

492. Hadden, Jeffrey K., et al., eds. METROPOLIS IN CRISIS: SOCIAL
AND POLITICAL PERSPECTIVES. 2nd ed. Itasca, Ill.: F.E. Peacock,
1971. xxii, 622 p.

> A collection of forty-four articles which discuss dimensions of
> crisis, such as poverty, crime, transportation, air pollution,
> and problems of reorganization of government.

493. Rossi, Peter H., and Dentler, Robert A. THE POLITICS OF URBAN
RENEWAL: THE CHICAGO FINDINGS. New York: Free Press of
Glencoe, 1961. 308 p.

> Reactions of Blacks and whites to the plans for renewal by the
> University of Chicago of the Hyde Park-Kenwood neighborhood.

494. Rossi, Peter H., et al. THE ROOTS OF URBAN DISCONTENT: PUBLIC
POLICY, MUNICIPAL INSTITUTIONS AND THE GHETTO. New York:
Wiley, 1974. xxv, 499 p. (A publication of the Center for Metropoli-
tan Planning and Research, Johns Hopkins University.)

495. United States National Commission on Urban Problems. BUILDING THE
AMERICAN CITY: REPORT OF THE NATIONAL COMMISSION ON

URBAN PROBLEMS TO THE CONGRESS AND TO THE PRESIDENT OF
THE UNITED STATES. Washington, D.C.: Government Printing Office,
1968. 504 p.

This report, issued under the chairmanship of Paul H. Douglas,
collected information on slums, urban decay, and inadequate
housing, and made recommendations on urban policies.

496. Weaver, Robert C. DILEMMAS OF URBAN AMERICA. Cambridge,
Mass.: Harvard University Press, 1965. ix, 138 p.

Discussion of urbanization, new communities, urban renewal,
and problems of race.

497. Wilson, James Q., ed. URBAN RENEWAL; THE RECORD AND THE
CONTROVERSY. Cambridge, Mass.: The M.I.T. Press, 1966. xix,
683 p. (Publication of the Joint Center for Urban Studies of the Massachusetts Institute of Technology and Harvard University.)

Twenty-six contributors discuss the issues of renewal programs
which have involved nearly 1,600 projects in more than 770
communities in forty-four states.

498. Wolf, Eleanor P., and Lebeaux, Charles N. CHANGE AND RENEWAL
IN AN URBAN COMMUNITY; FIVE CASE STUDIES OF DETROIT. New
York: Praeger, 1969. xxxiii, 574 p.

Failure of the promise of urban renewal is documented from
research on middle and lower class residential areas, the process of relocation, and the effects on small business.

H. SUBURBS

499. Berger, Bennett M. WORKING CLASS SUBURB; A STUDY OF AUTO
WORKERS IN SUBURBIA. Berkeley: University of California Press,
1960. xiii, 143 p. (Publication of the Institute of Industrial Relations,
University of California.)

A study of working class life in a California suburb, based on
interviews with 100 relocated factory workers. Bibliography
(pp. 139-43).

500. Dobriner, William M. CLASS IN SUBURBIA. Englewood Cliffs, N.J.:
Prentice-Hall, 1963. 166 p.

Discusses suburban development in relation to class structure and
the changes in Levittown over a ten-year period. Bibliography.

501. _____, ed. THE SUBURBAN COMMUNITY. New York: Putnam,

1958. 416 p.

Articles discuss the metropolitan area, its fringes, and the suburbs.

502. Gans, Herbert J. THE LEVITTOWNERS; WAYS OF LIFE AND POLITICS IN A NEW SUBURBAN COMMUNITY. New York: Pantheon Books, 1967. xxix, 474 p.

Description of the world of suburbia based on participant observation, a mail questionnaire, and interviews.

503. Kramer, John, ed. NORTH AMERICAN SUBURBS: POLITICS, DIVERSITY, AND CHANGE. Berkeley: Glendessary, 1972. 330 p.

Nineteen articles organized under five headings: beyond the suburban myth; suburbia past and present; suburban diversity examined; politics and suburbia; and towards suburbia's future.

504. Martin, Walter T. THE RURAL-URBAN FRINGE; A STUDY OF ADJUSTMENT TO RESIDENCE LOCATION. Eugene: University of Oregon Press, 1953. v, 109 p.

505. Sobin, Dennis P. DYNAMICS OF COMMUNITY CHANGE; THE CASE OF LONG ISLAND'S DECLINING "GOLD COAST." Port Washington, N.Y.: Ira J. Friedman, 1968. xv, 205 p.

A multidimensional analysis of Long Island's North Shore and changes in the upper class setting over a period of the last seventy years.

506. Wood, Robert C. SUBURBIA; ITS PEOPLE AND THEIR POLITICS. Boston: Houghton Mifflin, 1959. 340 p.

Discusses the ideal of local government and the development of suburban neighborhoods--politically autonomous, but economically dependent.

I. URBAN ADMINISTRATION

507. Aron, Joan B. THE QUEST FOR REGIONAL COOPERATION; A STUDY OF THE NEW YORK METROPOLITAN REGIONAL COUNCIL. Berkeley: University of California Press, 1969. vi, 225 p.

A study of the Council, established in 1956 to coordinate public agencies in nearly 1,500 distinct political units spread over parts of three states.

508. Eldredge, Hanford Wentworth, ed. TAMING MEGALOPOLIS. Vol. 1:

WHAT IS AND WHAT COULD BE; vol. 2: HOW TO MANAGE AN URBANIZED WORLD. Garden City, N.Y.: Doubleday, Anchor, 1967. xv, 1166 p.

509. Greer, Scott A. GOVERNING THE METROPOLIS. New York: Wiley, 1962. 153 p.

Sketches the economic and ecological processes which transform the city into a metropolis. Bibliography.

510. _____. THE URBANE VIEW: LIFE AND POLITICS IN METROPOLITAN AMERICA. New York: Oxford University Press, 1972. 355 p.

511. Janowitz, Morris, et al. PUBLIC ADMINISTRATION AND THE PUBLIC-- PERSPECTIVES TOWARD GOVERNMENT IN A METROPOLITAN COMMU- NITY. Ann Arbor: Institute of Public Administration, Bureau of Govern- ment, University of Michigan, 1958. vii, 140 p.

512. Moynihan, Daniel Patrick, ed. TOWARD A NATIONAL URBAN POLICY. New York: Basic Books, 1970. xiv, 348 p.

J. TEXTS AND READERS

513. Bernard, Jessie. THE SOCIOLOGY OF COMMUNITY. Glenview, Ill.: Scott, Foresman, 1973. 216 p.

Discussion of classic models of community and their validity today, when technology is erasing physical community bound- aries. Selected readings on pp. 193-208.

514. Boskoff, Alvin. THE SOCIOLOGY OF URBAN REGIONS. 2nd ed. New York: Appleton-Century-Crofts, 1970. xvi, 389 p.

515. Burgess, Ernest W., and Bogue, Donald J., eds. CONTRIBUTIONS TO URBAN SOCIOLOGY. Chicago: University of Chicago Press, 1964. xi, 673 p.

Forty-four reports on urban research undertaken by Chicago sociologists over a forty year period.

516. Gutman, Robert, and Popenoe, David, eds. NEIGHBORHOOD, CITY AND METROPOLIS; AN INTEGRATED READER IN URBAN SOCIOLOGY. New York: Random House, 1970. xii, 942 p.

Sixty articles on urbanism in America and some other western societies. Bibliography.

517. Hawley, Amos H. URBAN SOCIETY; AN ECOLOGICAL APPROACH.
New York: Ronald Press, 1971. 348 p.

Development of urban organization and dependence of social
life upon transportation and communication; historical and
cross-national comparisons.

518. Lewis, Michael. URBAN AMERICA; INSTITUTIONS AND EXPERIENCE.
New York: Wiley, 1973. xi, 276 p.

Discusses urban discontent and minority relations. Annotated
bibliography (pp. 255-69).

519. Palen, J. John, and Flaming, Karl H., eds. URBAN AMERICA: CON-
FLICT AND CHANGE. New York: Holt, Rinehart and Winston, 1972.
xi, 430 p.

A collection of articles and essays on the evolution of American urban society. Discusses historical perspectives, urban
structures, life styles, and urban crisis. Bibliography.

520. Park, Robert, et al. THE CITY. Chicago: University of Chicago
Press, 1925. 239 p.

This classic study of the city was jointly authored by Park,
Ernest W. Burgess, and Roderick McKenzie. The bibliography
of the urban community (pp. 161-228) was prepared by Louis
Wirth.

521. Schnore, Leo F., ed. SOCIAL SCIENCE AND THE CITY: A SURVEY
OF URBAN RESEARCH. New York: Praeger, 1968. 335 p.

These essays first appeared as Part I of URBAN RESEARCH AND
POLICY PLANNING, edited by Leo F. Schnore and Henry
Fagin (Urban Affairs Annual Reviews, vol. 1. Beverly Hills,
Calif.: Sage Publications, 1967). They survey some of the
major urban studies conducted by social scientists since World
War II. Bibliography (pp. 303-30).

522. Short, James F., Jr., ed. THE SOCIAL FABRIC OF THE METROPOLIS;
CONTRIBUTIONS OF THE CHICAGO SCHOOL OF URBAN SOCIOLOGY.
Chicago: University of Chicago Press, 1971. xlvi, 320 p.

Discussion of the Chicago approach to urban sociology and a
collection of classic studies. Bibliography.

523. Sweetser, Frank L., ed. STUDIES IN AMERICAN URBAN SOCIETY.
New York: Thomas Y. Crowell Co., 1970. viii, 272 p.

Six analytic studies of American urban society and metropolitan
development.

524. Thomlinson, Ralph. URBAN STRUCTURE; THE SOCIAL AND SPATIAL CHARACTER OF CITIES. New York: Random House, 1969. xiii, 335 p.

Focus on urban ecology; selected readings on pp. 306-17.

525. Warren, Roland L. THE COMMUNITY IN AMERICA. 2nd ed. Chicago: Rand McNally, 1972. 424 p.

A systematic approach to the study of community.

526. _____, ed. PERSPECTIVES ON THE AMERICAN COMMUNITY, A BOOK OF READINGS. Chicago: Rand McNally, 1966. xii, 618 p.

Fifty-eight selections on such topics as planned community change and citizen participation.

* * *

See also Chapter 9, Section C; Chapter 19, Section G; and Chapter 20, Section E.

Chapter 8

BLACK AMERICA

Chapter 8

BLACK AMERICA

A. REFERENCE WORKS AND BIBLIOGRAPHIES

527. Chicago Public Library. George Cleveland Hall Branch. Vivian Harsh Collection of Afro-American History and Literature. THE CHICAGO AFRO-AMERICAN UNION ANALYTIC CATALOG. 5 vols. Boston: G. K. Hall, 1972. 13,384 p.

> An index to materials on the Afro-American in the principal libraries of Chicago.

528. Davis, John P., ed. THE AMERICAN NEGRO REFERENCE BOOK. 2 vols. Yonkers, N.Y.: Educational Heritage, 1966. 886 p. Bibliography.

529. THE EBONY HANDBOOK. Rev. ed. Compiled by the editors of EBONY and Doris E. Saunders. Chicago: Johnson, 1974. 553 p.

> An earlier edition was compiled by the editors of EBONY and published as THE NEGRO HANDBOOK (Chicago: Johnson, 1966).

530. McPherson, James M., et al. BLACKS IN AMERICA; BIBLIOGRAPHICAL ESSAYS. Garden City, N.Y.: Doubleday, 1971. 430 p.

531. Miller, Elizabeth, and Fisher, Mary L., eds. THE NEGRO IN AMERICA: A BIBLIOGRAPHY. Rev. ed. Cambridge, Mass.: Harvard University Press, 1970. xx, 351 p.

532. New York Public Library. DICTIONARY CATALOG OF THE SCHOMBURG COLLECTION OF NEGRO LITERATURE AND HISTORY. 9 vols. Boston: G. K. Hall, 1962. 8,474 p.

> Followed by supplements in 1967 (2 vols., 1,769 p.) and 1972 (2 vols., 2,694 p.).

533. Porter, Dorothy B. THE NEGRO IN THE UNITED STATES: A SELECTED BIBLIOGRAPHY. Washington, D.C.: Library of Congress, sold by Government Printing Office, 1970. 313 p.

534. Thompson, Edgar, and Thompson, Alma Macy. RACE AND REGION, A DESCRIPTIVE BIBLIOGRAPHY COMPILED WITH SPECIAL REFERENCE TO THE RELATIONS BETWEEN WHITES AND NEGROES IN THE UNITED STATES. Chapel Hill: University of North Carolina Press, 1949. Reprint. New York: Kraus Reprint, 1971. 194 p.

B. BLACK AMERICANS

535. Blackwell, James E., and Janowitz, Morris, eds. BLACK SOCIOLO-GISTS: HISTORICAL AND CONTEMPORARY PERSPECTIVES. Heritage of Sociology Series. Chicago: University of Chicago Press, 1974. 384 p.

The outcome of a national conference convened in Chicago in 1972 by the Caucus of Black Sociologists.

536. Bracey, John H., Jr., et al., eds. THE BLACK SOCIOLOGISTS: THE FIRST HALF CENTURY. Belmont, Calif.: Wadsworth, 1971. 186 p.

Excerpts from representative works of Black sociologists such as W.E.B. Du Bois, G.E. Haynes, Charles Johnson, E. Frank-lin Frazier, St. Clair Drake, and Horace Cayton.

537. Broom, Leonard, and Glenn, Norval D. TRANSFORMATION OF THE NEGRO AMERICAN. New York: Harper & Row, Publishers, 1965. xi, 207 p.

A concise review of main trends in Black culture from the Civil War to Black activism of the 1960s. Bibliography.

538. DuBois, William E. Burghardt. THE PHILADELPHIA NEGRO. 1899. Reprint. Millwood, N.Y.: Kraus-Thompson, 1973. 520 p. Bibliography.

539. _____. THE SOULS OF BLACK FOLK. 1903. Reprint. Millwood, N.Y.: Kraus-Thompson, 1973. 264 p.

Early studies by the noted Black scholar.

540. Frazier, E. Franklin. THE NEGRO IN THE UNITED STATES. Rev. ed. New York: Macmillan, 1957. xxxiii, 769 p.

History, principal social institutions, and the Negro protest movement. Bibliography.

541. Lyman, Stanford M. THE BLACK AMERICAN IN SOCIOLOGICAL THOUGHT: THE FAILURE OF SOCIAL SCIENCE. New Perspectives on Black America. New York: Putnam, 1972. 220 p.

Traces the ways in which Black Americans have been viewed in the nineteenth and twentieth centuries and argues that the sociology of Black people has not begun. Bibliography (pp. 185–208).

542. Myrdal, Gunnar. AN AMERICAN DILEMMA; THE NEGRO PROBLEM AND MODERN DEMOCRACY. 2 vols. New York: Harper & Brothers, 1944. lix, 1483 p.

The most comprehensive study of the Negro in the United States. Bibliography (pp. 1144–80).

543. Pettigrew, Thomas F. A PROFILE OF THE NEGRO AMERICAN. Princeton, N.J.: Van Nostrand, 1964. 250 p.

Review of literature on the personality of Black Americans, racial differences, and the protest movement; 565-item bibliography (pp. 202–35).

544. Pinkney, Alphonso. BLACK AMERICANS. Ethnic Groups in American Life Series. Englewood Cliffs, N.J.: Prentice-Hall, 1969. xvii, 226 p.

The development of the Black community from the seventeenth to the mid-twentieth century; extensive bibliography.

545. Rose, Arnold Marshall. THE NEGRO IN AMERICA. New York: Harper & Brothers, 1948. 325 p.

A condensed version of Gunnar Myrdal's AN AMERICAN DILEMMA; THE NEGRO PROBLEM AND MODERN DEMOCRACY (see item 542). Bibliography.

546. Thompson, Daniel C. SOCIOLOGY OF THE BLACK EXPERIENCE. Westport, Conn.: Greenwood, 1974. x, 261 p. Bibliography pp. 245–54.

547. Yinger, J. Milton. A MINORITY GROUP IN AMERICAN SOCIETY. New York: McGraw-Hill, [c.1965]. xii, 143 p.

Study of the Negro minority as a social problem deriving from three patterns of stratification: caste, minority-majority, and social class systems.

C. BLACK COMMUNITIES

548. Burgess, M. Elaine. NEGRO LEADERSHIP IN A SOUTHERN CITY. Chapel Hill: University of North Carolina Press, 1962. 231 p.

    Community power analysis of a middle-sized southern city. Bibliography.

549. Carter, Wilmoth A. THE URBAN NEGRO IN THE SOUTH. New York: Vantage Press, 1962. 272 p.

    Based on 466 interviews conducted in the central Negro business street in Raleigh, North Carolina. Bibliography.

550. Drake, St. Clair, and Cayton, Horace R. BLACK METROPOLIS: A STUDY OF NEGRO LIFE IN A NORTHERN CITY. New York: Harcourt, Brace & World, 1945. 809 p. Rev. and enl. ed. 2 vols. New York: Harper & Row, Publishers, 1962. Vol. 1, 377 p.; vol. 2, 390 p.

    Classic study of the Black community in Chicago.

551. Hesslink, George K. BLACK NEIGHBORS; NEGROES IN A NORTHERN RURAL COMMUNITY. 2nd ed. Indianapolis: Bobbs-Merrill, 1973. xix, 325 p.

    Study of a stable biracial community in southwestern Michigan, where separation among three status groups persists. Bibliography.

552. Lee, Frank F. NEGRO AND WHITE IN CONNECTICUT TOWN. New York: Bookman Associates, 1961. 207 p.

    Patterns of race relations in an industrial town of 10,000 people in the early 1950s.

553. Lewis, Hylan. BLACKWAYS OF KENT. Field Studies in the Modern Culture of the South, vol. 2. Chapel Hill: University of North Carolina Press, 1955. 337 p.

    Analysis of the culture of Blacks in Kent, a town of 4,000 in the Piedmont south.

554. Thompson, Daniel C. THE NEGRO LEADERSHIP CLASS. Englewood Cliffs, N.J.: Prentice-Hall, 1963. 174 p.

    Change in New Orleans Negro leadership between 1940 and 1960.

555. Warren, Donald I. BLACK NEIGHBORHOODS: AN ASSESSMENT OF

COMMUNITY POWER. Ann Arbor: University of Michigan Press, 1974. 232 p.

556. Williams, Joyce E. BLACK COMMUNITY CONTROL: A STUDY OF TRANSITION IN A TEXAS GHETTO. Praeger Special Studies. New York: Praeger, 1973. 277 p.

Patterns of leadership in the Como Black community of Fort Worth, Texas.

D. SOCIAL CLASS AND OCCUPATIONS

557. Burkey, Richard M. RACIAL DISCRIMINATION AND PUBLIC POLICY IN THE UNITED STATES. Lexington, Mass.: D.C. Heath, Lexington Books, 1971. xx, 144 p.

Examines the effectiveness of governmental policy on race relations.

558. Cousens, Frances R. PUBLIC CIVIL RIGHTS AGENCIES AND FAIR EMPLOYMENT; PROMISE VS. PERFORMANCE. Praeger Special Studies. New York: Praeger, 1969. xviii, 162 p.

Data from ten states and District of Columbia and 800 interviews with executives of 623 companies reveal racial discrimination in all industries.

559. Edwards, G. Franklin. THE NEGRO PROFESSIONAL CLASS. Glencoe, Ill.: Free Press, 1959. 224 p.

Study of background and mobility of Black male professionals--physicians, lawyers, dentists, and college teachers--in Washington, D.C.

560. Ferman, Louis A. THE NEGRO AND EQUAL EMPLOYMENT OPPORTUNITIES; A REVIEW OF MANAGEMENT EXPERIENCES IN TWENTY COMPANIES. Praeger Special Studies in U.S. Economic and Social Development. New York: Praeger, 1968. xv, 195 p.

Universality of discrimination is reflected in placement, training, and promotion.

561. Ferman, Louis A., et al., eds. NEGROES AND JOBS: A BOOK OF READINGS. Ann Arbor: University of Michigan Press, 1968. 591 p.

Thirty-two selections, all published after 1960, by sociologists, economists, and civil rights leaders. Bibliography.

562. Frazier, E. Franklin. BLACK BOURGEOISIE. Glencoe, Ill.: Free Press, [c.1957]. 264 p.

> Discusses the objective situation and the social and psychological implications of the status of the American Negro middle class. Bibliography.

563. Kronus, Sidney. THE BLACK MIDDLE CLASS. Columbus: Charles E. Merrill, 1971. 182 p.

> Study of sixty white collar and twenty blue collar Black men in Chicago's South Side. Bibliography.

564. Ross, Arthur M., and Hill, Herbert, eds. EMPLOYMENT, RACE AND POVERTY. New York: Harcourt, Brace & World, 1967. ix, 598 p.

> Twenty articles on the status of Black workers between 1865 and 1965.

565. Ross, Jack C., and Wheeler, Raymond H. BLACK BELONGING; A STUDY OF THE SOCIAL CORRELATES OF WORK RELATIONS AMONG NEGROES. Westport, Conn.: Greenwood, 1971. 292 p.

> Study of the relationship between occupations and membership in voluntary associations. Bibliography.

566. Willhelm, Sidney M. WHO NEEDS THE NEGRO? Cambridge, Mass.: Schenkman, 1970. 266 p.

> Black rebellion of the 1960s is related to automation, which threatens the existence of the Black population as a source of cheap labor. Bibliography.

E. FAMILY

567. Bernard, Jessie. MARRIAGE AND FAMILY AMONG NEGROES. Englewood Cliffs, N.J.: Prentice-Hall, 1966. xi, 160 p.

> The author distinguishes two general value orientations: the acculturated who accept, and the externally adapted who reject many values of the dominant society.

568. Billingsley, Andrew, with Billingsley, Amy Tate. BLACK FAMILIES IN WHITE AMERICA. Englewood Cliffs, N.J.: Prentice-Hall, 1968. v, 218 p.

> Study of the interdependence between the Black family and the institutions of white society.

569. Billingsley, Andrew, and Giovannoni, Jeanne M. CHILDREN OF THE

STORM: BLACK CHILDREN AND AMERICAN CHILD WELFARE. New
York: Harcourt Brace Jovanovich, 1972. xvii, 263 p.

Historical information and contemporary social analysis. Bibliography.

570. Frazier, E. Franklin. THE NEGRO FAMILY IN THE UNITED STATES.
Rev. and abr. ed. Chicago: University of Chicago Press, 1966.
372 p.

Classic study of the Negro family, demonstrating its capacity
to persist even under most unfavorable conditions. Bibliography.

571. Moynihan, Daniel Patrick. THE NEGRO FAMILY, THE CASE FOR
NATIONAL ACTION. Washington, D.C.: U.S. Department of
Labor, 1965. 78 p.

The original "Moynihan report," published by the Office of
Policy Planning and Research, U.S. Department of Labor in
March 1965. Reprinted in Rainwater and Yancey's THE
MOYNIHAN REPORT AND THE POLITICS OF CONTROVERSY
(see item 573).

572. Rainwater, Lee. BEHIND GHETTO WALLS; BLACK FAMILIES IN A
FEDERAL SLUM. Chicago: Aldine, 1970. xi, 446 p.

Detailed account of the personal and family life of some
10,000 children and adults living in the Pruitt-Igoe public
housing project in St. Louis. Bibliography (pp. 427-40).

573. Rainwater, Lee, and Yancey, William L. THE MOYNIHAN REPORT
AND THE POLITICS OF CONTROVERSY. Cambridge, Mass.: The
M.I.T. Press, 1967. 493 p.

Reprint of the full text of the report and discussion of the role
of social scientists in policy making.

574. Scanzoni, John H. THE BLACK FAMILY IN MODERN SOCIETY.
Boston: Allyn & Bacon, 1971. xi, 353 p.

Discussion of relationships in Black families following a generational model: parents, husband-wife, and socialization of
children. Data derived from interviews in 400 Black households in 1968.

575. Schulz, David A. COMING UP BLACK; PATTERNS OF GHETTO SO-
CIALIZATION. Englewood Cliffs, N.J.: Prentice-Hall, 1969. 209 p.

Detailed study of ten Black families, comprising 108 persons,
half of them headed by women, residents in the Pruitt-Igoe
public housing project in St. Louis; six page bibliography.

576. Staples, Robert, ed. THE BLACK FAMILY; ESSAYS AND STUDIES. Belmont, Calif.: Wadsworth, 1971. 393 p.

> Forty-three essays and six research reports by thirty-two authors, primarily on low income Black families. Bibliography.

577. Willie, Charles V., ed. THE FAMILY LIFE OF BLACK PEOPLE. Columbus: Charles E. Merrill, 1970. x, 341 p.

> Twenty-six studies by thirty-one social scientists, many based on U.S. census data, present Black family life as integrative and functional.

F. BLACK-WHITE ATTITUDES

578. Brink, William, and Harris, Louis. BLACK AND WHITE: A STUDY OF U.S. RACIAL ATTITUDES TODAY. New York: Simon and Schuster, 1967. 285 p.

> Updates the 1963 NEWSWEEK-sponsored survey (see item 579).

579. _____. THE NEGRO REVOLUTION IN AMERICA. New York: Simon and Schuster, 1964. 249 p.

> NEWSWEEK-sponsored 1963 survey of more than 1,200 Blacks and 1,200 whites.

580. Campbell, Angus. WHITE ATTITUDES TOWARD BLACK PEOPLE. Ann Arbor, Mich.: Institute for Social Research, 1971. viii, 177 p.

> Reports on several nationwide studies of racial attitudes between 1964 and 1970. Bibliography.

581. Goldman, Peter. REPORT FROM BLACK AMERICA. New York: Simon and Schuster, 1970. 282 p.

> Data based on a nationwide poll of Black Americans, carried out by NEWSWEEK to update its 1963 and 1966 studies of Black opinion. Bibliography.

582. Goodman, Mary Ellen. RACE AWARENESS IN YOUNG CHILDREN. Cambridge, Mass.: Addison-Wesley, 1952. viii, 280 p.

> Quotations from children and parents of white and Black families who shared three urban nursery schools.

583. Porter, Judith D.R. BLACK CHILD, WHITE CHILD; THE DEVELOPMENT OF RACIAL ATTITUDES. Cambridge, Mass.: Harvard University Press, 1971. xi, 278 p.

Study of racial attitudes of 359 three- to five-year old children who attended kindergarten and nursery schools in Boston in 1965.

584. Schwartz, Mildred A. TRENDS IN WHITE ATTITUDES TOWARD NE-GROES. National Opinion Research Center Report, no. 119. Chicago: University of Chicago, National Opinion Research Center, 1967. 134 p.

Uses data from surveys done between 1942 and 1965; ten from the National Opinion Research Center, one Roper, five Gallup.

G. RACISM AND RACIAL CRISIS

585. Allen, Robert L. BLACK AWAKENING IN CAPITALIST AMERICA: AN ANALYTIC HISTORY. Garden City, N.Y.: Doubleday, 1969. 251 p. Bibliography.

586. Blauner, Robert. RACIAL OPPRESSION IN AMERICA. New York: Harper & Row, Publishers, 1972. x, 309 p.

Discusses the persistence of racism in American life, racial conflict, and militancy of minority groups.

587. Bromley, David G., and Longino, Charles F., Jr., eds. WHITE RACISM AND BLACK AMERICANS. Cambridge, Mass.: Schenkman, 1972. xxiii, 662 p.

Thirty-five selections from over 1,000 essays and research reports chosen by faculty and students at the University of Virginia in a seminar on racism.

588. Dixon, Vernon J., and Foster, Badi G., eds. BEYOND BLACK OR WHITE; AN ALTERNATE AMERICA. Boston: Little, Brown and Co., 1971. xii, 141 p.

Eight essays on the present racial crisis.

589. Franklin, Raymond S., and Resnik, Solomon. THE POLITICAL ECONOMY OF RACISM. New York: Holt, Rinehart and Winston, 1973. vii, 279 p.

Explores the economic and political foundations of racism in America.

590. Goldschmid, Marcel L., ed. BLACK AMERICANS AND WHITE RACISM; THEORY AND RESEARCH. New York: Holt, Rinehart and Winston, 1970. 434 p.

Thirty articles, mostly by social psychologists, more than half reporting on sponsored research. Bibliography.

591. Killian, Lewis [M.], and Grigg, Charles. RACIAL CRISIS IN AMERI-
CA; LEADERSHIP IN CONFLICT. Englewood Cliffs, N.J.: Prentice-
Hall, 1964. xiii, 144 p.

    Analysis of racial tensions resulting from differential life con-
    ditions, divergent perspectives, and conflicting goals. Solu-
    tions will not be found in education, interracial organization,
    or Negro moderates and white liberals as agents of change.

592. Knowles, Louis L., and Prewitt, Kenneth. INSTITUTIONAL RACISM
IN AMERICA. Englewood Cliffs, N.J.: Prentice-Hall, 1970. xii,
180 p.

    Based on papers prepared for the Stanford chapter of the Uni-
    versity Christian Movement.

593. Masotti, Louis H., et al. A TIME TO BURN? AN EVALUATION OF
THE PRESENT CRISIS IN RACE RELATIONS. Chicago: Rand McNally,
1969. xii, 187 p.

    Argues that civil disorder has occurred mainly as a consequence
    of the questioning of legitimacy of authority by Black and
    white protest groups.

594. Pettigrew, Thomas F. RACIALLY SEPARATE OR TOGETHER? McGraw-
Hill Series in Sociology. New York: McGraw-Hill, 1971. 371 p.

    Comments and recommendations on race, police, housing,
    employment, and educational problems. Bibliography.

595. Willie, Charles V., et al., eds. RACISM AND MENTAL HEALTH;
ESSAYS. Contemporary Community Health Series. Pittsburgh: University of Pittsburgh Press, 1973. 604 p.

    Fifteen multidisciplinary essays on the effect of bigotry on the
    psychological health of Black and white Americans.

596. Wilson, William J. POWER, RACISM, AND PRIVILEGE; RACE RELA-
TIONS IN THEORETICAL AND SOCIOHISTORICAL PERSPECTIVES.
New York: Macmillan, 1973. ix, 224 p. Bibliography pp. 203-16.

H. BLACK ACTIVISM AND CONFLICT

597. Bracey, John H., Jr., et al., eds. BLACK NATIONALISM IN AMERI-
CA. American Heritage Series. Indianapolis: Bobbs-Merrill, 1970.
lxx, 568 p.

Selected documents trace the course of Black nationalism
from 1787 to 1968; an eight-page bibliography follows the
introductory essay.

598. Carmichael, Stokely, and Hamilton, Charles V. BLACK POWER; THE
POLITICS OF LIBERATION IN AMERICA. New York: Vintage Books,
[c.1967]. xii, 198 p.

Expresses the dilemmas of a minority too small to achieve self-
government. Bibliography.

599. Demerath, Nicholas J. III, et al. DYNAMICS OF IDEALISM; WHITE
ACTIVISTS IN A BLACK MOVEMENT. San Francisco: Jossey-Bass,
1971. xxiii, 228 p.

Traces over a four-year period the impact on white students of
their participation in a 1965 voter registration drive in Atlanta.

600. Foner, Philip S., ed. THE BLACK PANTHERS SPEAK. Philadelphia:
Lippincott, 1970. xxx, 274 p.

This collection includes the party platform and statements from
prominent members.

601. Geschwender, James A. BLACK REVOLT: THE CIVIL RIGHTS MOVE-
MENT, GHETTO UPRISINGS AND SEPARATISM. Englewood Cliffs,
N.J.: Prentice-Hall, 1971. xi, 483 p.

Collection of articles by social scientists who analyze Black
protest from different frames of reference, and who comment on
the shift from the nonviolence of the civil rights movement,
through the militance of Black power, to the violence of
ghetto insurrections.

602. Grimshaw, Allen D., ed. RACIAL VIOLENCE IN THE UNITED STATES.
Chicago: Aldine, 1969. 553 p.

An anthology of the history of Negro-white violence, its
causes, patterns, and meaning. Bibliography.

603. Hare, Nathan. THE BLACK ANGLO-SAXONS. New York: Marzani
and Munsell, 1965. 124 p.

Criticism of Black leadership for its collaboration with white
leadership and imitation of dominant values.

604. Helmreich, William B. THE BLACK CRUSADERS: A CASE STUDY OF
A BLACK MILITANT ORGANIZATION. New York: Harper & Row,
Publishers, 1973. x, 186 p.

A study of the organizational structure and beliefs of a militant group in existence from August 1968 to February 1969 by a white participant-observer.

605. Killian, Lewis M. THE IMPOSSIBLE REVOLUTION? BLACK POWER AND THE AMERICAN DREAM. New York: Random House, 1968. xvi, 198 p.

Traces attitudes among Black Americans from the civil rights phase of the early 1960s to the more recent militant Black power movements.

606. Marx, Gary T. PROTEST AND PREJUDICE: A STUDY OF BELIEF IN THE BLACK COMMUNITY. New York: Harper & Row, Publishers, 1967. xxxviii, 228 p.

Study of Negro beliefs about the civil rights struggle, from interviews done in 1964 by the National Opinion Research Center.

607. _____. RACIAL CONFLICT: TENSION AND CHANGE IN AMERICAN SOCIETY. Boston: Little, Brown and Co., 1971. v, 489 p.

Text and reader with fifty-four selections.

I. ANTHOLOGIES

608. Endo, Russell K., and Strawbridge, William, eds. PERSPECTIVES ON BLACK AMERICA. Englewood Cliffs, N.J.: Prentice-Hall, 1970. 403 p. Bibliography.

609. Epps, Edgar G., ed. RACE RELATIONS: CURRENT PERSPECTIVES. Cambridge, Mass.: Winthrop Publishers, 1973. xi, 383 p.

610. Fisher, Sethard, ed. POWER AND THE BLACK COMMUNITY: A READER ON RACIAL SUBORDINATION IN THE UNITED STATES. New York: Knopf, 1970. 468 p.

Uses historical and contemporary works to show that Black adaptation to American life is essentially different from that of other ethnic groups.

611. Goldstein, Rhoda L., ed. BLACK LIFE AND CULTURE IN THE UNITED STATES. New York: Thomas Y. Crowell Co., 1971. 400 p.

A collection of previously unpublished essays written by a group of predominantly Black authors; history, sociology, Black art and drama, politics, and psychology are represented.

612. Ladner, Joyce A., ed. THE DEATH OF WHITE SOCIOLOGY. New York: Vintage Books, 1973. xxxiii, 476 p.

   Twenty-six contributors (including E. Franklin Frazier, Nathan Hare, Douglas Davidson, Kenneth B. Clark, and Andrew Billingsley attack American sociology for its tendency to regard Blacks as "deviants" from white middle-class standards.

613. Miller, Kent S., and Dreger, Ralph Mason, eds. COMPARATIVE STUDIES OF BLACKS AND WHITES IN THE UNITED STATES. Quantitative Studies in Social Relations. New York: Seminar Press, 1973. xiii, 572 p.

   Reviews recent psychological, sociological, and physiological studies of Black Americans.

614. Parsons, Talcott, and Clark, Kenneth B., eds. THE NEGRO AMERICAN. Boston: Houghton Mifflin Co., 1966. xxix, 781 p.

   Twenty-eight essays from a symposium on American race relations.

615. Rose, Peter I., ed. AMERICANS FROM AFRICA. Vol. 1: SLAVERY AND ITS AFTERMATH; vol. 2: OLD MEMORIES, NEW MOODS. New York: Atherton, 1970. Vol. 1, 459 p.; vol. 2, 452 p.

   Forty-five selections on the Afro-American experience from slavery to Black protest.

616. Rose, Peter I., et al., eds. THROUGH DIFFERENT EYES; BLACK AND WHITE PERSPECTIVES ON AMERICAN RACE RELATIONS. New York: Oxford University Press, 1973. xviii, 453 p.

617. Segal, Bernard E., ed. RACIAL AND ETHNIC RELATIONS: SELECTED READINGS. New York: Thomas Y. Crowell Co., 1966. 492 p. Bibliography.

618. Szwed, John F., ed. BLACK AMERICA. New York: Basic Books, 1970. 303 p. Bibliography.

619. Wilkinson, Doris Yvonne, ed. BLACK REVOLT: STRATEGIES OF PROTEST. Berkeley: McCutchan, 1969. vii, 146 p. Bibliography.

* * *

See also Chapter 7, Sections E and F; Chapter 10, Section H; Chapter 11, Section E; Chapter 17, Sections G and H; and Chapter 20, Section E.

Chapter 9

JEWISH COMMUNITY

Chapter 9

JEWISH COMMUNITY

A. REFERENCE WORKS

620. AMERICAN JEWISH YEARBOOK. Philadelphia: Jewish Publication Society of America and the American Jewish Committee, 1899--. Annual.

    Articles interpreting Jewish life and culture; statistical information; and directories of Jewish organizations. Beginning with volume fifty-one, the YEARBOOK includes a cumulative index to feature articles. This updates the "Index to Special Articles, Directory Lists, and Statistics in Volumes 1-50" in the 1949 YEARBOOK, volume 50, pp. 867-76.

621. ENCYCLOPEDIA JUDAICA. Cecil Roth, editor-in-chief. 16 vols. Jerusalem: Ktav; New York: Macmillan, 1972.

B. JEWISH LIFE

622. Doroshkin, Milton. YIDDISH IN AMERICA; SOCIAL AND CULTURAL FOUNDATIONS. Rutherford, N.J.: Fairleigh Dickinson University Press, 1972. 281 p.

    The role of Yiddish language among East European Jewish immigrants. Bibliography.

623. Glazer, Nathan. AMERICAN JUDAISM. 2nd ed. The Chicago History of American Civilization Series. Chicago: University of Chicago Press, 1972. 210 p.

    The course of Judaism from the mid-seventeenth to the mid-twentieth century.

624. Halpern, Ben. THE AMERICAN JEW: A ZIONIST ANALYSIS. New York: Theodore Herzl Foundation, 1956. 174 p. Bibliography.

625. Rose, Peter I., ed. THE GHETTO AND BEYOND; ESSAYS ON JEWISH LIFE IN AMERICA. New York: Random House, 1969. viii, 504 p.

 Twenty-six articles, six original, others from such sources as MIDSTREAM, COMMENTARY, JOURNAL OF JEWISH SOCIOLOGY, and JUDAISM.

626. Sherman, Charles Bezalel. THE JEW WITHIN AMERICAN SOCIETY; A STUDY IN ETHNIC INDIVIDUALITY. Detroit: Wayne State University Press, 1961. 260 p. Bibliography.

627. Sidorsky, David, ed. THE FUTURE OF THE JEWISH COMMUNITY IN AMERICA. New York: Basic Books, 1973. xxviii, 324 p.

 Essays on the future of the Jewish community in America, prepared for a task force of the American Jewish Committee.

628. Sklare, Marshall. AMERICA'S JEWS. Ethnic Groups in Comparative Perspective. New York: Random House, 1971. 234 p.

 Jewish social history, group identity, social characteristics, family, community, education, and interaction of Jew and Gentile. Bibliography.

629. _____. CONSERVATIVE JUDAISM; AN AMERICAN RELIGIOUS MOVEMENT. Glencoe, Ill.: Free Press, 1955. 298 p.

 Description of a religious movement which originated in the United States to preserve ethnic distinctiveness and prevent assimilation. The study focuses on Chicago.

630. _____, ed. THE JEWS; SOCIAL PATTERNS OF AN AMERICAN GROUP. Glencoe, Ill.: Free Press, 1958. 669 p.

 Thirty-three selections from the 1940s and 1950s. Bibliography.

C. COMMUNITY STUDIES

631. Bigman, Stanley K. THE JEWISH POPULATION OF GREATER WASHINGTON IN 1956. Washington, D.C.: Jewish Community Council of Greater Washington, 1957. 173 p.

 Size, social characteristics, residential mobility, community participation, and observance of traditional practices.

632. Goldstein, Sidney. THE GREATER PROVIDENCE JEWISH COMMUNITY; A POPULATION SURVEY. Providence, R.I.: General Jewish Community of Providence, 1964. xix, 256 p.

633. _____ . A POPULATION SURVEY OF THE GREATER SPRINGFIELD JEWISH COMMUNITY. Springfield, Mass.: Springfield Jewish Community Council, 1968. xv, 181 p.

634. Gordon, Albert I. JEWS IN SUBURBIA. Boston: Beacon Press, 1959. 264 p.

Study of eighty suburban Jewish communities; findings apply mainly to affiliated Jews. Bibliography.

635. _____ . JEWS IN TRANSITION. Minneapolis: University of Minnesota Press, 1949. xviii, 331 p.

Account of an immigrant community in Minneapolis and changes in its beliefs and practices.

636. Kaplan, Benjamin. THE ETERNAL STRANGER; A STUDY OF JEWISH LIFE IN THE SMALL COMMUNITY. New York: Bookman Associates, 1957. 198 p.

The author traces the development of Jewish group life in three small Louisiana towns. Bibliography.

637. Kranzler, George. WILLIAMSBURG: A JEWISH COMMUNITY IN TRANSITION; A STUDY OF THE FACTORS AND PATTERNS OF CHANGE IN THE ORGANIZATION AND STRUCTURE OF A COMMUNITY IN TRANSITION. New York: Feldheim, 1961. 310 p.

Sociohistorical analysis over a fifty year period in Brooklyn, New York.

638. Landesman, Alter F. BROWNSVILLE; THE BIRTH, DEVELOPMENT AND PASSING OF A JEWISH COMMUNITY IN NEW YORK. 2nd ed. New York: Bloch Publishing Co., 1971. xiv, 418 p. Bibliography.

639. Massarik, Fred. THE JEWISH POPULATION OF LOS ANGELES. Los Angeles: Los Angeles Jewish Community Council, 1953. 127 p.

640. _____ . THE JEWISH POPULATION OF SAN FRANCISCO, MARIN COUNTY AND THE PENINSULA, 1959. San Francisco: Jewish Welfare Federation, 1959. xi, 143 leaves.

641. Poll, Solomon. THE HASIDIC COMMUNITY OF WILLIAMSBURG. 2nd ed. New York: Schocken Books, 1969. x, 308 p.

Describes social, economic, and normative systems. Bibliography.

642. Rosenthal, Erich. THE JEWISH POPULATION OF CHICAGO, ILLINOIS. Chicago: The College of Jewish Studies, 1952. 128 p. Bibliography.

643. Rubin, Israel. SATMAR: AN ISLAND IN THE CITY. Chicago: Quadrangle Books, 1972. x, 272 p.

> Study of the Hasidic community of Satmar, located primarily in the Williamsburg section of Brooklyn, New York.

644. Sklare, Marshall, and Greenblum, Joseph. JEWISH IDENTITY ON THE SUBURBAN FRONTIER; A STUDY OF GROUP SURVIVAL IN THE OPEN SOCIETY. The Lakeville Studies, vol. 1. New York: Basic Books, 1967. xv, 362 p.

> Data gathered in the late 1950s through intensive interviews with 432 Jewish and 250 Gentile residents of Lakeville, a midwestern suburb.

D. MARRIAGE AND FAMILY

645. Cahnman, Werner J., ed. INTERMARRIAGE AND JEWISH LIFE; A SYMPOSIUM. New York: Herzl Press, 1963. 212 p. Bibliography.

646. Goldstein, Sidney, and Goldscheider, Calvin. JEWISH AMERICANS: THREE GENERATIONS IN A JEWISH COMMUNITY. Englewood Cliffs, N.J.: Prentice-Hall, 1968. xvii, 274 p.

> A survey of 1,500 Jewish families in Providence, Rhode Island; socioeconomic characteristics and analysis of changes from one generation to another. Bibliography.

647. Kaplan, Benjamin. THE JEW AND HIS FAMILY. Baton Rouge: Louisiana University Press, 1967. xv, 205 p.

> The Jewish family in biblical times, in the shtetl of Eastern Europe, and in modern America. Bibliography.

648. Kramer, Judith R., and Leventman, Seymour. CHILDREN OF THE GILDED GHETTO; CONFLICT RESOLUTIONS OF THREE GENERATIONS OF AMERICAN JEWS. New Haven: Yale University Press, 1961. xviii, 228 p.

> Effects of class and generational position in a midwest Jewish community. Bibliography.

649. Mayer, John E. JEWISH-GENTILE COURTSHIPS: AN EXPLORATORY STUDY OF A SOCIAL PROCESS. New York: Free Press, 1961. ix, 240 p.

Study of forty-five Jewish-Gentile couples in New York City, interviewed shortly after their marriages.

650. Rosen, Bernard C. ADOLESCENCE AND RELIGION; THE JEWISH TEEN-AGER IN AMERICAN SOCIETY. Cambridge, Mass.: Schenkman, 1965. xviii, 218 p. Bibliography.

651. Rosenthal, Erich. STUDIES OF JEWISH INTERMARRIAGE IN THE UNITED STATES. New York: American Jewish Committee, 1963. 53 p. Reprinted from AMERICAN JEWISH YEAR BOOK, vol. 64, 1963.

E. JEWISH-AMERICAN RELATIONS AND ANTI-SEMITISM

652. Berson, Lenora E. THE NEGROES AND THE JEWS. New York: Random House, 1971. 436 p.

Black-Jewish relationships depend upon America's response to the Black challenge.

653. Bettelheim, Bruno, and Janowitz, Morris. DYNAMICS OF PREJUDICE; A PSYCHOLOGICAL AND SOCIOLOGICAL STUDY OF VETERANS. New York: Harper & Brothers, 1950. xix, 227 p.

Based on in-depth interviews with 150 Chicago veterans.

654. _____. SOCIAL CHANGE AND PREJUDICE, INCLUDING "DYNAMICS OF PREJUDICE." New York: Free Press of Glencoe, 1964. xi, 337 p.

Reappraisal of their earlier research on the dynamics of prejudice.

655. Glock, Charles Y. CHRISTIAN BELIEFS AND ANTI-SEMITISM. New York: Harper & Row, Publishers, 1966. xxi, 266, 24 p.

First volume in a series from a five year study of anti-Semitism. Analyzes the ways in which the teachings of the Christian churches shape American attitudes towards Jews. The questionnaire used in the study is included as a twenty-four page appendix.

656. Glock, Charles Y., et al. THE APATHETIC MAJORITY; A STUDY BASED ON PUBLIC RESPONSES TO THE EICHMANN TRIAL. New York: Harper & Row, Publishers, 1966. xii, 222 p.

Second volume in a series from a five-year study of anti-Semitism in the United States. Data were obtained from 463 hour-long interviews with a sample of adults in Oakland, California, in 1961, shortly before the end of the trial.

657. Harris, Louis, and Swanson, Bert E. BLACK–JEWISH RELATIONS IN NEW YORK CITY. New York: Praeger, 1970. xxiii, 234 p.

A social attitude survey including 191 cross–tabulations indicates that education diminished unfavorable perception, but that Jewish liberalism may have declined.

658. Lowenthal, Leo, and Guterman, Norbert. PROPHETS OF DECEIT: A STUDY OF THE TECHNIQUES OF THE AMERICAN AGITATOR. New York: Harper & Brothers, 1949. 164 p.

Relates twenty–one themes in the spoken and written appeals of anti–Semitic and pro–Fascist agitators to the malaise which affects American society.

659. Ringer, Benjamin B. THE EDGE OF FRIENDLINESS; A STUDY OF JEWISH–GENTILE RELATIONS. The Lakeville Studies, vol. 2. New York: Basic Books, 1967. xii, 272 p.

Relationships in a high status suburb among Jews and Gentiles.

660. Selznick, Gertrude J., and Steinberg, Stephen. THE TENACITY OF PREJUDICE; ANTI–SEMITISM IN CONTEMPORARY AMERICA. Patterns of American Prejudice Series, vol. 4. New York: Harper & Row, Publishers, 1969. xxi, 248 p.

Measures anti–Semitic beliefs routine in American society, derived from 1,913 informants.

661. Stark, Rodney, et al. WAYWARD SHEPHERDS: PREJUDICE AND THE PROTESTANT CLERGY. Patterns of American Prejudice Series, vol. 6. New York: Harper & Row, Publishers, 1971. 138 p.

Information derived from questionnaries sent to California parish clergymen in the nine largest Protestant denominations in the spring of 1968. Bibliography.

662. Stember, Charles Herbert, et al. JEWS IN THE MIND OF AMERICA. New York: Basic Books, 1966. xiv, 413 p.

Discusses public opinion polls concerning Jews, conducted between 1937 and 1962.

663. Tumin, Melvin M. AN INVENTORY AND APPRAISAL OF RESEARCH ON AMERICAN ANTI–SEMITISM. New York: Freedom Books, 1961. v, 185 p.

Discussion of social and psychological factors in anti–Semitism.

664. Weintraub, Ruth G. HOW SECURE THESE RIGHTS? ANTI–SEMITISM IN THE UNITED STATES IN 1948: AN ANTI–DEFAMATION LEAGUE

SURVEY. Garden City, N.Y.: Doubleday, 1949. vii, 215 p.

An analysis of discriminatory practices directed against Jews, Negroes, and other minorities and an appraisal of the civil status of the Jews in the United States.

665. Weisbord, Robert G., and Stein, Arthur. BITTERSWEET ENCOUNTER; THE AFRO-AMERICAN AND THE AMERICAN JEW. Westport, Conn.: Negro Universities Press, 1970. xxvii, 242 p.

Surveys the historical relationship between Blacks and Jews in the United States. Bibliography.

* * *

See also Chapter 11, Section E.

Chapter 10

ETHNIC GROUPS

Chapter 10

ETHNIC GROUPS

A. REFERENCE WORKS AND BIBLIOGRAPHIES

666. Bravo, Enrique, ed. AN ANNOTATED SELECTED PUERTO RICAN BIBLIOGRAPHY. New York: Urban Center of Columbia University, 1972. 114 p.

667. Cordasco, Francesco, and LaGumina, Salvatore. ITALIANS IN THE UNITED STATES: A BIBLIOGRAPHY OF REPORTS, TEXTS, CRITICAL STUDIES AND RELATED MATERIALS. New York: Oriole Editions, 1972. xvi, 137 p.

668. Cordasco, Francesco, et al. PUERTO RICANS ON THE UNITED STATES MAINLAND; A BIBLIOGRAPHY OF REPORTS, TEXTS, CRITICAL STUDIES AND RELATED MATERIALS. Totowa, N.J.: Rowman and Littlefield, 1972. xiv, 146 p.

669. Institute of Labor and Industrial Relations. University of Michigan-Wayne State University. Research Division. DOCUMENT AND REFERENCE TEXT; AN INDEX TO MINORITY GROUP EMPLOYMENT INFORMATION. Ann Arbor, Mich.: 1967. 602 p. (Produced under contract with the Equal Employment Opportunity Commission.)

    Lists 4,000 publications on employment problems of minority workers, their employers, and the public.

670. Kinton, Jack F. AMERICAN ETHNIC GROUPS AND THE REVIVAL OF CULTURAL PLURALISM: EVALUATIVE SOURCEBOOK FOR THE 1970'S. 4th ed. Aurora, Ill.: Social Science and Sociological Resources, 1974. 206 p.

    This bibliography lists books, journal articles, and reference works on ethnic groups and immigration; it also includes films and a list of ethnic studies centers.

671. Matsuda, Mitsugu. THE JAPANESE IN HAWAII, 1868-1967: A BIBLI-
     OGRAPHY OF THE FIRST HUNDRED YEARS. Honolulu: University of
     Hawaii Press, 1968. xi, 222 p.

672. Nogales, Luis G., ed. THE MEXICAN AMERICAN; A SELECTED AND
     ANNOTATED BIBLIOGRAPHY. 2nd ed. Stanford: Center for Latin
     American Studies, Stanford University, 1971. 162 p.

     Contains 444 annotated entries, predominantly in the social
     sciences; includes a list of Chicano periodicals.

673. Vivo, Paquita, ed. THE PUERTO RICANS: AN ANNOTATED BIBLI-
     OGRAPHY. New York: Bowker, 1973. xv, 299 p. (Published for
     the Puerto Rican Research and Resources Center.)

B. AMERICAN INDIANS

674. Bahr, Howard M., et al., eds. NATIVE AMERICANS TODAY: SO-
     CIOLOGICAL PERSPECTIVES. New York: Harper & Row, Publishers,
     1972. xii, 547 p.

     Forty-two recent articles, some previously unpublished, on
     prejudice, education, acculturation, urban problems, and red
     power.

675. Cahn, Edgar S., ed. OUR BROTHERS' KEEPER: THE INDIAN IN
     WHITE AMERICA. New York: World Publishing Co., 1970. ix,
     193 p.

     Criticism of the Bureau of Indian Affairs.

676. Deloria, Vine, Jr. CUSTER DIED FOR YOUR SINS; AN INDIAN
     MANIFESTO. New York: Macmillan, 1969. 279 p.

677. _____. WE TALK, YOU LISTEN; NEW TRIBES, NEW TURF. New
     York: Macmillan, 1970. 227 p.

     Analysis of white power and institutional racism by a leader of
     the National Congress of American Indians.

678. Levine, Stuart, and Lurie, Nancy O., eds. THE AMERICAN INDIAN
     TODAY. Rev. ed. Baltimore: Penguin Books, 1970. 352 p.

     Thirteen Indian and white anthropologists discuss contemporary
     Indian life.

679. Sasaki, Tom T. FRUITLAND, NEW MEXICO: A NAVAHO COMMU-

NITY IN TRANSITION. Ithaca, N.Y.: Cornell University Press, 1960. xvii, 217 p.

> Study of cultural change among the Navahos between 1930 and 1956, initiated by a forced livestock reduction program.

680. Steiner, Stan. THE NEW INDIANS. New York: Harper & Row, Publishers, 1968. xiii, 348 p.

> The emergence of Indian activism.

681. Vogt, Evan Z., and Albert, Ethel M. PEOPLE OF RIMROCK: A STUDY OF VALUES IN FIVE CULTURES. Cambridge, Mass.: Harvard University Press, 1966. xiv, 342 p.

> Zuni and Navaho Indians studied in their relationship to their Hispanic, Mormon, and Texan neighbors.

682. Waddell, Jack O., and Watson, O. Michael, eds. THE AMERICAN INDIAN IN URBAN SOCIETY. Boston: Little, Brown and Co., 1971. xiv, 414 p.

> An anthology on the urbanization of Indians, 350,000 of whom live in towns and cities.

683. Wax, Murray L. INDIAN AMERICANS; UNITY AND DIVERSITY. Englewood Cliffs, N.J.: Prentice-Hall, 1971. xix, 236 p.

> Indian history, demography, and community life, and typology of Indian-white relations.

C. ASIAN-AMERICANS

684. Broom, Leonard, and Kitsuse, John I. THE MANAGED CASUALTY: THE JAPANESE-AMERICAN FAMILY IN WORLD WAR II. University of California Publications in Culture and Society, vol. 6. Berkeley: University of California Press, 1956. iv, 226 p.

685. Broom, Leonard, and Riemer, Ruth. REMOVAL AND RETURN: THE SOCIOECONOMIC EFFECTS OF THE WAR ON JAPANESE AMERICANS. Berkeley: University of California Press, 1949. x, 259 p.

686. Conroy, Hilary, and Miyakawa, T. Scott, eds. EAST ACROSS THE PACIFIC: HISTORICAL AND SOCIOLOGICAL STUDIES OF JAPANESE IMMIGRATION AND ASSIMILATION. Santa Clara, Calif.: American Bibliographical Center/Clio Press, 1972. xviii, 322 p.

687. Hagopian, Elaine C., and Paden, Ann, eds. THE ARAB-AMERICANS; STUDIES IN ASSIMILATION. Wilmette, Ill.: Medina University Press International, 1969. viii, 111 p.

> A monograph by seven members of the Association of Arab-American University Graduates, organized in 1968.

688. Lee, Rose Hum. THE CHINESE IN THE UNITED STATES OF AMERICA. Hong Kong: Hong Kong University Press, 1960. 465 p.

> Description of Chinatown life styles and three subgroups: the sojourners, the students and intellectuals, and the American-Chinese, with a plea for integration.

689. Loewen, James W. THE MISSISSIPPI CHINESE: BETWEEN BLACK AND WHITE. Cambridge, Mass.: Harvard University Press, 1971. 237 p.

> Focuses on the triangular relationship between Chinese, whites, and Blacks within the social and economic structure of the delta.

690. Petersen, William. JAPANESE AMERICANS: OPPRESSION AND SUC-CESS. Ethnic Groups in Comparative Perspective. New York: Random House, 1971. 268 p.

> Discrimination and adversity have reinforced the group solidarity of a "subnation." Bibliography (pp. 237-54).

691. Samuels, Frederick. THE JAPANESE AND THE HAOLES OF HONOLU-LU: DURABLE GROUP INTERACTION. New Haven: College and University Press, 1970. 206 p.

> Research on perception, attitudes, and behavior patterns distinguishes three groups of Haoles: Kamaaina (long-time resident white), Malihina (relative newcomer from the mainland), and tourist.

692. Thomas, Dorothy S. THE SALVAGE. Japanese American Evacuation and Resettlement, vol. 2. Berkeley: University of California Press, 1952.

> Describes the 36,000 Japanese-Americans classified as "loyal" and discharged from evacuation camps before December 1944.

693. Thomas, Dorothy S., and Nishimoto, Richard S. THE SPOILAGE. Japanese American Evacuation and Resettlement, vol. 1. Berkeley: University of California Press, 1946. xx, 388 p.

> Study of those Japanese who, after evacuation, renounced their American citizenship.

D. MEXICAN-AMERICANS

694. Burma, John H. MEXICAN-AMERICANS IN THE UNITED STATES: A READER. Cambridge, Mass.: Schenkman, 1970. xviii, 487 p.

695. Duran, Livie Isauro, and Bernard, Russell H. INTRODUCTION TO CHICANO STUDIES; A READER. New York: Macmillan, 1973. v, 585 p.

    Sociological, psychological, and historical aspects of Chicano life.

696. Grebler, Leo, et al. THE MEXICAN-AMERICAN PEOPLE: THE NATION'S SECOND LARGEST MINORITY. New York: Free Press, 1970. xvii, 777 p.

    UCLA (University of California, Los Angeles) Project 1964-1968 based on interview survey in Los Angeles and San Antonio.

697. Heller, Celia S. MEXICAN AMERICAN YOUTH: FORGOTTEN YOUTH AT THE CROSSROADS. New York: Random House, 1966. viii, 113 p.

    Review of literature; opportunities for the younger generation.

698. _____. NEW CONVERTS TO THE AMERICAN DREAM? MOBILITY ASPIRATIONS OF YOUNG MEXICAN AMERICANS. New Haven: College and University Press, 1971. 287 p.

    Based on 1955 questionnaires of Los Angeles white and Mexican high school seniors and eighteen interviews taped just prior to the 1965 Watts riot.

699. Moore, Joan W., with Cuellar, Alfredo. MEXICAN AMERICANS. Englewood Cliffs, N.J.: Prentice-Hall, 1970. xii, 172 p.

    Examines factors which reduced Mexican-Americans to landless labor by 1900 and determined their present status.

700. Nava, Julian, ed. VIVA LA RAZA! READINGS ON MEXICAN AMERICANS. New York: Van Nostrand, 1973. xiv, 169 p.

701. Penalosa, Fernando. CLASS CONSCIOUSNESS AND SOCIAL MOBILITY IN A MEXICAN-AMERICAN COMMUNITY. San Francisco: R. and E. Research Associates, 1971. ix, 145 p.

    Based on 147 interviews in Pomona, California, with 114 American-born and 32 Mexican-born persons.

702. Rendon, Armando B. CHICANO MANIFESTO: THE HISTORY AND ASPIRATIONS OF THE SECOND LARGEST MINORITY IN AMERICA. New York: Macmillan, 1971. vii, 337 p.

703. Samora, Julian. LOS MOJADOS: THE WETBACK STORY. Notre Dame, Ind.: University of Notre Dame Press, 1971. xi, 205 p.

    Based on interviews with 494 wetbacks in detention centers.

704. _____, ed. LA RAZA: FORGOTTEN AMERICANS; PAPERS IN MEMORY OF CHARLES DE YOUNG ELKUS. Notre Dame, Ind.: University of Notre Dame Press, 1966. xvii, 218 p.

705. Samora, Julian, and Lamanna, Richard A. MEXICAN-AMERICANS IN A MIDWEST METROPOLIS: A STUDY OF EAST CHICAGO. Advance Report, no. 8. Los Angeles: Mexican American Study Project, University of California, 1967. x, 164 p.

706. Shannon, Lyle, and Shannon, Magdaline. MINORITY MIGRANTS IN THE URBAN COMMUNITY; MEXICAN-AMERICAN AND NEGRO ADJUSTMENT TO INDUSTRIAL SOCIETY. Beverly Hills: Sage Publications, 1973. 352 p.

    Research in Racine, a small industrial city in Wisconsin, in the 1950s.

707. Steiner, Stan. LA RAZA: THE MEXICAN AMERICANS. New York: Harper & Row, Publishers, 1970. xii, 418 p.

    Confrontation with the power structure in the American southwest, and growth of self-awareness and militancy. Bibliography (pp. 393–406).

708. Wagner, Nathaniel N., and Haus, Marsha J., eds. CHICANOS; SOCIAL AND PSYCHOLOGICAL PERSPECTIVES. St. Louis, Mo.: C.V. Mosby, 1971. xxvii, 303 p.

    Twenty-eight readings mostly published in the mid-sixties on interethnic perceptions, family, law, and mental health. Bibliography.

E. PUERTO RICANS

709. Fitzpatrick, Joseph P. PUERTO RICAN AMERICANS: THE MEANING OF MIGRATION TO THE MAINLAND. Englewood Cliffs, N.J.: Prentice-Hall, 1971. xvi, 192 p.

    Interpretation of the Puerto Rican community in New York

City based on participant observation.

710. Mills, C. Wright, et al. THE PUERTO RICAN JOURNEY; NEW YORK'S NEWEST MIGRANTS. New York: Harper & Brothers, 1950. xi, 238 p.

Report based on an area sample study of about 5,000 Puerto Ricans in some 1,100 households in New York City; examines problems of migration and group relations.

711. Padilla, Elena. UP FROM PUERTO RICO. New York: Columbia University Press, 1958. xiii, 317 p.

Intensive interviews of forty-eight Puerto Rican families in an East Harlem slum.

712. Rogler, Lloyd. MIGRANT IN THE CITY: THE LIFE OF A PUERTO RICAN ACTION GROUP. New York: Basic Books, 1972. xvi, 251 p.

Analyzes the experience of a forty-two-member Hispanic confederation in a middle-sized Northeastern city.

713. Senior, Clarence. THE PUERTO RICANS: STRANGERS, THEN NEIGH-BORS. Chicago: Quadrangle Books, 1965. 128 p.

Describes the Puerto Rican migration; 200-item bibliography.

714. Sexton, Patricia Cayo. SPANISH HARLEM; AN ANATOMY OF POVERTY. New York: Harper & Row, Publishers, 1965. xiii, 208 p.

Puerto Rican family life in New York City.

F. EURO-AMERICANS

715. Gans, Herbert J. THE URBAN VILLAGERS: GROUP AND CLASS IN THE LIFE OF ITALIAN-AMERICANS. New York: Free Press of Glencoe, 1962. xvi, 367 p.

An analysis of second-generation Italian-Americans based on eight months of participant observation in Boston's west end.

716. Greeley, Andrew M. THAT MOST DISTRESSFUL NATION: THE TAMING OF THE AMERICAN IRISH. Chicago: Quadrangle Books, 1972. xxviii, 281 p.

Historical and mainly contemporary analysis of Irish ethnicity, styles of life, and values and attitudes; discussion of Irish stereotypes.

717. _____ . WHY CAN'T THEY BE LIKE US? New York: Dutton, 1971.

223 p.

Discussion of the Irish and other Catholic groups in the process of acculturation.

718. Iorizzo, Luciano J., and Mondello, Salvatore. THE ITALIAN AMERI-CANS. New York: Twayne, 1971. 273 p.

Analysis of the Italian-American experience which seeks to correct misleading stereotypes.

719. Lopreato, Joseph. ITALIAN AMERICANS. Ethnic Groups in Comparative Perspective. New York: Random House, 1970. xiv, 204 p.

Individual and collective responses to American life.

720. Novak, Michael. THE RISE OF THE UNMELTABLE ETHNICS. New York: Macmillan, 1971. 321 p.

Discussion of the position of white non-WASP ethnics, descendants of immigrants from Southern and Eastern Europe, and their relationship to other minorities.

721. Simirenko, Alex. PILGRIMS, COLONISTS AND FRONTIERSMEN: AN ETHNIC COMMUNITY IN TRANSITION. New York: Free Press of Glencoe, 1964. xvi, 232 p.

An analysis of generational changes in social stratification in the Russian community in Minneapolis.

722. Thomas, W. I., and Znaniecki, Florian. THE POLISH PEASANT IN EUROPE AND THE UNITED STATES. 2 vols. New York: Dover Books, 1958. xv, 2250 p.

A classic study of attitudes and values, first published in 1918-20.

723. Tomasi, Silvano M., and Engel, Madeline H., eds. THE ITALIAN EXPERIENCE IN THE UNITED STATES. New York: Center for Migration Studies, 1970. vii, 239 p.

Essays on the more recent (post-World War II) immigration.

724. Wood, Arthur Evans. HAMTRAMCK THEN AND NOW: A SOCIOLOG-ICAL STUDY OF A POLISH-AMERICAN COMMUNITY. New York: Bookman Associates, 1955. 253 p.

Describes an immigrant community of 45,000 in a small independent municipality in the Detroit area.

G. IMMIGRANTS

725. Davie, Maurice R., et al. REFUGEES IN AMERICA. Report of the Commission for the Study of Recent Immigration from Europe. New York: Harper & Brothers, 1947. ix, 125 p.

    Data obtained from 638 communities in forty-three states.

726. Handlin, Oscar. THE UPROOTED; THE EPIC STORY OF THE GREAT MIGRATIONS THAT MADE THE AMERICAN PEOPLE. New York: Grosset and Dunlap, 1957. 310 p.

    The migration experience in the nineteenth and twentieth centuries.

727. _____, ed. CHILDREN OF THE UPROOTED. New York: George Braziller, 1966. xxii, 551 p.

    Examination of the Americanization process from the 1840s to the 1920s.

728. Kent, Donald Peterson. THE REFUGEE INTELLECTUAL: THE AMERICAN-IZATION OF THE IMMIGRANT OF 1933-41. New York: Columbia University Press, 1953. xx, 317 p.

    Study of the adjustment of refugees from Germany and Austria.

729. Kosa, John, ed. THE HOME OF THE LEARNED MAN: A SYMPOSIUM ON THE IMMIGRANT SCHOLAR IN AMERICA. New Haven: College and University Press, 1968. 192 p.

    Twelve contributors discuss the role of the scholar immigrant in the United States.

730. Wheeler, Thomas C., ed. THE IMMIGRANT EXPERIENCE; THE AN-GUISH OF BECOMING AMERICAN. New York: Dial Press, 1971. 212 p.

    Nine autobiographical essays.

H. MINORITY RELATIONS, ASSIMILATION, AND CONFLICT

731. Bayley, David H., and Mendelsohn, Harold. MINORITIES AND THE POLICE: CONFRONTATION IN AMERICA. New York: Free Press, 1969. xii, 209 p.

    Based on 1966 public opinion surveys in Denver, Colorado. Minorities (Negroes and Spanish-named), policemen, members

of the dominant community (non-Mexican whites), and community leaders were surveyed to explore relations between police
and community.

732. Berry, Brewton. ALMOST WHITE: A STUDY OF CERTAIN RACIAL
HYBRIDS IN THE EASTERN UNITED STATES. New York: Macmillan,
1963. viii, 212 p.

The product of twenty years of study of isolated settlements of
part Negro, part Indian, and part white people.

733. Blalock, Herbert. TOWARD A THEORY OF MINORITY GROUP RELA-
TIONS. New York: Wiley, 1967. x, 227 p.

General theoretical propositions about minority-group relations
based on competition, status, and economic factors related to
discrimination.

734. Glazer, Nathan, and Moynihan, Daniel Patrick. BEYOND THE MELT-
ING POT: THE NEGROES, PUERTO RICANS, JEWS, ITALIANS, AND
IRISH OF NEW YORK CITY. 2nd ed. Cambridge, Mass.: The M.I.T.
Press, 1970. xcviii, 363 p.

Explores the meaning and persistence of ethnicity in a multi-
ethnic context.

735. Gordon, Milton M. ASSIMILATION IN AMERICAN LIFE: THE ROLE
OF RACE, RELIGION AND NATIONAL ORIGINS. New York: Oxford University Press, 1964. iv, 276 p.

Examination of the theories of assimilation process and of
ethnic and class stratification in American society.

736. Greeley, Andrew M. ETHNICITY IN THE UNITED STATES: A PRE-
LIMINARY RECONNAISSANCE. New York: Wiley-Interscience, 1974.
384 p.

737. Greer, Colin, ed. DIVIDED SOCIETY: THE ETHNIC EXPERIENCE IN
AMERICA. New York: Basic Books, 1974. 405 p.

Contributions by Andrew Greeley, Marc Fried, Michael Novak,
and others indicate that the class structure rather than ethnic
identity is at the root of the American social reality of discrimination.

738. Hughes, Everett C., and Hughes, Helen MacGill. WHERE PEOPLES
MEET: RACIAL AND ETHNIC FRONTIERS. Glencoe, Ill.: Free Press,
1952. 204 p.

Discusses ethnic relations and competition for status.

739. Kramer, Judith R. THE AMERICAN MINORITY COMMUNITY. New York: Thomas Y. Crowell Co., 1970. x, 293 p.

   Analysis of minority membership and the function of minority communities; ethnic enclaves and consequences of deculturation; eight pages of bibliography.

740. Light, Ivan H. ETHNIC ENTERPRISE IN AMERICA; BUSINESS AND WELFARE AMONG CHINESE, JAPANESE, AND BLACKS. Berkeley: University of California Press, 1972. 209 p.

   Studies the problem of some ethnic groups in the creation of a business class. Bibliography (pp. 193-99).

741. Newman, William M. AMERICAN PLURALISM: A STUDY OF MINORITY GROUPS AND SOCIOLOGICAL THEORY. New York: Harper & Row, Publishers, 1973. ix, 307 p.

   Intergroup relations are analyzed in the framework of the theory of social conflict. Annotated bibliographies.

742. Stonequist, E. V. THE MARGINAL MAN; A STUDY IN PERSONALITY AND CULTURE CONFLICT. New York: Scribner, 1937. xviii, 228 p.

   A classic study of marginality in America and in cross-cultural context.

743. Warner, W. Lloyd, and Srole, Leo. THE SOCIAL SYSTEMS OF AMERICAN ETHNIC GROUPS. Yankee City Series, vol. 3. New Haven: Yale University Press, 1945. xii, 318 p.

   Ethnic patterns in Newburyport, Massachusetts.

I. TEXTBOOKS AND READERS

744. Barron, Milton L., ed. MINORITIES IN A CHANGING WORLD. New York: Knopf, 1967. xiii, 481 p.

   Thirty-three articles in seven sections, five of which are directly concerned with the United States. Bibliographic notes are included.

745. Berry, Brewton. RACE AND ETHNIC RELATIONS. 3rd ed. Boston: Houghton Mifflin Co., 1965. ix, 435 p. Bibliography.

746. Blauner, Robert, et al., eds. THE THIRD WORLD WITHIN. Belmont, Calif.: Wadsworth, 1973. 384 p.

   Presents the experiences of American Indians, Chicanos, Afro-

Americans, and Asian-Americans as groups which have shared a colonial-type heritage.

747. Freedman, Morris, and Banks, Carolyn, eds. AMERICAN MIX: THE MINORITY EXPERIENCE IN AMERICA. Philadelphia: Lippincott, 1972. 453 p.

A collection of materials on Blacks, Indians, Chicanos, Japanese-Americans, Polish-Americans, Jews, Catholics, the blind, the old, the poor, the young, and women.

748. Hunt, Chester L., and Walker, Lewis. ETHNIC DYNAMICS: PATTERNS OF INTERGROUP RELATIONS IN VARIOUS SOCIETIES. Homewood, Ill.: Dorsey Press, 1974. xiv, 463 p.

Touches on American society, but most of the text deals with ethnic relations in a global perspective. Bibliography (pp. 446-52).

749. Kurokawa, Minako, ed. MINORITY RESPONSES; COMPARATIVE VIEWS OF REACTIONS TO SUBORDINATION. New York: Random House, 1970. vii, 376 p.

750. Mack, Raymond W. RACE, CLASS AND POWER. 2nd ed. New York: American Book Co., 1968. x, 468 p.

751. Marden, Charles F., and Meyer, Gladys. MINORITIES IN AMERICAN SOCIETY. 3rd ed. New York: American Book Co., 1968. xxi, 486 p.

752. Rose, Arnold M[arshall], and Rose, Caroline, eds. MINORITY PROBLEMS. 2nd ed. New York: Harper & Row, Publishers, 1972. x, 483 p.

753. Rose, Peter I. THEY AND WE: RACIAL AND ETHNIC RELATIONS IN THE UNITED STATES. New York: Random House, 1964. xi, 177 p.

754. _____, ed. NATION OF NATIONS: THE ETHNIC EXPERIENCE AND THE RACIAL CRISIS. New York: Random House, 1972. xv, 351 p.

Autobiographical, literary, and sociological accounts of the heterogeneity of American society.

755. Simpson, George Eaton, and Yinger, J. Milton. RACIAL AND CULTURAL MINORITIES: AN ANALYSIS OF PREJUDICE AND DISCRIMINATION. 4th ed. New York: Harper & Row, Publishers, 1972. viii, 775 p.

756. Thompson, Edgar T., and Hughes, Everett C., eds. RACE: INDIVID-
UAL AND COLLECTIVE BEHAVIOR. Glencoe, Ill.: Free Press, 1958.
619 p.

   A reader of 139 selections, some literary; the forty-three-page
   bibliography has nearly 1,500 references.

757. Vander Zanden, James W. AMERICAN MINORITY RELATIONS: THE
SOCIOLOGY OF RACE AND ETHNIC GROUPS. 3rd ed. New York:
Ronald Press, 1972. vii, 494 p.

758. Yetman, Norman R., and Steele, C. Hoyt, eds. MAJORITY AND
MINORITY: THE DYNAMICS OF RACIAL AND ETHNIC RELATIONS.
Boston: Allyn & Bacon, 1971. xiii, 621 p.

* * *

See also Chapter 8; Chapter 9; and Chapter 11, Section F.

Chapter 11

RELIGION

Chapter 11

RELIGION

A. REFERENCE WORKS AND BIBLIOGRAPHIES

759. Berkowitz, Morris I., and Johnson, J. Edmund. SOCIAL SCIENTIFIC STUDIES OF RELIGION: A BIBLIOGRAPHY. Pittsburgh: University of Pittsburgh Press, 1967. xvii, 258 p.

     More than 6,000 items, arranged in a 132-division classification scheme.

760. Burr, Nelson Rollin. A CRITICAL BIBLIOGRAPHY OF RELIGION IN AMERICA. 2 vols. Religion in American Life, edited by James W. Smith and A. Leland Jamison, vol. 4. Princeton, N.J.: Princeton University Press, 1961.

761. _____. RELIGION IN AMERICAN LIFE. Goldentree Bibliographies in American Life Series. New York: Appleton-Century-Crofts, 1971. xix, 171 p.

762. Mead, Frank S., ed. HANDBOOK OF DENOMINATIONS IN THE UNITED STATES. 5th ed. New York: Abingdon Press, 1970. 265 p.

     Lists major denominations and sects; includes glossary of terms, addresses, and bibliography (pp. 235-45).

763. NEW CATHOLIC ENCYCLOPEDIA. 15 vols. New York: McGraw-Hill, 1967.

     An international work of reference on the teachings, history, organization, and activities of the Catholic church and on related topics.

764. OFFICIAL CATHOLIC DIRECTORY. New York: P. J. Kenedy and Son, 1822--. Annual.

     Directory information and religious statistics of the Catholic church; international in scope.

765. Rosten, Leo, ed. RELIGIONS IN AMERICA; A COMPLETELY REVISED AND UP-TO-DATE GUIDE TO CHURCHES AND RELIGIOUS GROUPS IN THE UNITED STATES. New York: Simon and Schuster, 1963. 415 p.

> First published in 1955 as A GUIDE TO THE RELIGIONS OF AMERICA (New York: Simon and Schuster, 1955).

766. Williams, Ethel L., and Brown, Clifton F., comp. AFRO-AMERICAN RELIGIOUS STUDIES: A COMPREHENSIVE BIBLIOGRAPHY WITH LO-CATIONS IN AMERICAN LIBRARIES. Metuchen, N.J.: Scarecrow Press, 1972. 454 p.

767. YEARBOOK OF AMERICAN AND CANADIAN CHURCHES. New York: Abingdon Press, 1916--. Annual. (For the National Council of Churches.)

> Denominational statistics on churches, church membership, religious education, clergymen, and finances as reported by more than 220 religious groups. Until 1972 the title was YEARBOOK OF AMERICAN CHURCHES.

B. GENERAL WORKS AND MONOGRAPHS

768. Berger, Peter L. THE NOISE OF SOLEMN ASSEMBLIES; CHRISTIAN COMMITMENT AND THE RELIGIOUS ESTABLISHMENT IN AMERICA. Garden City, N.Y.: Doubleday, 1961. 189 p.

> Critical examination of the religious revival of the 1950s. Bibliography.

769. Demerath, Nicholas J. III, and Hammond, Phillip E. RELIGION IN SOCIAL CONTEXT; TRADITION AND TRANSITION. New York: Random House, 1968. ix, 246 p.

> Part I deals with the history and development of the sociology of religion, especially the classic writings. Part II examines the present and future of religion in the United States. Selected annotated bibliography (pp. 233-38).

770. Glock, Charles Y., and Stark, Rodney. RELIGION AND SOCIETY IN TENSION. Chicago: Rand McNally, 1965. xii, 316 p.

> A new typological structure of religious beliefs, practices, experiences, and institutions.

771. Gordon, Albert I. THE NATURE OF CONVERSION; A STUDY OF FORTY-FIVE MEN AND WOMEN WHO CHANGED THEIR RELIGION. Boston: Beacon Press, 1967. xii, 333 p.

> A study of forty-five converts, thirty to Judaism, nine to Roman Catholicism, two to Protestantism, and one to Unitarian Universalism.

772. Greeley, Andrew M. THE DENOMINATIONAL SOCIETY; A SOCIO-LOGICAL APPROACH TO RELIGION IN AMERICA. Glenview, Ill.: Scott, Foresman, 1972. 266 p. Bibliography.

773. Hargrove, Barbara W. REFORMATION OF THE HOLY; A SOCIOLOGY OF RELIGION. Philadelphia: F.A. Davis, 1971. x, 315 p.

> Focuses on the wide range of American religious orientations and practices and their significance. Bibliography.

774. Herberg, Will. PROTESTANT, CATHOLIC, JEW; AN ESSAY IN AMER-ICAN RELIGIOUS SOCIOLOGY. Rev. ed. Garden City, N.Y.: Doubleday, Anchor Books, 1960. 309 p.

> Church membership and religious beliefs are related to the proposition of the "triple melting pot" whereby the immigrant is expected to give up language, nationality, and culture, but not religion. Bibliography.

775. Lenski, Gerhard E. THE RELIGIOUS FACTOR; A SOCIOLOGICAL STUDY OF RELIGION'S IMPACT ON POLITICS, ECONOMICS AND FAMILY LIFE. Garden City, N.Y.: Doubleday, 1961. xvi, 381 p.

> Data from four groups: white Protestants, Black Protestants, Catholics, and Jews in Detroit in 1958 test the hypothesis that each group develops a certain orientation toward all aspects of life.

776. Moberg, David O. THE CHURCH AS A SOCIAL INSTITUTION; THE SOCIOLOGY OF AMERICAN RELIGION. Englewood Cliffs, N.J.: Prentice-Hall, 1962. 569 p.

> A systematic sociological description of religion in the United States with an extensive bibliography.

777. Nottingham, Elizabeth K. RELIGION: A SOCIOLOGICAL VIEW. New York: Random House, 1971. xiii, 332 p.

> Based on the author's RELIGION AND SOCIETY (New York: Random House, 1954). Includes an annotated bibliography.

778. Salisbury, William Seward. RELIGION IN AMERICAN CULTURE: A

SOCIOLOGICAL INTERPRETATION. Homewood, Ill.: Dorsey Press, 1964. ix, 538 p.

Religious statistics, normative structures of major denominations, and relations between religious institutions and family, education, and government; twenty-four page annotated bibliography.

779. Schneider, Louis, and Dornbusch, Sanford M. POPULAR RELIGION: INSPIRATIONAL BOOKS IN AMERICA. Chicago: University of Chicago Press, 1958. xi, 173 p.

Examines forty-six best-selling inspirational books published between 1875 and 1955 and their common themes of pragmatism, optimism, and individualism.

780. Schroeder, W. Widick, and Obenhaus, Victor. RELIGION IN AMERICAN CULTURE: UNITY AND DIVERSITY IN A MIDWESTERN COUNTY. New York: Free Press of Glencoe, 1964. xxiii, 254 p.

A study of religious beliefs and behavior in selected communities of the corn belt area.

781. Stark, Rodney, and Glock, Charles Y. AMERICAN PIETY, THE NATURE OF RELIGIOUS COMMITMENT. Patterns of Religious Commitment, vol. 1. Berkeley: University of California Press, 1968. x, 230 p.

Based on a 1963 questionnaire survey of church members in northern California and on a 1964 national sample of adults. The measurement of commitment follows Glock and Stark's RELIGION AND SOCIETY IN TENSION (see item 770).

782. Underwood, Kenneth Wilson. PROTESTANT AND CATHOLIC: RELIGIOUS AND SOCIAL INTERACTION IN AN INDUSTRIAL COMMUNITY. Boston: Beacon Press, 1957. xxi, 484 p.

A study of Protestant-Catholic relations in Paper City (Holyoke, Massachusetts) around 1940. Bibliography.

783. Whitley, Oliver Read. THE CHURCH: MIRROR OR WINDOW? IMAGES OF THE CHURCH IN AMERICAN SOCIETY. St. Louis, Mo.: Bethany Press, 1969. 189 p.

Offers a guide to the sociological literature which describes modern church life.

784. Yinger, J. Milton. THE SCIENTIFIC STUDY OF RELIGION. New York: Macmillan, 1970. x, 593 p.

Revision of his RELIGION, SOCIETY AND THE INDIVIDUAL (New York: Macmillan, 1957). Treats the basic topics in the sociology of religion. Bibliography.

C. ROMAN CATHOLICISM

785. Abramson, Harold J. ETHNIC DIVERSITY IN CATHOLIC AMERICA. New York: Wiley, 1973. xvi, 207 p.

> Persistence of ethnic diversity among white Catholics, in contradiction to Herberg's thesis that ethnic groups merge into religious groupings (see item 774). Intermarriage is associated with higher levels of education.

786. Dohen, Dorothy. NATIONALISM AND AMERICAN CATHOLICISM. New York: Sheed & Ward, 1967. xiv, 210 p.

> Examines statements of seven leaders of the American Catholic hierarchy for evidence of nationalism. Bibliography.

787. Fichter, Joseph H. AMERICA'S FORGOTTEN PRIESTS; WHAT THEY ARE SAYING. New York: Harper & Row, Publishers, 1968. 254 p.

> Results of a 1966 national survey of attitudes of priests at the bottom of the Roman Catholic system of stratification; three-fifths favored the option of marriage and only 7 percent felt that there was open communication between them and the hierarchy.

788. _____. PRIEST AND PEOPLE. New York: Sheed & Ward, 1965. xiv, 203 p.

> Based on questionnaires sent to a national sample of 2,183 diocesan priests and 2,216 of their parishioners.

789. _____. RELIGION AS AN OCCUPATION: A STUDY IN THE SOCIOLOGY OF PROFESSIONS. Notre Dame, Ind.: University of Notre Dame Press, 1961. 295 p.

> Study of the employment practices of the American Catholic Church and its 250,000 full-time professionals. Bibliography.

790. _____. SOCIAL RELATIONS IN THE URBAN PARISH. Chicago: University of Chicago Press, 1960. vii, 263 p.

> Essays on Catholic parish life, some based on original field research, distinguish nuclear, modal, marginal, and dormant types of parishioners.

791. _____. SOUTHERN PARISH. Vol. 1: THE DYNAMICS OF A CITY CHURCH. Chicago: University of Chicago Press, 1951. ix, 283 p.

> Study of 6,127 practicing parishioners in an established neighborhood of a large southern city which focuses on the relations

between clergy and laity.

792. Greeley, Andrew M. THE CHURCH AND THE SUBURBS. Rev. ed. New York: Paulist Press, 1963. 192 p.

Adjustment of Catholicism to suburban life.

793. _____. PRIESTS IN THE UNITED STATES: REFLECTIONS ON A SURVEY. Garden City, N.Y.: Doubleday, 1972. 213 p.

An account for the layman of the results of the National Opinion Research Center study of the American Catholic priesthood, prepared for the National Conference of Catholic Bishops.

794. Kane, John J. CATHOLIC-PROTESTANT CONFLICTS IN AMERICA. Chicago: Regnery, 1955. 244 p.

Study of Protestant–Catholic tension on issues of school, politics, authoritarianism, and dogma.

795. Liu, William T., and Pallone, Nathaniel J. CATHOLICS/U.S.A.: PERSPECTIVES ON SOCIAL CHANGE. New York: Wiley, 1970. 529 p.

A collection of research studies, dating from the middle 1950s and early 1960s.

796. McAvoy, Thomas T., ed. ROMAN CATHOLICISM AND THE AMERICAN WAY OF LIFE. Grand Forks: University of North Dakota Press, 1960. viii, 248 p.

Essays concerning the status of Roman Catholics in America and the adjustment of Catholic immigrants to the American scene; eighteen contributors of three religious denominations from various social sciences.

797. Nuesse, Celestine J., and Harte, Thomas J., eds. THE SOCIOLOGY OF THE PARISH; AN INTRODUCTORY SYMPOSIUM. Milwaukee: Bruce Publishing Co., 1951. xii, 354 p.

Fifteen articles examine the parish, the literature on American church structure, and report on original field research. Bibliography.

798. Osborne, William Audley. THE SEGREGATED COVENANT; RACE RELATIONS AND AMERICAN CATHOLICS. New York: Herder and Herder, 1967. 252 p.

799. Schuyler, Joseph B., S.J. NORTHERN PARISH: A SOCIOLOGICAL

AND PASTORAL STUDY. Chicago: Loyola University Press, 1960. xxi, 360 p.

Descriptive study of a Roman Catholic parish in the Bronx, New York. Bibliography.

800. Thomas, John Lawrence. RELIGION AND THE AMERICAN PEOPLE. Westminster, Md.: Newman Press, 1963. 307 p.

Analyzes responses to a survey questionnaire on religious beliefs, practices, and attitudes of "average" adults.

801. Wakin, Edward, and Scheuer, Joseph F. THE DE-ROMANIZATION OF THE AMERICAN CATHOLIC CHURCH. New York: Macmillan, 1966. 318 p.

Analysis of traditional attitudes and practices in conflict with the layman's view.

D. PROTESTANTISM

802. Anderson, Charles H. WHITE PROTESTANT AMERICANS: FROM NATIONAL ORIGINS TO RELIGIOUS GROUP. Ethnic Groups in American Life Series. Englewood Cliffs, N.J.: Prentice-Hall, 1970. xx, 188 p.

Common religious heritage replaced distinct ethnic backgrounds and aided assimilation of Anglo-Saxon and Northern European immigrants. Bibliography.

803. Culver, Dwight W. NEGRO SEGREGATION IN THE METHODIST CHURCH. Yale Studies in Religious Education, no. 22. New Haven: Yale University Press, 1953. xii, 218 p.

Based on study of historical records, official church documents, and a series of questionnaires.

804. Demerath, Nicholas J. III. SOCIAL CLASS IN AMERICAN PROTESTANTISM. Chicago: Rand McNally, 1965. xxvi, 228 p.

Analyzes questionnaires collected from members of selected congregations by the National Council of Churches of Christ in 1957.

805. Glock, Charles Y., et al. TO COMFORT AND TO CHALLENGE; A DILEMMA OF THE CONTEMPORARY CHURCH. Berkeley: University of California Press, 1967. 268 p.

Studies of the attitudes and opinions of clergy and parishioners of the Protestant Episcopal Church.

806. Hadden, Jeffrey K. THE GATHERING STORM IN THE CHURCHES: THE WIDENING GAP BETWEEN CLERGY AND LAYMEN. Garden City, N.Y.: Doubleday, 1969. xxix, 257 p.

> Surveys from 1965 and 1967 of clergy and laymen about attitudes on the civil rights issues and the role of the clergy.

807. Hammond, Phillip E. THE CAMPUS CLERGYMAN. New York: Basic Books, 1966. xvi, 171 p.

> Nine hundred ninety-seven responses to a questionnaire mailed to all full-time Protestant campus clergymen suggest the lack of institutionalization of the campus ministry.

808. Harrison, Paul M. AUTHORITY AND POWER IN THE FREE CHURCH TRADITION; A SOCIAL CASE STUDY OF THE AMERICAN BAPTIST CONVENTION. Princeton, N.J.: Princeton University Press, 1959. 248 p.

> Explores the consequences of the clash between local churches and the authority of their national leadership. Bibliography.

809. Kersten, Lawrence L. THE LUTHERAN ETHIC; THE IMPACT OF RELIGION ON LAYMEN AND CLERGY. Detroit: Wayne State University Press, 1970. 309 p.

> Tests the thesis that the social consequences of Lutheranism are different from those of ascetic forms of Protestantism.

810. Metz, Donald L. NEW CONGREGATIONS; SECURITY AND MISSION IN CONFLICT. Philadelphia: Westminster Press, 1967. 170 p.

> A study of six newly established United Presbyterian congregations in suburbs of a West coast metropolitan area. Bibliography.

811. Pope, Liston. MILLHANDS AND PREACHERS: A STUDY OF GASTONIA. Yale Studies in Religious Education, no. 15. New Haven: Yale University Press, 1942. xvi, 369 p.

> Study of the transformation of sects into denominations in a North Carolina mill town. Bibliography.

812. Seger, Imogen. RESPONSIBILITY FOR THE COMMUNITY: A NEW NORM CONFRONTS TRADITION IN LUTHERAN CITY CHURCHES. Totowa, N.J.: Bedminster Press, 1963. viii, 366 p.

> American Protestantism has embraced the "social gospel" which conflicts with Lutheran religious traditions. Bibliography.

813. Shippey, Frederick A. PROTESTANTISM IN SUBURBAN LIFE. New

York: Abingdon Press, 1964. 221 p.

Discusses trends since 1945, especially relations with minorities; nine page bibliography.

814. Tapp, Robert B. RELIGION AMONG THE UNITARIAN UNIVERSALISTS: CONVERTS IN THE STEPFATHERS' HOUSE. Quantitative Studies in Social Relations. New York: Seminar Press, 1973. xii, 268 p.

Based on questionnaire responses of over 12,000 members of a representative sample of Unitarian Universalists living in the United States and Canada. Bibliography.

E. THE BLACK CHURCH

815. Brotz, Howard. THE BLACK JEWS OF HARLEM: NEGRO NATIONALISM AND THE DILEMMA OF NEGRO LEADERSHIP. New York: Schocken Books, 1970. 144 p.

A study of a religious community which traces its origins to the Ethiopian Hebrews or Falashas.

816. Frazier, E. Franklin. THE NEGRO CHURCH IN AMERICA. New York: Schocken Books, 1963. xii, 92 p.

The church plays an important part in social cohesion and functioning of the group.

817. Hamilton, Charles V. THE BLACK PREACHER IN AMERICA. New York: William Morrow, 1972. 246 p.

Discussion of the role and activities of Black ministry which historically ranked above other Black professionals; interviews with preachers of seven different denominations.

818. Lincoln, C. Eric. THE BLACK MUSLIMS IN AMERICA. Rev. ed. Boston: Beacon Press, 1973. xxxi, 302 p.

Studies tensions in the Black Muslim community and its relationship to Eastern Muslims, to other Black religions, and to the white community. Bibliography.

819. Nelsen, Hart M., et al., comp. THE BLACK CHURCH IN AMERICA. New York: Basic Books, 1971. vii, 375 p.

Essays on the history and differentiation of the Black church and alternatives to traditional Protestantism.

820. Washington, Joseph R., Jr. BLACK RELIGION: THE NEGRO AND

CHRISTIANITY IN THE UNITED STATES. Boston: Beacon Press, 1964. ix, 308 p.

821. _____. BLACK SECTS AND CULTS. Garden City, N.Y.: Doubleday, 1972. xii, 176 p.

Argues that the underlying theme of Black religion is the acquisition of power for a people blocked from many secular avenues of power. Bibliography.

F. OTHER RELIGIOUS COMMUNITIES, SECTS, CULTS

822. Braden, Charles S. THESE ALSO BELIEVE: A STUDY OF MODERN AMERICAN CULTS AND MINORITY RELIGIOUS MOVEMENTS. New York: Macmillan, 1949. xv, 491 p.

Discusses thirteen groups, such as Father Divine, Christian Science, Jehovah's Witnesses, Anglo-Israel, and the Oxford Group Movement.

823. Carden, Maren Lockwood. ONEIDA: UTOPIAN COMMUNITY TO MODERN CORPORATION. Baltimore: The Johns Hopkins University Press, 1969. xx, 228 p.

An account of the original Christian utopian settlement established by John Humphrey Noyes and its transformation into the present Kenwood community. Bibliography.

824. Clark, Elmer Talmage. THE SMALL SECTS IN AMERICA. Rev. ed. New York: Abingdon Press, 1949. 256 p.

Discusses the sectarian spirit in American Christianity and distinguishes five sect-types: pessimistic or adventist; perfectionist or subjectivist; charismatic or pentecostal; communistic; and legalistic or objectivist.

825. Dohrman, H. Theodore. CALIFORNIA CULT; THE STORY OF "MANKIND UNITED." Beacon Series in the Sociology of Religion, vol. 2. Boston: Beacon Press, 1958. 163 p.

Examines an economic-religious-utopian cult which had followers in California between 1934 and 1951.

826. Elkholy, Abdo A. THE ARAB MOSLEMS IN THE UNITED STATES; RELIGION AND ASSIMILATION. New Haven: College and University Press, [c.1966]. 176 p.

A study of Arab Moslems based on field research in 1959 in Toledo, Ohio, and Detroit, Michigan. Bibliography.

827. Hostetler, John A. AMISH SOCIETY. Rev. ed. Baltimore: The Johns Hopkins University Press, 1968. xviii, 369 p.

Observations of many communities, especially the Old Order Amish in Pennsylvania, Ohio, Indiana, Iowa, and Ontario, with discussion of conflicts and customs. Bibliography.

828. Hostetler, John A., and Huntington, Gertrude. CHILDREN IN AMISH SOCIETY: SOCIALIZATION AND COMMUNITY EDUCATION. New York: Holt, Rinehart and Winston, 1971. 119 p.

829. _____. THE HUTTERITES IN NORTH AMERICA. New York: Holt, Rinehart and Winston, 1967. viii, 119 p. Bibliography.

830. Lofland, John. DOOMSDAY CULT: A STUDY OF CONVERSION, PROSELYTIZATION AND MAINTENANCE OF FAITH. Englewood Cliffs, N.J.: Prentice-Hall, 1966. x, 276 p.

Intensive case study of a semi-Christian adventist sect, Divine Precepts or DP cult.

831. Needleman, Jacob. THE NEW RELIGIONS. Garden City, N.Y.: Doubleday, 1970. xii, 245 p.

Description of some of the Oriental religions to which an increasing number of Americans are attached.

832. Nelson, Lowry. THE MORMON VILLAGE: A PATTERN AND TECHNIQUE OF LAND SETTLEMENT. Salt Lake City: University of Utah Press, 1952. xvii, 296 p.

The development and structure of Mormon villages in the United States and Canada. Bibliography.

833. O'Dea, Thomas F. THE MORMONS. Chicago: University of Chicago Press, 1957. 288 p.

Describes the rise and expansion of the Mormon church.

834. Rowley, Peter. NEW GODS IN AMERICA. New York: David McKay, 1971. 208 p.

Examines the rise of new unconventional religious activity in the United States.

835. Schwartz, Gary. SECT IDEOLOGIES AND SOCIAL STATUS. Chicago: University of Chicago Press, 1970. x, 260 p.

A study of Seventh-Day Adventist and Pentecostal groups in an urban context in the United States.

836. Stroup, Herbert H. THE JEHOVAH'S WITNESSES. New York: Columbia University Press, 1945. vii, 180 p.

    Reviews history, organization, and relations with American society. Bibliography.

G. ANTHOLOGIES

837. Glock, Charles Y., comp. RELIGION IN SOCIOLOGICAL PERSPECTIVE: ESSAYS IN THE EMPIRICAL STUDY OF RELIGION. Belmont, Calif.: Wadsworth, 1973. ix, 315 p.

838. Hammond, Phillip E., and Johnson, Benton, eds. AMERICAN MOSAIC: SOCIAL PATTERNS OF RELIGION IN THE UNITED STATES. New York: Random House, 1970. xi, 342 p.

839. Knudten, Richard D., ed. THE SOCIOLOGY OF RELIGION: AN ANTHOLOGY. New York: Appleton-Century-Crofts, 1967. xiii, 560 p.

840. McLoughlin, William Gerald, and Bellah, Robert N., eds. RELIGION IN AMERICA. Boston: Houghton Mifflin Co., 1968. xxiv, 433 p.

    A symposium on the current religious revival, the secularization of society, and the activism of the clergy.

841. McNamara, Patrick H., ed. RELIGION AMERICAN STYLE: A SOCIOLOGICAL VIEW. New York: Harper & Row, Publishers, 1974. xiv, 408 p.

842. Smith, James Ward, and Jamison, A. Leland, eds. RELIGION IN AMERICAN LIFE. Vol. 1: THE SHAPING OF AMERICAN RELIGION; vol. 2: RELIGIOUS PERSPECTIVES IN AMERICAN CULTURE. Princeton, N.J.: Princeton University Press, 1961. Vol. 1, 514 p.; vol. 2, 427 p.

    Historical analyses of the interaction between religion and various phases of secular culture.

* * *

See also Chapter 9.

Chapter 12

SOCIAL STRATIFICATION

Chapter 12

SOCIAL STRATIFICATION

A. BIBLIOGRAPHIES

843. Blum, Zahava D., and Rossi, Peter H. SOCIAL CLASS RESEARCH AND IMAGES OF THE POOR: A BIBLIOGRAPHIC REVIEW. Baltimore: Johns Hopkins University, Center for the Study of Social Organization of Schools, 1968. 94 p. Bibliography pp. 71-94.

844. Glenn, Norval D., et al. SOCIAL STRATIFICATION: A RESEARCH BIBLIOGRAPHY. Berkeley: Glendessary Press, 1970. xi, 466 p.

    Entries are divided into sixty-five topics (eleven of which are geographical) with an author index.

845. Tompkins, Dorothy C. POVERTY IN THE UNITED STATES DURING THE SIXTIES: A BIBLIOGRAPHY. Berkeley: Institute of Governmental Studies, University of California, 1970. 542 p.

B. AMERICAN CLASS STRUCTURE

846. Centers, Richard. THE PSYCHOLOGY OF SOCIAL CLASSES; A STUDY OF CLASS CONSCIOUSNESS. Princeton, N.J.: Princeton University Press, 1949. xii, 244 p.

    Social class is treated as a psychological, subjective phenomenon determined by the person's awareness of membership in a class.

847. Dollard, John. CASTE AND CLASS IN A SOUTHERN TOWN. 3rd ed. Garden City, N.Y.: Doubleday, Anchor, 1957. xii, 466 p.

    Study based on observations and interviews in a small town in the southeastern region of the Deep South; first published in 1937.

848. Galbraith, John Kenneth. THE AFFLUENT SOCIETY. Boston: Houghton Mifflin Co., 1958. xii, 368 p.

   An analysis of preconditions and consequences of affluence, and the social and cultural context within which it occurs. Concern with production and marketing in private industry is contrasted to neglect in the sphere of public interest, such as education and social science.

849. Gordon, Milton M. SOCIAL CLASS IN AMERICAN SOCIOLOGY. Durham, N.C.: Duke University Press, 1958. xiii, 281 p.

   A critical evaluation of the major contributions to the study of class in the United States since the end of World War I.

850. Hodge, Robert W. TRENDS IN SOCIAL STRATIFICATION. Chicago: Markham, 1973. 150 p.

851. Kerckhoff, Alan C. SOCIALIZATION AND SOCIAL CLASS. Englewood Cliffs, N.J.: Prentice-Hall, 1972. vi, 170 p.

   Reviews the research literature on the socialization process within the context of the American stratification system.

852. Kohn, Melvin L. CLASS AND CONFORMITY: A STUDY IN VALUES. Homewood, Ill.: Dorsey Press, 1969. xxiii, 315 p.

   Explores the relationships among social structure, socialization, and personality.

853. Kolko, Gabriel. WEALTH AND POWER IN AMERICA: AN ANALYSIS OF SOCIAL CLASS AND INCOME DISTRIBUTION. New York: Praeger, 1962. xii, 178 p.

   Analysis of economic and social structure of America and maldistribution of wealth.

854. Laumann, Edward O. PRESTIGE AND ASSOCIATION IN AN URBAN COMMUNITY; AN ANALYSIS OF AN URBAN STRATIFICATION SYSTEM. Indianapolis: Bobbs-Merrill, 1966. viii, 218 p.

   A study of the stratification system in two urban communities-- Cambridge and Belmont, Massachusetts.

855. _____, ed. SOCIAL STRATIFICATION: RESEARCH AND THEORY FOR THE 1970'S. Indianapolis: Bobbs-Merrill, 1970. 280 p.

   Reprint of the special spring 1970 issue of SOCIOLOGICAL INQUIRY devoted entirely to social stratification.

856. McKinley, Donald G. SOCIAL CLASS AND FAMILY LIFE. New York: Free Press of Glencoe, 1964. xii, 306 p.

Socialization in an achievement-oriented society.

857. Miller, Herman P. RICH MAN, POOR MAN. New York: Thomas Y. Crowell Co., 1964. xxvi, 260 p.

Summarizes 1960 U.S. census data concerning the distribution of income and documents the persistence of inequality in American life.

858. Miller, S.M., and Roby, Pamela A. THE FUTURE OF INEQUALITY. New York: Basic Books, 1970. xvi, 272 p.

Presents data on unequal distribution of social goods--income, assets, basic services, education, power, status, life style, and respect. Analyzes the extent of inequality and the characteristics of the deprived. Discusses ameliorative policies concerning poverty in the context of social stratification.

859. Packard, Vance. THE STATUS SEEKERS; AN EXPLORATION OF CLASS BEHAVIOR IN AMERICA AND THE HIDDEN BARRIERS THAT AFFECT YOU, YOUR COMMUNITY, YOUR FUTURE. New York: David McKay, 1959. 376 p.

A popular presentation of militarization and bureaucratization of American society, stiffening of class boundaries, and decline in primary relationships.

860. Warner, W. Lloyd, and Lunt, Paul S. THE STATUS SYSTEM OF A MODERN COMMUNITY. Yankee City Series, vol. 2. New Haven: Yale University Press, 1942. xx, 246 p.

861. Warner, W. Lloyd, et al. DEMOCRACY IN JONESVILLE; A STUDY IN QUALITY AND INEQUALITY. New York: Harper & Brothers, 1949. xviii, 313 p.

862. _____. SOCIAL CLASS IN AMERICA: A MANUAL OF PROCEDURE FOR THE MEASUREMENT OF SOCIAL STATUS. New York: Harper & Row, Publishers, 1960. 298 p.

First published in 1949 in Chicago by Science Research Associates. The Harper Torchbook edition of 1960 includes two additional chapters. Bibliography.

C. TEXTBOOKS AND READERS

863. Barber, Bernard. SOCIAL STRATIFICATION: A COMPARATIVE ANAL-

YSIS OF STRUCTURE AND PROCESS. New York: Harcourt, Brace, 1957. 540 p.

864. Blumberg, Paul, ed. THE IMPACT OF SOCIAL CLASS; A BOOK OF READINGS. New York: Thomas Y. Crowell Co., 1972. x, 544 p.

Thirty-two selections from major historical and contemporary works and reprints from sociological journals.

865. Cuber, John F., and Kenkel, William F. SOCIAL STRATIFICATION IN THE UNITED STATES. New York: Appleton-Century-Crofts, 1954. x, 359 p.

866. Hodges, Harold M., Jr., and Lane, W. Clayton. SOCIAL STRATIFICA-TION: CLASS IN AMERICA. New York: Harper & Row, Publishers, 1970. 632 p.

A one-volume edition of Hodges' text, SOCIAL STRATIFICA-TION (Cambridge: Schenkman, 1964) and Lane's collection of readings, PERMANENCE AND CHANGE IN SOCIAL CLASS (New York: Harper & Row, Publishers, 1970).

867. Kahl, Joseph A. THE AMERICAN CLASS STRUCTURE. New York: Rinehart, 1957. 310 p.

Existence of stratification contrary to dominant American ide-ology; causes of mobility and changes in occupational opportu-nity.

868. Lasswell, Thomas E. CLASS AND STRATUM; AN INTRODUCTION TO CONCEPTS AND RESEARCH. Boston: Houghton Mifflin Co., 1965. xiv, 497 p.

A text on social stratification with a sociopsychological frame-work.

869. Lejeune, Robert, ed. CLASS AND CONFLICT IN AMERICAN SOCIETY. Chicago: Markham, 1972. vii, 310 p.

A collection of twenty-three articles, some from popular peri-odicals.

870. Mayer, Kurt B., and Buckley, Walter. CLASS AND SOCIETY. 3rd rev. ed. New York: Random House, 1970. x, 179 p.

871. Roach, Jack L., et al. SOCIAL STRATIFICATION IN THE UNITED STATES. Englewood Cliffs, N.J.: Prentice-Hall, 1969. xi, 621 p.

This text-reader presents a survey and critique of sociological writing on stratification.

872. Tumin, Melvin M. SOCIAL STRATIFICATION; THE FORMS AND FUNCTIONS OF INEQUALITY. Englewood Cliffs, N.J.: Prentice-Hall, 1967. ix, 118 p.

873. _____, ed. READINGS ON SOCIAL STRATIFICATION. Englewood Cliffs, N.J.: Prentice-Hall, 1970. ix, 454 p.

D. UPPER CLASS AND ELITES

874. Baltzell, Edward Digby. PHILADELPHIA GENTLEMEN: THE MAKING OF A NATIONAL UPPER CLASS. Glencoe, Ill.: Free Press, 1958. 440 p.

Also published as AN AMERICAN BUSINESS ARISTOCRACY (New York: Collier, 1962).

875. _____. THE PROTESTANT ESTABLISHMENT: ARISTOCRACY AND CASTE IN AMERICA. New York: Random House, 1964. xviii, 429 p.

Historical analysis of old-stock upper-class values from the late nineteenth century to the 1960s.

876. Domhoff, G. William. THE HIGHER CIRCLES: THE GOVERNING CLASS IN AMERICA. New York: Random House, 1970. 367 p.

Establishes a set of indicators by which to identify the upper class as the governing class.

877. _____. WHO RULES AMERICA? Englewood Cliffs, N.J.: Prentice-Hall, 1967. 184 p.

Argues that an upper class controls various institutions of American society.

878. Domhoff, G. William, and Ballard, Hoyt B., comp. C. WRIGHT MILLS AND THE POWER ELITE. Boston: Beacon Press, 1968. viii, 278 p.

Fifteen articles by sociologists, economists, and other social scientists.

879. Hunter, Floyd. THE BIG RICH AND THE LITTLE RICH. Garden City, N.Y.: Doubleday, 1965. ix, 101 p.

The dysfunctional consequences of excessive compensation of directorates of industry and commerce.

880. _____. TOP LEADERSHIP, U.S.A. Chapel Hill: University of North Carolina Press, 1959. 268 p.

Sociometric data on 106 influential national associations.

881. Keller, Suzanne. BEYOND THE RULING CLASS; STRATEGIC ELITES IN MODERN SOCIETY. New York: Random House, 1963. 354 p.

Differentiates between ruling classes and elites and argues that interdependent strategic elites emerge to take the place of a ruling class.

882. Lundberg, Ferdinand. THE RICH AND THE SUPER-RICH; A STUDY IN THE POWER OF MONEY TODAY. New York: Lyle Stuart, 1968. 812 p.

Analyzes the American oligarchy and its impact upon all of American life.

883. Mills, C. Wright. THE POWER ELITE. New York: Oxford University Press, 1956. 423 p.

Top executives in large corporations, government, and the armed forces form a "power elite" which collectively controls American society.

E. WORKING AND MIDDLE CLASSES

884. Fellman, Gordon, and Brandt, Barbara. THE DECEIVED MAJORITY; POLITICS AND PROTEST IN MIDDLE AMERICA. New York: Transaction Books, 1973. ix, 265 p.

Participant-observation study of blue-collar homeowners in Cambridge, Massachusetts, and an analysis of a conflict between working class and "organization class."

885. Fried, Marc. WORLD OF THE URBAN WORKING CLASS. Cambridge, Mass.: Harvard University Press, 1973. ix, 410 p.

Daily lives of residents of Boston's West End before its demolition in 1958 urban renewal. Bibliography (pp. 329-69).

886. Howell, Joseph T. HARD LIVING ON CLAY STREET; A STUDY OF BLUE COLLAR FAMILIES. Chapel Hill: University of North Carolina Press, 1972. vii, 405 p.

Participant-observation study of working class neighborhood in Washington, D.C.

887. Leggett, John C. CLASS, RACE AND LABOR: WORKING-CLASS CONSCIOUSNESS IN DETROIT. New York: Oxford University Press, 1968. xvii, 252 p.

A study of a random sample of 375 blue collar workers interviewed in 1960; two-thirds were found militant, especially better-off whites and Negroes. Bibliography (pp. 228-38).

888. Mills, C. Wright. WHITE COLLAR; THE AMERICAN MIDDLE CLASSES. New York: Oxford University Press, 1951. xx, 378 p.

Uses census and other data to show the decline of the old and the growth of the new middle class.

889. Mizruchi, Ephraim. SUCCESS AND OPPORTUNITY; A STUDY OF ANOMIE. New York: Free Press of Glencoe, 1964. xiii, 204 p.

Study of anomie which in the middle class results from the disparity of aspiration and achievement (boundlessness) and in the lower class from limits on occupational attainment and community integration (bondlessness). Bibliography.

890. Sexton, Patricia Cayo, and Sexton, Brendan. BLUE COLLARS AND HARD HATS: THE WORKING CLASS AND THE FUTURE OF AMERICAN POLITICS. New York: Random House, 1971. xii, 327 p.

891. Shostak, Arthur B. BLUE-COLLAR LIFE. New York: Random House, 1969. xvi, 299 p.

Systematic analysis of the life style and problems of the urban, male, Caucasian, union-affiliated, blue-collar worker.

892. Shostak, Arthur B., and Gomberg, William, eds. BLUE-COLLAR WORLD. Englewood Cliffs, N.J.: Prentice-Hall, 1964. xviii, 622 p.

Reader of sixty-one articles, most published previously, on life styles and conditions of the working class.

F. POVERTY

893. Caplovitz, David. THE POOR PAY MORE; CONSUMER PRACTICES OF LOW-INCOME FAMILIES. New York: Free Press of Glencoe, 1963. 220 p.

Study by the Columbia University Bureau of Applied Social Research of consumer practices of people in low-income housing projects in the 1960s.

894. Deutscher, Irwin, and Thompson, Elizabeth J., eds. AMONG THE PEOPLE: ENCOUNTERS WITH THE POOR. New York: Basic Books, 1968. xvii, 408 p.

895. Ferman, Louis A., et al., eds. POVERTY IN AMERICA; A BOOK OF READINGS. Rev. ed. Ann Arbor: University of Michigan Press, 1968. xxxiii, 669 p.

896. Gans, Herbert J. MORE EQUALITY. New York: Pantheon Books, 1973. xx, 261 p.

Suggests that American society may become more egalitarian by virtue of income redistribution and other economic policies.

897. Gitlin, Todd, and Hollander, Nanci. UPTOWN; POOR WHITES IN CHICAGO. New York: Harper & Row, Publishers, 1970. xxxii, 435 p.

The struggle of southern whites in Chicago, based on direct observation.

898. Glazer, Nona Y., and Creedon, Carol F., eds. CHILDREN AND POVERTY; SOME SOCIOLOGICAL AND PSYCHOLOGICAL PERSPEC-TIVES. Chicago: Rand McNally, 1968. vii, 328 p.

A sociologist and a psychologist describe the social and psychological characteristics of the more than fourteen million children who grow up in poverty in an affluent society.

899. Goldstein, Bernard. LOW INCOME YOUTH IN URBAN AREAS; A CRITICAL REVIEW OF THE LITERATURE. New York: Holt, Rinehart and Winston, 1967. vii, 280 p.

A survey of research and 230 annotated references to articles.

900. Harrington, Michael. THE OTHER AMERICA; POVERTY IN THE UNITED STATES. New York: Macmillan, 1962. 191 p.

Reveals the emergence of a culture of poverty.

901. Huber, Joan, and Chalfont, Peter, eds. SOCIOLOGY OF AMERICAN POVERTY. Cambridge, Mass.: Schenkman, distributed by General Learning Press, Morristown, N.J., 1974. x, 408 p. Bibliography pp. 345-406.

902. Kramer, Ralph M. PARTICIPATION OF THE POOR; COMPARATIVE COMMUNITY CASE STUDIES IN THE WAR ON POVERTY. Englewood Cliffs, N.J.: Prentice-Hall, 1969. xii, 273 p.

Community action programs in the San Francisco Bay area.

903. Kriesberg, Louis. MOTHERS IN POVERTY: A STUDY OF FATHERLESS
FAMILIES. Chicago: Aldine, 1970. x, 356 p.

Interviews with a cross-section of households in four low-income
public housing projects and their neighborhoods in Syracuse,
New York.

904. Miller, S.M., and Riessman, Frank. SOCIAL CLASS AND SOCIAL
POLICY. New York: Basic Books, 1968. 302 p.

A collection of essays on the concept of a "new working
class"--the poor and the underprivileged. This class has much
strength and many positive features, such as strong ethnic
traditions, extended cooperative family, humor, sense of
equality, and avoidance of competition. Social and welfare
policies should reflect these values.

905. Moynihan, Daniel Patrick, ed. ON UNDERSTANDING POVERTY:
PERSPECTIVES FROM THE SOCIAL SCIENCES. New York: Basic
Books, 1969. xviii, 425 p.

906. Pinkney, Alphonso, and Woock, Roger R. POVERTY AND POLITICS
IN HARLEM; REPORT ON PROJECT UPLIFT, 1965. New Haven:
College and University Press, 1970. 191 p.

Critical view of the "War on Poverty" as administered by the
Office of Economic Opportunity, and the implementation of
Project Uplift in Harlem in the summer of 1965.

907. Roby, Pamela [A.], ed. THE POVERTY ESTABLISHMENT. Englewood
Cliffs, N.J.: Prentice-Hall, 1974. 217 p.

A collection of recent articles, some previously unpublished,
on the power structure which regulates the poor and preserves
inequality by increasing the profits of the rich. Bibliography.

908. Seligman, Ben B. PERMANENT POVERTY; AN AMERICAN SYNDROME.
Chicago: Quadrangle, 1968. 238 p.

909. Shostak, Arthur B., and Gomberg, William, eds. NEW PERSPECTIVES
ON POVERTY. Englewood Cliffs, N.J.: Prentice-Hall, 1965. vi,
185 p.

910. Will, Robert E., and Vatter, Harold G. POVERTY IN AFFLUENCE;
THE SOCIAL, POLITICAL AND ECONOMIC DIMENSIONS OF POVERTY
IN THE UNITED STATES. 2nd ed. New York: Harcourt, Brace and
World, 1970. xi, 243 p.

911. Zurcher, Louis A., Jr. POVERTY WARRIORS: THE HUMAN EXPERIENCE OF PLANNED SOCIAL INTERVENTION. Austin: University of Texas Press, 1970. xxiii, 442 p.

   Account of the first eighteen months of operation of the Topeka Office of Economic Opportunity; participation by the poor in antipoverty programs; eighteen-page bibliography.

* * *

See also Chapter 7, Section E; Chapter 13; and Chapter 23, Section G.

Chapter 13

WORK AND OCCUPATIONS

Chapter 13

WORK AND OCCUPATIONS

A. REFERENCE WORKS AND BIBLIOGRAPHIES

912. Cornell University. New York State School of Industrial and Labor Relations. Library. CATALOG OF THE MARTIN P. CATHERWOOD LIBRARY. 12 vols. Boston: G.K. Hall, 1967. 9,632 p. Supplements, 6 vols., 1967-73. 5,269 p.

   Includes material on labor-management relations, human relations in industry, personnel, social insurance and employee welfare, and related topics.

913. Overs, Robert P., and Deutsch, Elizabeth C. SOCIOLOGICAL STUDIES OF OCCUPATIONS: A BIBLIOGRAPHY. Washington, D.C.: U.S. Department of Labor, Office of Manpower, Automation and Training, Manpower Administration, 1965. 85 p.

914. United States Employment Service. DICTIONARY OF OCCUPATIONAL TITLES. 3rd ed. Vol 1: DEFINITIONS OF TITLES; vol. 2: OCCUPATIONAL CLASSIFICATION AND INDUSTRY. Washington, D.C.: U.S. Department of Labor, Manpower Administration, Bureau of Employment Security, sold by Government Printing Office, 1965. Vol. 1, xxiv, 809 p.; vol. 2, vii, 656 p. (A revised edition is in preparation.)

915. Wasserman, Paul, et al., eds. ENCYCLOPEDIA OF BUSINESS INFORMATION SOURCES. Vol. 1: GENERAL SUBJECTS; vol. 2: GEOGRAPHIC SOURCES. Detroit: Gale Research Co., 1970. 689 p.

   A detailed listing of primary subjects of interest to managerial personnel, with a record of sourcebooks, periodicals, organizations, directories, handbooks, bibliographies, and other sources of information on each topic. Volume one covers the United States, volume two, other countries.

B. WORK AND OCCUPATIONAL STRUCTURE

916. Berger, Peter L., ed. THE HUMAN SHAPE OF WORK: STUDIES IN THE SOCIOLOGY OF OCCUPATIONS. New York: Macmillan, 1964. vii, 241 p.

    Five essays and an editorial summary explore the meaning of work in modern society.

917. Blau, Peter M[ichael], and Duncan, Otis Dudley. THE AMERICAN OCCUPATIONAL STRUCTURE. New York: Wiley, 1967. xvii, 520 p.

    A modern classic, based on a 1962 quantitative analysis of 20,700 males between the ages of twenty and sixty-four, which measured five variables: father's education, father's occupation, respondent's education, his first job, and his occupation in 1962.

918. Glaser, Barney G., ed. ORGANIZATIONAL CAREERS; A SOURCE-BOOK FOR THEORY. Chicago: Aldine, 1968. ix, 468 p.

    Collection of sixty-four articles discussing organizational life--recruitment, motivation, commitment, promotion, and career patterns.

919. Morse, Dean. THE PERIPHERAL WORKER. New York: Columbia University Press, 1969. xvi, 202 p.

    Data from Bureau of Labor Statistics showing that of the seventy-six million persons in the labor force in 1965, twenty-five to thirty million worked less than full time for a full year.

920. Mott, Paul E., et al. SHIFT WORK; THE SOCIAL, PSYCHOLOGICAL AND PHYSICAL CONSEQUENCES. Ann Arbor: University of Michigan Press, 1965. vi, 351 p.

    Based on responses to more than 1,000 questionnaires. Bibliography (pp. 339-46).

921. Patchen, Martin. PARTICIPATION, ACHIEVEMENT, AND INVOLVEMENT ON THE JOB. Englewood Cliffs, N.J.: Prentice-Hall, 1970. xvi, 285 p.

    A study of workers in three power plants and two engineering divisions of the Tennessee Valley Authority.

922. Reiss, Albert J., Jr., et al. OCCUPATIONS AND SOCIAL STATUS. New York: Free Press of Glencoe, 1962. vii, 305 p.

Critical evaluation of the 1947 National Opinion Research
Center study upon which the North-Hatt occupational prestige
scale was based; includes Duncan's new occupational index,
based on census data.

923. Wilensky, Harold L. SYLLABUS OF INDUSTRIAL RELATIONS; A GUIDE
TO READING AND RESEARCH. Chicago: University of Chicago Press,
1954. xi, 305 p.

Emphasizes issues related to unionism and the economic, social,
and psychological aspects of the organization of work; selected
bibliography of 1,000 titles (pp. 200-305).

924. Zald, Mayer N. OCCUPATIONS AND ORGANIZATIONS IN AMERI-
CAN SOCIETY; THE ORGANIZATION-DOMINATED MAN? Chicago:
Markham, 1971. xii, 108 p. Bibliography.

C. TEXTS AND READINGS

925. Caplow, Theodore. SOCIOLOGY OF WORK. Minneapolis: University of Minnesota Press, 1957; New York: McGraw-Hill, 1964.
330 p. Bibliography.

926. Hall, Richard H. OCCUPATIONS AND THE SOCIAL STRUCTURE.
Englewood Cliffs, N.J.: Prentice-Hall, 1969. xi, 393 p.

927. Hughes, Everett C. MEN AND THEIR WORK. Glencoe, Ill.: Free
Press, 1958. 184 p.

A collection of thirteen of Hughes' essays on work, the organization of work, and the nature of work experience. Bibliography.

928. Krause, Elliott A. THE SOCIOLOGY OF OCCUPATIONS. Boston:
Little, Brown and Co., 1971. xiv, 398 p. Bibliographic notes pp.
357-87.

929. Pavalko, Ronald M. SOCIOLOGY OF OCCUPATIONS AND PROFES-
SIONS. Itasca, Ill.: F.E. Peacock, 1971. x, 234 p.

930. _____, ed. SOCIOLOGICAL PERSPECTIVES ON OCCUPATIONS.
Itasca, Ill.: F.E. Peacock, 1972. xi, 388 p.

Twenty-nine selections to accompany his textbook (see item
929).

931. Schneider, Eugene V. INDUSTRIAL SOCIOLOGY; THE SOCIAL RELA-

TIONS OF INDUSTRY AND THE COMMUNITY. 2nd ed. New York: McGraw-Hill, 1969. xii, 637 p. Bibliography pp. 561-611.

932. Slocum, Walter L. .OCCUPATIONAL CAREERS; A SOCIOLOGICAL PERSPECTIVE. 2nd ed. Chicago: Aldine, 1974. 324 p.

Contemporary work and occupations, career-related problems of women and minority groups.

933. Taylor, Lee. OCCUPATIONAL SOCIOLOGY. New York: Oxford University Press, 1968. xiv, 591 p.

Relates occupations to social organization.

934. Whyte, William Foote. ORGANIZATIONAL BEHAVIOR: THEORY AND APPLICATION. Homewood, Ill.: Richard D. Irwin, 1969. xiv, 807 p.

A revision of his MEN AT WORK (Homewood, Ill.: Dorsey, 1961); case studies, analysis of labor and industrial organizations. Bibliography.

D. LABOR FORCE AND UNIONS

935. Blumberg, Paul. INDUSTRIAL DEMOCRACY: THE SOCIOLOGY OF PARTICIPATION. New York: Schocken Books, 1969. viii, 278 p.

Workers' management and decision-making powers are discussed as a realistic answer to the problem of worker alienation.

936. Dubin, Robert. WORKING UNION-MANAGEMENT RELATIONS; THE SOCIOLOGY OF INDUSTRIAL RELATIONS. Englewood Cliffs, N.J.: Prentice-Hall, 1958. 291 p.

Industrial unions and management in the role of antagonistic cooperators in the contemporary United States; twenty-three-page bibliography.

937. Dubin, Robert, et al. LEADERSHIP AND PRODUCTIVITY; SOME FACTS OF INDUSTRIAL LIFE. San Francisco: Chandler, 1965. ix, 138 p.

Four essays on the supervisor and the performance of his unit.

938. Karsh, Bernard. DIARY OF A STRIKE. Urbana: University of Illinois Press, 1958. 180 p.

Study of the organization of a 200-member, mostly female, local union in a town of 14,000 people. Bibliography.

939. Miller, Robert W., et al. THE PRACTICE OF LOCAL UNION LEADER-SHIP; A STUDY OF FIVE LOCAL UNIONS. Columbus: Ohio State University Press, 1965. xiv, 282 p.

Study of leaders and members of five middle-sized local industrial union organizations in Columbus, Ohio. Bibliography (pp. 269-76).

940. Peck, Sidney M. THE RANK-AND-FILE LEADER: A STUDY OF THE SOCIAL AND POLITICAL IDEOLOGY OF THE INDUSTRIAL UNION STEWARD. New Haven: College and University Press, 1963. 398 p.

Investigates the job and class-consciousness among union stewards in the Milwaukee area. Bibliography (pp. 364-92).

941. Rose, Arnold Marshall. UNION SOLIDARITY; THE INTERNAL CO-HESION OF A LABOR UNION. Minneapolis: University of Minnesota Press, 1952. xx, 209 p.

A 1948 study of attitudes of the members of Local 688 of the Teamsters Union in St. Louis.

942. Rosenblum, Gerald. IMMIGRANT WORKERS; THEIR IMPACT ON AMERICAN LABOR RADICALISM. New York: Basic Books, 1973. vi, 189 p.

An examination of immigrant influence on U.S. labor politics and the conservative posture of the American labor movement.

943. Seidman, Joel, et al. THE WORKER VIEWS HIS UNION. Chicago: University of Chicago Press, 1958. xi, 299 p.

Six case studies of different unions.

944. Shostak, Arthur B. AMERICA'S FORGOTTEN LABOR ORGANIZATION; A SURVEY OF THE ROLE OF THE SINGLE-FIRM INDEPENDENT UNION IN AMERICAN INDUSTRY. Princeton University Industrial Relations Section, Research Report Series, no. 103. Princeton, N.J.: Princeton University Press, 1962. 141 p.

A study of forty independent single firm trade unions in New Jersey.

945. Wilensky, Harold L. INTELLECTUALS IN LABOR UNIONS; ORGANI-ZATIONAL PRESSURES ON PROFESSIONAL ROLES. Glencoe, Ill.: Free Press, 1956. 336 p.

The sample included 298 staff experts drawn from the international headquarters of twenty-eight unions with at least 50,000 members.

E. BLUE COLLAR WORK

946. Blauner, Robert. ALIENATION AND FREEDOM; THE FACTORY WORKER AND HIS INDUSTRY. Chicago: University of Chicago Press, 1964. xvi, 222 p.

> Hypothesizes that the degree of freedom or alienation is a function of four stages of technology: craft, machine tending, assembly line, and automation.

947. Gilman, Glenn. HUMAN RELATIONS IN THE INDUSTRIAL SOUTH-EAST; A STUDY OF THE TEXTILE INDUSTRY. Chapel Hill: University of North Carolina Press, 1956. xii, 327 p.

> Discusses the importance of folkways in evolution of industrial relations in the Piedmont region.

948. Kornhauser, Arthur William. MENTAL HEALTH OF THE INDUSTRIAL WORKER; A DETROIT STUDY. New York: Wiley, 1965. xi, 354 p.

> Study of auto factory workers.

949. Lipset, Seymour Martin, et al. UNION DEMOCRACY: THE INTERNAL POLITICS OF THE INTERNATIONAL TYPOGRAPHICAL UNION. New York: Free Press, 1956. xxviii, 455 p.

950. Meissner, Martin. TECHNOLOGY AND THE WORKER; TECHNICAL DEMANDS AND SOCIAL PROCESSES IN INDUSTRY. San Francisco: Chandler, 1969. xiii, 264 p.

951. Walker, Charles R. STEELTOWN, AN INDUSTRIAL CASE HISTORY OF THE CONFLICT BETWEEN PROGRESS AND SECURITY. New York: Harper & Brothers, 1950. xv, 284 p.

> A Yale study of changes experienced by management, union, workers, and community when a long-established factory was transplanted from a Pennsylvania town to Gary, Indiana.

952. Walker, Charles R., and Guest, Robert H. THE MAN ON THE ASSEM-BLY LINE. Cambridge, Mass.: Harvard University Press, 1952. 180 p.

> A 1949 Yale study of 180 workers in a New England automobile assembly plant.

953. Warner, W. Lloyd, and Low, J.O. THE SOCIAL SYSTEM OF THE MODERN FACTORY. THE STRIKE: A SOCIAL ANALYSIS. Yankee City Series, vol. 4. New Haven: Yale University Press, 1947. 245 p.

Study of a strike in a shoe factory in the 1930s and ten years later.

954. Zaleznik, Abraham. WORKER SATISFACTION AND DEVELOPMENT: A CASE STUDY OF WORK AND SOCIAL BEHAVIOR IN A FACTORY GROUP. Cambridge, Mass.: Harvard University Graduate School of Business Administration, 1956. 148 p.

Analysis of a small work group using Homans' model from THE HUMAN GROUP (see item 1796).

F. PROFESSIONS AND SEMIPROFESSIONS

955. Abrahamson, Mark. THE PROFESSIONAL IN THE ORGANIZATION. Chicago: Rand McNally, 1967. ix, 158 p.

Discusses professionals, such as scientists, ministers, nurses, physicians, and psychologists.

956. Carlin, Jerome E. LAWYERS' ETHICS; A SURVEY OF THE NEW YORK CITY BAR. New York: Russell Sage Foundation, 1966. xxix, 267 p.

Stratification of metropolitan legal profession and social controls within it. Professional norms are related to organizational context.

957. _____. LAWYERS ON THEIR OWN; A STUDY OF INDIVIDUAL PRACTITIONERS IN CHICAGO. New Brunswick, N.J.: Rutgers University Press, 1962. 234 p.

958. Cole, Stephen. THE UNIONIZATION OF TEACHERS; A CASE STUDY OF THE UFT. New York: Praeger, 1969. ix, 245 p.

Study of conditions that led to teacher militancy in New York City.

959. Etzioni, Amitai, ed. THE SEMI-PROFESSIONS AND THEIR ORGANI-ZATION; TEACHERS, NURSES, SOCIAL WORKERS. New York: Free Press, 1969. xix, 328 p.

Analysis from the perspective of conflict resulting from the incompatibility of administrative and professional authority.

960. Hirsch, Walter, SCIENTISTS IN AMERICAN SOCIETY. New York: Random House, 1968. xii, 174 p.

961. Hughes, Everett C., et al. TWENTY THOUSAND NURSES TELL THEIR STORY; A REPORT ON STUDIES OF NURSING FUNCTIONS. Philadel-

phia: Lippincott, 1958. xi, 280 p.

962. Kornhauser, William. SCIENTISTS IN INDUSTRY: CONFLICT AND ACCOMMODATION. Berkeley: University of California Press, Institute of Industrial Relations, 1962. xii, 230 p.

Based on interviews with scientists in various laboratories, universities, and government positions; includes bibliography.

963. Marcson, Simon. THE SCIENTIST IN AMERICAN INDUSTRY; SOME ORGANIZATIONAL DETERMINANTS IN MANPOWER UTILIZATION. New York: Harper & Row, Publishers, 1960. 158 p.

Case study of engineers, chemists, and physicists in one laboratory that is part of a larger business organization.

964. Moore, Wilbert E. THE PROFESSIONS: ROLES AND RULES. New York: Russell Sage Foundation, 1970. 303 p.

The emergence of professionalism: the clients, self-regulation, prestige, organization, complementary occupations, and social responsibilities of the professions. Bibliography (pp. 245-301).

965. Perrucci, Robert, and Gerstl, Joel E. PROFESSION WITHOUT COMMUNITY; ENGINEERS IN AMERICAN SOCIETY. Studies in Occupations and Professions. New York: Random House, 1969. 194 p.

Data from a national survey of engineers in government and industry.

966. _____, eds. THE ENGINEERS AND THE SOCIAL SYSTEM. New York: Wiley, 1969. xii, 344 p.

Education, work, family roles, and social class.

967. Smigel, Erwin O. THE WALL STREET LAWYER: PROFESSIONAL ORGANIZATION MAN? New York: Free Press, 1964. ix, 369 p.

968. Strauss, Anselm L., and Rainwater, Lee. THE PROFESSIONAL SCIENTIST; A STUDY OF AMERICAN CHEMISTS. Social Research Studies in Contemporary Life. Chicago: Aldine, 1962. xiii, 282 p.

A study commissioned by the American Chemical Society.

969. Warkov, Seymour, and Zelan, J. LAWYERS IN THE MAKING. National Opinion Research Center, Monographs in Social Research, no. 7. Chicago: Aldine, 1965. xxii, 180 p.

Recruitment of lawyers and their occupational values; the sample was drawn from 33,782 college seniors at 135 colleges who received B.A. degrees in 1961. Bibliography.

970. Wood, Arthur Lewis. CRIMINAL LAWYER. New Haven: College and University Press, 1967. 335 p.

> Attitudes and behavior of criminal vs. civil lawyers; 101 attorneys from Brooklyn, Jersey City, Birmingham, Madison, and New London were interviewed.

G. MANAGEMENT

971. Bendix, Reinhard. HIGHER CIVIL SERVANTS IN AMERICAN SOCIETY; A STUDY OF THE SOCIAL ORIGINS, THE CAREERS AND THE POWER-POSITION OF HIGHER FEDERAL ADMINISTRATION. University of Colorado Studies, Series in Sociology, no. 2. Boulder: University of Colorado Press, 1949. 129 p.

> Investigation of a sample of higher governmental administrators lends support to Myrdal's thesis that American civil servants have not been neutral in the implementation of legislative policies (see item 542).

972. Hackett, Bruce M. HIGHER CIVIL SERVANTS IN CALIFORNIA: A SOCIAL AND POLITICAL PORTRAIT. Berkeley: University of California, Institute of Governmental Affairs, 1967. 141 p.

> Examination of 850 higher civil servants in 1963-64.

973. Jennings, Eugene E. THE MOBILE MANAGER: A STUDY OF THE NEW GENERATION OF TOP EXECUTIVES. Ann Arbor: Bureau of Industrial Relations, University of Michigan Press, 1967. viii, 135 p.

> Ambitions of executives in 500 largest industrial firms.

974. Warner, W. Lloyd, and Abegglen, James C. OCCUPATIONAL MOBILITY IN AMERICAN BUSINESS AND INDUSTRY, 1928-1952. Minneapolis: University of Minnesota Press, 1955. xxi, 315 p.

> Replication of AMERICAN BUSINESS LEADERS: A STUDY IN SOCIAL ORIGINS AND SOCIAL STRATIFICATION, by Frank W. Taussig and Carl S. Joslyn (New York: Macmillan, 1932). Bibliography (pp. 305-11).

975. Warner, W. Lloyd, and Martin, Norman H., eds. INDUSTRIAL MAN; BUSINESSMEN AND BUSINESS ORGANIZATIONS. New York: Harper & Brothers, 1959. 580 p.

> Study of personality and role of business leaders, their relationships with workers and supervisors, and their ideologies. Bibli-

ography.

976. Warner, W. Lloyd, et al. THE AMERICAN FEDERAL EXECUTIVE; A STUDY OF THE SOCIAL AND PERSONAL CHARACTERISTICS OF THE CIVILIAN AND MILITARY LEADERS OF THE UNITED STATES FEDERAL GOVERNMENT. New Haven: Yale University Press, 1963. xvii, 405 p.

H. AUTOMATION AND UNEMPLOYMENT

977. Aiken, Michael, et al. ECONOMIC FAILURE, ALIENATION AND EXTREMISM. Ann Arbor: University of Michigan Press, 1968. vi, 213 p.

A report on the unemployment and reemployment experiences of 300 former employees of the Packard Motor Company.

978. Mann, Floyd Christopher, and Hoffman, L. Richard. AUTOMATION AND THE WORKER; A STUDY OF SOCIAL CHANGE IN POWER PLANTS. New York: Holt, 1960. xiv, 272 p. Bibliography.

979. Marcson, Simon, comp. AUTOMATION, ALIENATION, AND ANOMIE. New York: Harper & Row, Publishers, 1970. xii, 479 p.

Twenty-eight selections on the nature and consequences of automation.

980. Shepard, Jon M. AUTOMATION AND ALIENATION; A STUDY OF OFFICE AND FACTORY WORKERS. Cambridge, Mass.: The M.I.T. Press, 1971. 163 p.

Automated technology reduces the level of alienation of factory and office workers; eleven-page bibliography (pp. 145-55).

981. Sheppard, Harold L., and Belitsky, A. Harvey. THE JOB HUNT: JOB-SEEKING BEHAVIOR OF UNEMPLOYED WORKERS IN A LOCAL ECONOMY. Baltimore: The Johns Hopkins University Press, 1966. xiii, 270 p.

Study in Erie, Pennsylvania, based on questionnaires and interviews with 473 blue collar and 77 white collar workers.

982. Sheppard, Harold L., and Herrick, Neal Q. WHERE HAVE ALL THE ROBOTS GONE? WORKER DISSATISFACTION IN THE 70'S. New York: Free Press, 1972. xxxiv, 222 p.

Three surveys of workers including national sample of 1,533
employed workers, blue and white collar, male and female.

983. Walker, Charles R.   TOWARD THE AUTOMATIC FACTORY; A CASE
STUDY OF MEN AND MACHINES.   New Haven: Yale University
Press, 1957.   xv, 232 p.

A case study of automation in a new continuous seamless
pipe mill.

* * *

See also Chapter 12; and Chapter 19, Section D.

Chapter 14

MARRIAGE AND FAMILY

Chapter 14

MARRIAGE AND FAMILY

A. REFERENCE WORKS AND BIBLIOGRAPHIES

984. Aldous, Joan, and Hill, Reuben. INTERNATIONAL BIBLIOGRAPHY OF RESEARCH IN MARRIAGE AND THE FAMILY, 1900-1964. Minneapolis: Distributed by the University of Minnesota Press for the Minnesota Family Study Center and the Institute of Life Insurance, 1967. 508 p.

985. Aldous, Joan, and Dahl, Nancy. INTERNATIONAL BIBLIOGRAPHY OF RESEARCH IN MARRIAGE AND THE FAMILY, VOL. 2: 1965-1972. Minneapolis: University of Minnesota Press, in association with the Institute of Life Insurance, for the Minnesota Family Study Center, 1974. 1519 p.

986. Christensen, Harold T., ed. HANDBOOK OF MARRIAGE AND THE FAMILY. Chicago: Rand McNally, 1964. 1028 p. Bibliography.

987. Ellis, Albert, and Abarbanel, Albert, eds. THE ENCYCLOPEDIA OF SEXUAL BEHAVIOR. 2nd ed. New York: Hawthorn Books, 1967. 1072 p.

988. Goode, William J., et al. SOCIAL SYSTEMS AND FAMILY PATTERNS: A PROPOSITIONAL INVENTORY. Indianapolis: Bobbs-Merrill, 1971. xxix, 779 p. Bibliography pp. 733-79.

989. Goslin, David A., ed. HANDBOOK OF SOCIALIZATION THEORY AND RESEARCH. Chicago: Rand McNally, 1969. xiii, 1182 p. Bibliography.

990. Schlesinger, Benjamin. THE ONE-PARENT FAMILY: PERSPECTIVES AND ANNOTATED BIBLIOGRAPHY. Toronto: University of Toronto Press, 1970. xiii, 138 p.

B. TEXTS

991. Adams, Bert N. THE AMERICAN FAMILY: A SOCIOLOGICAL INTER-
PRETATION. Chicago: Markham, 1971. xv, 378 p.

    History of the family; subcultures, adolescence, mate selection,
    and the marital relationship.

992. Bell, Robert R. MARRIAGE AND FAMILY INTERACTION. 3rd ed.
Homewood, Ill.: Dorsey Press, 1971. xii, 573 p.

    Focuses on the middle-class family, dating and courtship,
    marriage, and parenthood.

993. Benson, Leonard. THE FAMILY BOND: MARRIAGE, LOVE, AND
SEX IN AMERICA. New York: Random House, 1971. xi, 431 p.

    Studies the family in terms of four processes: anticipation,
    formation, accommodation, and dissolution. Bibliography
    (pp. 397–422).

994. Blood, Robert O., Jr. THE FAMILY. New York: Free Press, 1972.
viii, 694 p. Bibliography pp. 630–48.

995. Burgess, Ernest W., et al. THE FAMILY: FROM TRADITION TO
COMPANIONSHIP. 4th ed. New York: Van Nostrand, 1971. xii,
644 p. Bibliography.

996. Cavan, Ruth S. THE AMERICAN FAMILY. 4th ed. New York:
Thomas Y. Crowell Co., 1969. xi, 556 p. Bibliography.

997. Christensen, Harold T., and Johnsen, Kathryn P. MARRIAGE AND
THE FAMILY. 3rd ed. New York: Ronald Press, 1971. viii, 546 p.

    First and second editions published as MARRIAGE ANAL-
    YSIS. Bibliography (pp. 523–36).

998. Duberman, Lucile. MARRIAGE AND ITS ALTERNATIVES. New York:
Praeger, 1974. xvii, 238 p.

    Discussion of trends in family life and the future of marriage.
    Bibliography (pp. 217–31).

999. Eshleman, J. Ross. THE FAMILY: AN INTRODUCTION. Boston:
Allyn & Bacon, 1974. 698 p.

    Family systems, marital status, sexual norms, and interaction
    throughout life cycles.

1000. Kephart, William M. THE FAMILY, SOCIETY, AND THE INDIVIDUAL. 3rd ed. Boston: Houghton Mifflin Co., 1972. viii, 628 p. Bibliography.

1001. Reiss, Ira L. THE FAMILY SYSTEM IN AMERICA. New York: Holt, Rinehart and Winston, 1971. xvi, 493 p. Bibliography pp. 455-80.

1002. Skolnick, Arlene. THE INTIMATE ENVIRONMENT; EXPLORING MARRIAGE AND THE FAMILY. Boston: Little, Brown and Co., 1973. 478 p.

> Discusses ideal and reality in family life, social change, couples, communes, generational conflict, prospects, and policies of the family.

1003. Winch, Robert F. THE MODERN FAMILY. 3rd ed. New York: Holt, Rinehart and Winston, 1971. xviii, 654 p.

C. READERS

1004. Bell, Norman W., and Vogel, Ezra F., eds. A MODERN INTRODUCTION TO THE FAMILY. Rev. ed. New York: Free Press, 1968. xi, 758 p.

> Seven introductory selections and forty-four readings on the relationships between family and society.

1005. Glasser, Paul H., and Glasser, Lois N., eds. FAMILIES IN CRISIS. New York: Harper & Row, Publishers, 1970. vi, 405 p.

> Twenty selections grouped in three topical sections: poverty, disorganization, and illness and disability.

1006. Gordon, Michael, ed. THE AMERICAN FAMILY IN SOCIAL-HISTORICAL PERSPECTIVE. New York: St. Martin's Press, 1973. xv, 428 p.

> Twenty selections focus upon the American scene--ethnic variation, youth, women, sexual behavior, and demographic trends.

1007. Hadden, Jeffrey K., and Borgatta, Marie L., eds. MARRIAGE AND THE FAMILY; A COMPREHENSIVE READER. Itasca, Ill.: F.E. Peacock, 1969. xi, 667 p.

> Sixty-five selections under sixteen topical headings. Majority date from 1965 or later. Bibliography.

1008. Kline, Arthur F., and Medley, Morris. DATING AND MARRIAGE; AN INTERACTIONIST PERSPECTIVE. Boston: Holbrook Press, 1973. iv, 506 p.

Twenty-five readings on the dyadic relationship between men and women.

1009. Lopata, Helena Z., ed. MARRIAGE AND FAMILIES. New York: Van Nostrand, 1973. xi, 417 p.

1010. Otto, Herbert A., ed. THE FAMILY IN SEARCH OF A FUTURE: ALTERNATE MODELS FOR MODERNS. New York: Appleton-Century-Crofts, 1970. xiv, 204 p.

Fifteen articles discuss alternate forms of marriage.

1011. Schulz, David A., and Wilson, Robert A. READINGS ON THE CHANGING FAMILY. Englewood Cliffs, N.J.: Prentice-Hall, 1973. vi, 313 p.

Alternatives to the style of the middle-class monogamous family. Articles on sexual revolution, generation gap, and women's liberation.

1012. Sussman, Marvin B. SOURCEBOOK IN MARRIAGE AND THE FAMILY. 4th ed. Boston: Houghton Mifflin Co., 1974. vii, 389 p.

An anthology of thirty-six articles, seventeen from the third edition and nineteen new selections, on trends in marriage styles, sex roles, and socialization.

D. MARRIAGE AND DIVORCE

1013. Bernard, Jessie. THE FUTURE OF MARRIAGE. New York: World Publishing Co., 1972. xvi, 367 p.

Survey of research on mental health and happiness of single and married men and women. Bibliography (pp. 333-60).

1014. _____. REMARRIAGE: A STUDY OF MARRIAGE. New York: Dryden Press, 1956. 372 p.

Based on census data, intensive case studies, and 2,009 cases gathered by questionnaires. Outlines the extent and nature of remarriage in the United States.

1015. _____. THE SEX GAME: COMMUNICATION BETWEEN THE SEXES. New York: Atheneum, 1972. 372 p.

Analysis of husband-wife interaction, problems of communication, and the female role in the occupational structure.

1016. Blood, Robert O., Jr., and Wolfe, Donald M. HUSBANDS AND

WIVES: THE DYNAMICS OF MARRIED LIVING. Glencoe, Ill.: Free Press, 1960. xxi, 293 p.

Findings based on a probability sample of 731 urban (Detroit) and suburban wives, and 178 farm wives. Focuses on the dyadic components of decision making--division of labor, the economic function, children, companionship, emotional understanding, and love.

1017. Burgess, Ernest W., and Wallin, Paul W. ENGAGEMENT AND MARRIAGE. Philadelphia: Lippincott, 1953. xii, 819 p.

Information derived from a large-scale research project with engaged couples. Bibliography (pp. 789-800).

1018. Carter, Hugh, and Glick, Paul C. MARRIAGE AND DIVORCE: A SOCIAL AND ECONOMIC STUDY. Cambridge, Mass.: Harvard University Press, 1970. xxix, 451 p.

Analyzes significant trends and variations in the demographic aspects of marital behavior in the United States. Bibliography.

1019. Constantine, Larry L., and Constantine, Joan M. GROUP MARRIAGE: A STUDY OF CONTEMPORARY MULTILATERAL MARRIAGE. New York: Macmillan, 1973. xii, 299 p.

Reports on three years of research on thirty marriages in which there were more than two partners. Bibliography (pp. 291-99).

1020. DeLora, Joann S., and DeLora, Jack R., eds. INTIMATE LIFE STYLES: MARRIAGE AND ITS ALTERNATIVES. Pacific Palisades, Calif.: Goodyear, 1972. xv, 421 p.

About fifty selections on the contemporary family, alternatives to marriage, and future lifestyles.

1021. Goode, William J. AFTER DIVORCE. Glencoe, Ill.: Free Press, 1956. xv, 381 p.

Four hundred twenty-five mothers, twenty to thirty-eight years of age, were interviewed at intervals of two months, eight months, fourteen months, or twenty-six months after their divorces. Reissued in a paperbound edition as WOMEN IN DIVORCE (New York: Free Press, 1965).

1022. Jacobson, Paul H., with Jacobson, Pauline F. AMERICAN MARRIAGE AND DIVORCE. New York: Holt, Rinehart and Winston, 1959. xviii, 188 p.

Statistical overview, covering the period from 1860 to mid-1950s.

1023. Komarovsky, Mirra, with Philips, Jane H. BLUE-COLLAR MARRIAGE. New York: Random House, Vintage, 1967. xv, 395 p.

   A study of fifty-eight marriages in a working class community of 50,000. Bibliography (pp. 380-97).

1024. Monahan, Thomas P. THE PATTERN OF AGE AT MARRIAGE IN THE UNITED STATES. 2 vols. Philadelphia: Stephenson-Brothers, 1951. vi, 451 p.

   Determines the pattern of age at marriage and its trend over the years. Bibliography (pp. 397-451).

1025. O'Neill, Nena, and O'Neill, George. OPEN MARRIAGE: A NEW LIFE STYLE FOR COUPLES. New York: Evans, 1972. 287 p.

   Discussion of open marriage of companionship versus closed marriage of full commitment; based on interviews with white middle-class couples. Bibliography.

1026. Rogers, Carl R. BECOMING PARTNERS; MARRIAGE AND ITS ALTERNATIVES. New York: Delacorte Press, 1972. 243 p. Bibliography.

1027. Scanzoni, John H. SEXUAL BARGAINING: POWER POLITICS IN THE AMERICAN MARRIAGE. Englewood Cliffs, N.J.: Prentice-Hall, 1972. viii, 180 p.

   Examines male-female, husband-wife relationships, social exchanges, conflicts, and changes within marriage.

1028. Winch, Robert F. MATE-SELECTION; A STUDY OF COMPLEMENTARY NEEDS. New York: Harper & Brothers, 1958. 349 p.

E. INTERMARRIAGE

1029. Barron, Milton L. PEOPLE WHO INTERMARRY; INTERMARRIAGE IN A NEW ENGLAND INDUSTRIAL COMMUNITY. Syracuse, N.Y.: Syracuse University Press, 1947. xii, 389 p.

   Intermarriage, as studied in 1929-30 and 1940, occurs most often between ethnic groups, less often between religious groups, and least often between racial groups. Bibliography (pp. 355-66).

1030. _____, ed. THE BLENDING AMERICAN; PATTERNS OF INTERMARRIAGE. Chicago: Quadrangle, 1972. xiv, 357 p. Bibliography.

1031. Besanceney, Paul H. INTERFAITH MARRIAGES: WHO AND WHY.

New Haven: College and University Press, 1970. 223 p. Bibliography pp. 184-217.

1032. Gordon, Albert I. INTERMARRIAGE: INTERFAITH, INTERRACIAL, INTERETHNIC. Boston: Beacon Press, 1964. xiii, 420 p.

A study of the attitudes toward intermarriage of 5,407 college students; an extensive review of the literature. Greatest increase is likely in interethnic marriages.

1033. Washington, Joseph R., Jr. MARRIAGE IN BLACK AND WHITE. Boston: Beacon Press, 1971. 358 p.

A study of attitudes toward interracial marriage.

F. PARENTHOOD AND CHILDREARING

1034. Benson, Leonard. FATHERHOOD: A SOCIOLOGICAL PERSPECTIVE. New York: Random House, 1968. xii, 371 p. Bibliography pp. 325-59.

1035. Bossard, James Herbert Siward. PARENT AND CHILD; STUDIES IN FAMILY BEHAVIOR. Philadelphia: University of Pennsylvania Press, 1953. 308 p.

Based on 500 case studies of students attending colleges in the Northeast.

1036. Bossard, James Herbert Siward, and Boll, Eleanor Stoker. THE SOCIOLOGY OF CHILD DEVELOPMENT. 4th ed. New York: Harper & Row, Publishers, 1966. x, 566 p.

Revision of a text originally published in 1948.

1037. Bossard, James Herbert Siward, with Boll, Eleanor Stoker. THE LARGE FAMILY SYSTEM; AN ORIGINAL STUDY IN THE SOCIOLOGY OF FAMILY BEHAVIOR. Philadelphia: University of Pennsylvania Press, 1956. 325 p.

A pioneering study of one hundred large families, each with at least six children.

1038. Bowerman, Charles, et al. UNWED MOTHERHOOD: PERSONAL AND SOCIAL CONSEQUENCES. Chapel Hill: Institute for Research in Social Science, University of North Carolina Press, 1963-66. xi, 410 p.

1039. Ginzberg, Eli, ed. THE NATION'S CHILDREN. Vol. 1: THE FAMI-

LY AND SOCIAL CHANGE; vol. 2: DEVELOPMENT AND EDUCATION;
vol. 3: PROBLEMS AND PROSPECTS. New York: Columbia University
Press, 1960. Vol. 1, 252 p.; vol. 2, 242 p.; vol. 3, 242 p.

> Thirty-one reports prepared for the 1960 White House Conference
> on Children and Youth. Bibliography (vol. one, pp. 249-52;
> vol. two, pp. 239-42; vol. three, pp. 239-42).

1040. LeMasters, E.E. PARENTS IN MODERN AMERICA; A SOCIOLOGICAL
ANALYSIS. Homewood, Ill.: Dorsey Press, 1970. xiii, 232 p.

1041. Miller, Daniel R., and Swanson, Guy E. THE CHANGING AMERICAN
PARENT; A STUDY IN THE DETROIT AREA. New York: Wiley, 1958.
302 p.

> Tests the hypothesis that goals and methods of childrearing
> among middle-class parents have changed as a direct result of
> the bureaucratization of American economic enterprise.

1042. Ritchie, Oscar W., and Koller, Marvin R. SOCIOLOGY OF CHILD-
HOOD. New York: Meredith, 1964. x, 333 p.

> Discusses in twenty chapters social settings for childhood,
> means, models, and problems of socialization.

1043. Sexton, Patricia Cayo. THE FEMINIZED MALE: CLASSROOMS,
WHITE COLLARS AND THE DECLINE OF MANLINESS. New York:
Random House, 1969. 240 p.

> The influence of major social institutions--family, school, and
> occupation based on study of school children in a small city.
> School reform and integration of women at all economic and
> political levels are suggested.

1044. Vincent, Clark E. UNMARRIED MOTHERS. New York: Free Press
of Glencoe, 1961. x, 308 p.

> Empirical research primarily based on data concerning 539
> illegitimate births in Alameda County, California, in 1954.
> Bibliography (pp. 291-301).

1045. Winch, Robert F. IDENTIFICATION AND ITS FAMILIAL DETERMI-
NANTS; EXPOSITION OF THEORY AND RESULTS OF PILOT STUDIES.
Indianapolis: Bobbs-Merrill, 1962. 223 p. Bibliography.

G. FAMILY LIVING AND KINSHIP

1046. Adams, Bert N. KINSHIP IN AN URBAN SETTING. Chicago: Markham, 1968. xvii, 228 p.

Interviews of 799 young, white, married adults in Greensboro, North Carolina; kin recognized by 30 percent of respondents. Bibliography (pp. 213-20).

1047. Aldous, Joan, et al., eds. FAMILY PROBLEM SOLVING; A SYMPOSI-UM ON THEORETICAL, METHODOLOGICAL, AND SUBSTANTIVE CONCERNS. Hinsdale, Ill.: Dryden Press, 1971. xii, 452 p.

Based on a 1969 symposium held at the University of California at Riverside. An annotated bibliography (pp. 353-77) gives abstracts of relevant research published from 1950 to 1970.

1048. Bossard, James Herbert Siward, and Boll, Eleanor Stoker. RITUAL IN FAMILY LIVING; A CONTEMPORARY STUDY. Philadelphia: University of Pennsylvania Press, 1950. 228 p.

Information from interviews and published autobiographies reveal the importance of rituals and their social, racial, and religious backgrounds in the American family.

1049. Calhoun, Arthur W. A SOCIAL HISTORY OF THE AMERICAN FAMILY FROM COLONIAL TIMES TO THE PRESENT. Vol. 1: COLONIAL PERIOD; vol. 2: FROM INDEPENDENCE THROUGH THE CIVIL WAR; vol. 3: SINCE THE CIVIL WAR. Cleveland: Arthur H. Clark Co., 1917-19. Vol. 1, 348 p.; vol. 2, 390 p; vol. 3, 411 p.

1050. Farber, Bernard. KINSHIP AND CLASS, A MIDWESTERN STUDY. New York: Basic Books, 1971. xii, 210 p.

Data obtained from long interviews with 239 families with preschool children in Champaign-Urbana, Illinois. Bibliography (pp. 191-97).

1051. Ferriss, Abbott L. INDICATORS OF CHANGE IN THE AMERICAN FAMILY. New York: Russell Sage Foundation, 1970. xii, 145 p.

Time series data on marriage, marital status, households, fertility, dependency, divorce, work and income, and poverty. Contains numerous graphs, charts, and tables. Bibliography (pp. 130-45).

1052. Hill, Reuben, et al. FAMILY DEVELOPMENT IN THREE GENERA-TIONS; A LONGITUDINAL STUDY OF CHANGING FAMILY PATTERNS OF PLANNING AND ACHIEVEMENT. Cambridge, Mass.: Schenkman, 1970. xix, 424 p. Bibliography pp. 358-69.

1053. Holmstrom, Lynda L. THE TWO-CAREER FAMILY. Cambridge, Mass.:

Schenkman, distributed by General Learning Press, Morristown, N.J., 1972. 203 p.

> Married couples pursuing professional careers are compared with traditional families.

1054. Parsons, Talcott, and Bales, Robert F. FAMILY, SOCIALIZATION, AND INTERACTION PROCESS. Glencoe, Ill.: Free Press, 1960. 422 p. Bibliography pp. 409-11.

1055. Rosenberg, George S., and Anspach, Donald F. WORKING-CLASS KINSHIP. Lexington, Mass.: D.C. Heath, 1973. 224 p.

> Authors propose a definition of kinship which includes four subtypes and offer a new model of kindred interaction. Bibliography.

1056. Scanzoni, John H. OPPORTUNITY AND THE FAMILY. New York: Free Press, 1970. vi, 247 p.

> A study of the conjugal family within the economic opportunity structure of American society, based on a survey of 900 households. Bibliography (pp. 241-44).

1057. Shanas, Ethel, and Streib, Gordon F. SOCIAL STRUCTURE AND THE FAMILY: GENERATIONAL RELATIONS. Englewood Cliffs, N.J.: Prentice-Hall, 1965. xii, 394 p.

> Papers presented at a symposium on the family, intergenerational relations, and social structure, held at Duke University in November 1963.

1058. Turner, Ralph H. FAMILY INTERACTION. New York: Wiley, 1970. x, 505 p.

> Microsociological analysis of the social-psychological aspects of the contemporary American family. Bibliography.

1059. Yorburg, Betty. THE CHANGING FAMILY. New York: Columbia University Press, 1973. viii, 230 p.

> Discusses ethnic and class differences and the future of the American family.

1060. Zimmerman, Carle C., and Cervantes, Lucius F. SUCCESSFUL AMERICAN FAMILIES. New York: Pageant Press, 1960. 226 p.

> Based on a statistical study of about 10,000 families in eight cities who were designated successful.

H. SEXUAL BEHAVIOR

1061. Bartell, Gilbert D. GROUP SEX; A SCIENTIST'S EYEWITNESS REPORT ON THE AMERICAN WAY OF SWINGING. New York: Wyden, 1971. x, 298 p.

> Based on more than 100 interviews with swingers, described as middle-class couples, typically conservative socially and politically for whom sex is a substitute for lack of genuine intimacy and whose aesthetic concepts are shaped by television.

1062. Bell, Robert R., and Gordon, Michael, eds. THE SOCIAL DIMENSION OF HUMAN SEXUALITY. Boston: Little, Brown and Co., 1972. vii, 290 p.

> An introductory essay is followed by seventeen selections, arranged under these headings: premarital sex, marital sexuality, extramarital sex, female sexuality and the liberated woman, homosexuality, and commercialized sex. Bibliography.

1063. Cuber, John F., and Harroff, Peggy B. THE SIGNIFICANT AMERICANS: A STUDY OF SEXUAL BEHAVIOR AMONG THE AFFLUENT. New York: Appleton-Century-Crofts, 1965. xi, 204 p.

> Interviews with 437 men and women.

1064. Henslin, James M., ed. STUDIES IN THE SOCIOLOGY OF SEX. New York: Appleton-Century-Crofts, 1971. vi, 410 p.

> Articles by eighteen contributors. Bibliography.

1065. Himelhoch, Jerome, and Fava, Sylvia F., eds. SEXUAL BEHAVIOR IN AMERICAN SOCIETY; AN APPRAISAL OF THE FIRST TWO KINSEY REPORTS. New York: Norton, 1955. xvii, 446 p.

> Thirty-eight articles with 260-item bibliography (pp. 417-35).

1066. Kinsey, Alfred C., et al. SEXUAL BEHAVIOR IN THE HUMAN FEMALE. Philadelphia: Saunders, 1953. 842 p.

1067. _____. SEXUAL BEHAVIOR IN THE HUMAN MALE. Philadelphia: Saunders, 1948. xv, 804 p.

1068. Packard, Vance. THE SEXUAL WILDERNESS; THE CONTEMPORARY UPHEAVAL IN MALE-FEMALE RELATIONSHIPS. New York: David McKay, 1968. xi, 553 p.

> Based on a mail questionnaire sent to some 100 students at each of twenty-one colleges, with comparable research at four

European colleges.

1069. Reiss, Ira L. PREMARITAL SEXUAL STANDARDS IN AMERICA; A SOCIOLOGICAL INVESTIGATION OF THE RELATIVE SOCIAL AND CULTURAL INTEGRATION OF AMERICAN SEXUAL STANDARDS. Glencoe, Ill.: Free Press, 1960. 286 p.

Classifies premarital sex standards under four headings: abstinence, double standard, permissiveness without affection, and permissiveness with affection.

1070. _____. THE SOCIAL CONTEXT OF PREMARITAL SEXUAL PERMISSIVENESS. New York: Holt, Rinehart and Winston, 1967. xiv, 256 p. Bibliography pp. 234-45.

1071. Sorensen, Robert C. ADOLESCENT SEXUALITY IN CONTEMPORARY AMERICA: PERSONAL VALUES AND SEXUAL BEHAVIOR, AGES 13-19. New York: World Publishing Co., 1972. 549 p.

Study using data from 200 personal interviews and 411 self-administered questionnaires. Appendixes include "A Note on the Methodology" by Jiri Nehnevajsa, and samples of the survey questionnaires.

1072. Sorokin, Pitirim A. THE AMERICAN SEX REVOLUTION. Boston: Porter Sargent, 1956. 186 p.

Argues that there is a decline of parental love, proliferating promiscuity, and growing sex addiction.

1073. Winick, Charles. THE NEW PEOPLE: DESEXUALIZATION IN AMERICAN LIFE. New York: Pegasus, 1968. xii, 384 p.

Discussion of sexual depolarization and decrease in sexual interest and activity, documented in the arts, interior decoration, and dress.

I. FAMILY PLANNING

1074. Gebhard, Paul H., et al. PREGNANCY, BIRTH AND ABORTION. New York: Harper & Brothers, 1958. xix, 282 p.

A report from the Indiana Institute for Sex Research, based on personal interviews gathered mostly between 1940 and 1949. Bibliography (pp. 249-65).

1075. Hill, Reuben, et al. THE FAMILY AND POPULATION CONTROL: A PUERTO RICAN EXPERIMENT IN SOCIAL CHANGE. Chapel Hill:

University of North Carolina Press, 1959. xxvi, 481 p.

The culmination of seven years of work which used techniques of psychological research to investigate the decisions of husbands and wives who claim small family goals but have large families.

1076. Lee, Nancy H. THE SEARCH FOR AN ABORTIONIST. Chicago: University of Chicago Press, 1969. 207 p.

A study of 114 middle and upper-middle class women, with 60 percent of the sample from the Northeast.

1077. Rainwater, Lee. AND THE POOR GET CHILDREN: SEX, CONTRACEPTION, AND FAMILY PLANNING IN THE WORKING CLASS. Social Research Studies in Contemporary Life. Chicago: Quadrangle, 1960. 202 p.

Based on in-depth interviews with forty-six lower-class men and fifty women in Chicago and Cincinnati.

1078. _____. FAMILY DESIGN; MARITAL SEXUALITY, FAMILY SIZE, AND CONTRACEPTION. Social Research Studies in Contemporary Life. Chicago: Aldine, 1965. 349 p.

A sample of 409 individuals in 257 families, mainly from Chicago, was selected for a study of differences in fertility rates and family planning by class, religion, and race. Bibliography.

1079. Sarvis, Betty, and Rodman, Hyman. THE ABORTION CONTROVERSY. 2nd ed. New York: Columbia University Press, 1974. ix, 207 p.

Discusses public attitudes, court cases, statistics of legal and illegal abortions, and laws; surveys the implications of the January 1973 Supreme Court ruling. Bibliography.

1080. Stuart, Martha, with Liu, William T., eds. THE EMERGING WOMAN: THE IMPACT OF FAMILY PLANNING; AN INFORMAL SHARING OF INTERESTS, IDEAS AND CONCERNS. Boston: Little, Brown and Co., 1970. xxiii, 329 p.

Eleven discussions at a conference at the University of Notre Dame in November 1967.

* * *

See also Chapter 8, Section E; Chapter 9, Section D; and Chapter 11, Section F.

Chapter 15

WOMEN

Chapter 15

WOMEN

A. REFERENCE WORKS AND BIBLIOGRAPHIES

1081. Astin, Helen S., et al. WOMEN; A BIBLIOGRAPHY ON THEIR EDUCA-
TION AND CAREERS. Washington, D.C.: Human Service Press, 1971.
v, 243 p.

1082. Rosenberg, Marie B., and Bergstrom, Len V. WOMEN AND SOCIETY:
A CRITICAL REVIEW OF THE LITERATURE WITH A SELECTED ANNO-
TATED BIBLIOGRAPHY. Beverly Hills: Sage Publications, in prepara-
tion.

Includes over 3,500 citations in sociology, political science,
and history.

1083. United States Women's Bureau. HANDBOOK ON WOMEN WORKERS.
Washington, D.C.: U.S. Department of Labor, sold by Government
Printing Office, 1969. 384 p.

B. GENERAL WORKS

1084. Amundsen, Kirsten. THE SILENCED MAJORITY; WOMEN AND AMERI-
CAN DEMOCRACY. Englewood Cliffs, N.J.: Prentice-Hall, 1971.
v, 184 p.

Explores the relationship between the sexes in the American
"democratic" system and the need for influencing legislation
by reshaping the stereotype of the American woman.

1085. Bernard, Jessie. WOMEN AND THE PUBLIC INTEREST; AN ESSAY
ON POLICY AND PROTEST. Chicago: Aldine, 1971. viii, 279 p.

Analyzes women's status and problems relating to public policy;
sees sexual division of labor as dysfunctional for general welfare.

1086. Chafe, William H. THE AMERICAN WOMAN; HER CHANGING SOCIAL, ECONOMIC AND POLITICAL ROLES, 1920-1970. New York: Oxford University Press, 1972. xiii, 352 p.

Discusses political, economic, and professional interests, the impact of World War II, and the revival of familism. Bibliography (pp. 321-41).

1087. Chafetz, Janet Saltzman. MASCULINE/FEMININE OR HUMAN? AN OVERVIEW OF THE SOCIOLOGY OF SEX ROLES. Itasca, Ill.: F.E. Peacock, 1974. 242 p.

1088. Glazer-Malbin, Nona, and Waehrer, Helen Youngelson, eds. WOMAN IN A MAN-MADE WORLD; A SOCIOECONOMIC HANDBOOK. Chicago: Rand McNally, 1972. xi, 316 p.

Forty articles and excerpts provide an interdisciplinary introduction to some of the problems facing modern women.

1089. Hogeland, Ronald W., ed. WOMEN AND WOMANHOOD IN AMERICA. Lexington, Mass.: D.C. Heath, 1973. xi, 183 p.

A collection of essays, articles, and bibliographic notes, many from a historical perspective. Bibliography (pp. 181-82).

1090. Ladner, Joyce A. TOMORROW'S TOMORROW: THE BLACK WOMAN. Garden City, N.Y.: Doubleday, 1971. xxvi, 304 p.

The meaning of womanhood in the Black community, especially during the period of adolescence. Bibliography (pp. 289-97).

1091. Lopata, Helena Z. WIDOWHOOD IN AN AMERICAN CITY. Morristown, N.J.: General Learning Press, 1972. xii, 369 p.

Study focuses on widows past fifty who live in major urban centers; discusses roles of wife and mother, kin groups, friendship, and involvement in the community. Bibliography (pp. 347-56).

1092. Mead, Margaret, and Kaplan, Frances. AMERICAN WOMEN; THE REPORT OF THE PRESIDENT'S COMMISSION ON THE STATUS OF WOMEN AND OTHER PUBLICATIONS OF THE COMMISSION. New York: Scribner, 1965. xi, 274 p.

1093. Reeves, Nancy. WOMANKIND, BEYOND THE STEREOTYPES. Chicago: Aldine, 1971. xii, 434 p.

Images of women in this century and an anthology of parallel readings. Bibliography (pp. 419-24).

1094. Riegel, Robert E. AMERICAN WOMEN; A STORY OF SOCIAL CHANGE. Rutherford, N.J.: Fairleigh Dickinson University Press, 1970. 376 p.

    Historical analysis which covers the nineteenth and twentieth centuries. Bibliographic notes (pp. 350–72).

1095. Staples, Robert. THE BLACK WOMAN IN AMERICA: SEX, MARRIAGE, AND THE FAMILY. Chicago: Nelson Hall, 1973. 269 p. Bibliography pp. 243–59.

1096. Yorburg, Betty. SEXUAL IDENTITY: SEX ROLES AND SOCIAL CHANGE. New York: Wiley, 1974. x, 227 p.

    An interdisciplinary analysis. Uses role and exchange theories to describe historical, biological, and other correlates of sexual identity.

C. STATUS OF WOMEN

1097. Andreas, Carol. SEX AND CASTE IN AMERICA. Englewood Cliffs, N.J.: Prentice-Hall, 1971. xiv, 146 p.

    Discusses socialization, sex, the labor market, family structure and its impact on women, and the legal status of women.

1098. Bird, Caroline, with Briller, Sara W. BORN FEMALE; THE HIGH COST OF KEEPING WOMEN DOWN. Rev. ed. New York: David McKay, 1970. xiv, 302 p.

    Social waste of talent due to educational and occupational discrimination against women.

1099. Bullough, Vern, with Bullough, Bonnie. THE SUBORDINATE SEX; A HISTORY OF ATTITUDES TOWARD WOMEN. Urbana: University of Illinois Press, 1973. viii, 375 p. Bibliography pp. 353–66.

1100. Carden, Maren Lockwood. THE NEW FEMINIST MOVEMENT. New York: Russell Sage Foundation, 1974. 226 p.

    Study of the new women's movement and its organizations from small action groups to the National Organization for Women.

1101. Epstein, Cynthia Fuchs, and Goode, William J., eds. THE OTHER HALF; ROADS TO WOMEN'S EQUALITY. Englewood Cliffs, N.J.: Prentice-Hall, 1971. viii, 207 p.

    Articles from academic and women's movement publications, with editorial introductions.

1102. Ferriss, Abbott L. INDICATORS OF TRENDS IN THE STATUS OF AMERICAN WOMEN. New York: Russell Sage Foundation, 1971. xx, 451 p.

Trend data on education, married status and fertility, labor force, employment and income, and health and recreation. Other volumes prepared by Ferris deal with trends in the American family (see item 1051) and in American education (see item 1181). Bibliography (pp. 433-51).

1103. Flexner, Eleanor. CENTURY OF STRUGGLE; THE WOMEN'S RIGHTS MOVEMENT IN THE UNITED STATES. Cambridge, Mass.: Belknap Press of Harvard University, 1959. 384 p.

Analysis of opposition to women's suffrage and documentation of intense resistance to the movement, which gained acceptance between 1848 and 1910. Bibliography.

1104. Harbeson, Gladys E. CHOICE AND CHALLENGE FOR THE AMERICAN WOMAN. 2nd ed. Cambridge, Mass.: Schenkman, 1972. xvii, 185 p.

Discussion of new life patterns, feminism, choice of careers, and achievement of integrated life.

1105. Hole, Judith, and Levine, Ellen. REBIRTH OF FEMINISM. New York: Quadrangle, 1971. xiii, 488 p.

Discussion touches upon the first feminist movement, but is devoted mainly to the contemporary women's movement. Selected and annotated bibliography (pp. 453-74).

1106. Huber, Joan. CHANGING WOMEN IN A CHANGING SOCIETY. Chicago: University of Chicago Press, 1973. vi, 295 p.

Contributions by twenty-six women sociologists; first appeared as Vol. 78, January issue of AMERICAN JOURNAL OF SOCIOLOGY.

1107. Kanowitz, Leo. SEX ROLES IN LAW AND SOCIETY: CASES AND MATERIALS. Albuquerque: University of New Mexico Press, 1974. xiv, 706 p.

1108. _____. WOMEN AND THE LAW; THE UNFINISHED REVOLUTION. Albuquerque: University of New Mexico Press, 1969. ix, 312 p.

An analysis of the legal discrepancies which concern women; includes detailed documentation.

1109. Sinclair, Andrew. THE EMANCIPATION OF THE AMERICAN WOMAN.

2nd ed. New York: Harper & Row, Publishers, 1965. xxix, 410 p.

History of emancipation from early Puritanism.

1110. Ware, Cellestine. WOMAN POWER: THE MOVEMENT FOR WOMEN'S LIBERATION. New York: Tower Publications, 1970. 176 p.

Discussion of feminist leaders and groups; the relationship between radical feminism and the old and the new left. Bibliography (pp. 175-76).

D. WORKING WOMEN

1111. Ginzberg, Eli, and Yohalem, Alice M., eds. CORPORATE LIB: WOMEN'S CHALLENGE TO MANAGEMENT. Policy Studies in Employment and Welfare, no. 17. Baltimore: The Johns Hopkins University Press, 1973. x, 153 p.

Thirteen contributors discuss the implications of female competition for more responsible positions in business and management.

1112. Kreps, Juanita. SEX IN THE MARKETPLACE; AMERICAN WOMEN AT WORK. Policy Studies in Employment and Welfare, no. 11. Baltimore: The Johns Hopkins University Press, 1971. x, 117 p. Bibliography pp. 109-17.

1113. Lopata, Helena Z. OCCUPATION: HOUSEWIFE. New York: Oxford University Press, 1971. xvi, 387 p.

Based on in-depth interviews with nearly 1,000 women in the Chicago metropolitan area over a five-year period in the 1960s.

1114. Nye, Francis Ivan, and Hoffman, Lois Wladis, eds. THE EMPLOYED MOTHER IN AMERICA. Chicago: Rand McNally, 1963. x, 406 p.

Twenty-two empirical studies on the effects of maternal employment upon children, upon husband-wife relationships, and upon the adjustment of the working mother.

1115. Smuts, Robert W. WOMEN AND WORK IN AMERICA. New York: Columbia University Press, 1959. 180 p.

Study of women in the labor force since 1890; greatest change has been in age and in marital status of women workers rather than in the kinds of occupations women choose. Bibliography.

1116. Sweet, James A. WOMEN IN THE LABOR FORCE. Studies in Population. New York: Seminar Press, 1973. viii, 211 p.

A study, based on 1960 U.S. census figures, of the influence of family composition on the labor force activity of wives.

E. ACADEMIC AND PROFESSIONAL WOMEN

1117. Astin, Helen S. THE WOMAN DOCTORATE IN AMERICA; ORIGINS, CAREER, AND FAMILY. New York: Russell Sage Foundation, 1969. xii, 196 p.

Based on an 80 percent mail sample of all female doctorates awarded in 1957 and 1958 in the United States.

1118. Bernard, Jessie. ACADEMIC WOMEN. University Park: Pennsylvania State University Press, 1964. xxv, 331 p.

Official statistics, published and unpublished research, personal documents, and case histories.

1119. Cussler, Margaret. THE WOMAN EXECUTIVE. New York: Harcourt, Brace, 1958. xxi, 165 p.

Interviews with and observations of fifty-five women who had at least three persons working under them.

1120. Epstein, Cynthia Fuchs. WOMAN'S PLACE; OPTIONS AND LIMITS IN PROFESSIONAL CAREERS. Berkeley: University of California Press, 1970. x, 221 p.

Women's access to American professions; discussion of the self-image of the working woman and of institutions, such as child care facilities. Bibliography (pp. 203-13).

1121. Furniss, W. Todd, and Graham, Patricia Albjerg, eds. WOMEN IN HIGHER EDUCATION. Washington, D.C.: American Council on Education, 1974. xiv, 336 p.

Essays on topics from undergraduate admissions to affirmative action, job security, and advancement.

1122. Ginzberg, Eli, and Yohalem, Alice M. EDUCATED AMERICAN WOMEN: SELF-PORTRAITS. New York: Columbia University Press, 1966. xii, 198 p.

Third and final volume of the results of studies of talented persons started by the Human Resources Project at Columbia University in 1960. Self-portraits are composed from information derived from questionnaires.

1123. Ginzberg, Eli, et al. LIFE STYLES OF EDUCATED WOMEN. New

York: Columbia University Press, 1966. ix, 224 p.

Three hundred eleven women who had done graduate work
at Columbia between 1945 and 1951 answered a thirty-nine-
item questionnaire for the Conservation of Human Resources
Project at Columbia. Bibliography (pp. 209-12).

1124. Hughes, Helen MacGill, ed. THE STATUS OF WOMEN IN SOCIOLOGY
1968-1972. Washington, D.C.: American Sociological Association,
1973. iv, 60 p.

Report to the American Sociological Association of the Ad
Hoc Committee on the Status of Women in the Profession.

1125. Komarovsky, Mirra. WOMEN IN THE MODERN WORLD; THEIR EDU-
CATION AND THEIR DILEMMAS. Boston: Little, Brown and Co.,
1953. Reprint. Dubuque, Iowa: W.C. Brown Reprints, 1972. xv,
319 p.

Examines the malaise of the middle-class, college educated
woman and relates this to stresses derived from inconsistencies
in role patterns.

1126. Mattfeld, Jacquelyn A., and Van Aken, Carol G., eds. WOMEN
AND THE SCIENTIFIC PROFESSIONS; PROCEEDINGS OF THE 1961
M.I.T. SYMPOSIUM ON WOMEN IN SCIENCE AND ENGINEERING.
Cambridge, Mass.: The M.I.T. Press, 1965. xvii, 250 p.

Personal, social, and economic factors in women's professional
careers. Decline in professional degrees and participation in
scientific and industrial work.

1127. Rossi, Alice, and Calderwood, Ann, eds. ACADEMIC WOMEN ON
THE MOVE. New York: Russell Sage Foundation, [c.1973]. xv, 560 p.

Twenty-one chapters summarize research on women in higher
education and discuss the rise of political activism among
women between 1968 and 1972.

1128. Theodore, Athena, ed. THE PROFESSIONAL WOMAN. Cambridge,
Mass.: Schenkman, 1971. xi, 769 p.

Fifty-three articles, most previously published, arranged under
such headings as sexual structure of professions, cultural
definitions of the female professional, career patterns and
marriage, and female professionalism and social change.

Chapter 16

YOUTH

Chapter 16

YOUTH

A. BIBLIOGRAPHIES

1129. Gottlieb, David, and Reeves, Jon. ADOLESCENT BEHAVIOR IN URBAN AREAS: A BIBLIOGRAPHIC REVIEW AND DISCUSSION OF THE LITERATURE. New York: Free Press of Glencoe, 1963. 244 p.

1130. Gottlieb, David, et al. THE EMERGENCE OF YOUTH SOCIETIES; A CROSS-CULTURAL APPROACH. New York: Free Press, 1966. xii, 416 p.

> Forty-seven-page introduction and over 350 pages of bibliography, half of it annotated.

B. YOUTH AND ADOLESCENCE

1131. Coleman, James S. THE ADOLESCENT SOCIETY; THE SOCIAL LIFE OF THE TEENAGER AND ITS IMPACT ON EDUCATION. New York: Free Press of Glencoe, 1961. xvi, 368 p.

> Study of the social systems of ten high schools in northern Illinois from 1957 to 1958 shows emphasis on nonacademic, especially athletic interests, and downgrading of intellectual values.

1132. Cottle, Thomas J. TIME'S CHILDREN; IMPRESSIONS OF YOUTH. Boston: Little, Brown and Co., 1971. xxviii, 354 p.

> Essays on youth, education, and politics. Bibliography.

1133. Friedenberg, Edgar Z. COMING OF AGE IN AMERICA: GROWTH AND ACQUIESCENCE. New York: Random House, 1965. xii, 300 p.

> Study of adolescence in high school years.

1134. _____. THE DIGNITY OF YOUTH AND OTHER ATAVISMS. Boston: Beacon Press, 1965. 254 p.

1135. _____. THE VANISHING ADOLESCENT. Boston: Beacon Press, 1959. 144 p.

> Analysis of pressures to create conformity and uniformity in adolescent behavior.

1136. Ginzberg, Eli. THE OPTIMISTIC TRADITION AND AMERICAN YOUTH. New York: Columbia University Press, 1962. x, 160 p.

> Discussion of the improvement of the position of youth, aid to handicapped families, strengthening of the school system, and provision of job opportunities. Bibliography (pp. 159-60).

1137. Goodman, Paul. GROWING UP ABSURD; PROBLEMS OF YOUTH IN THE ORGANIZED SYSTEM. New York: Random House, Vintage, 1960. 296 p.

> The plight of the youthful dissenter and the youthful conformist, and the waste of human resources in America today.

1138. Gottlieb, David, and Ramsey, Charles [E.] THE AMERICAN ADOLESCENT. Homewood, Ill.: Dorsey Press, 1964. viii, 281 p.

1139. Gottlieb, David, and Heinsohn, Anne L., eds. AMERICA'S OTHER YOUTH; GROWING UP POOR. Englewood Cliffs, N.J.: Prentice-Hall, 1971. 206 p.

> Examines situation of Puerto Rican, migrant worker, Mexican-American, American Indian, Appalachian, and Black youth. Bibliography.

1140. Hollingshead, August de Belmont. ELMTOWN'S YOUTH, THE IMPACT OF SOCIAL CLASS ON ADOLESCENTS. New York: Wiley, 1949. xi, 480 p.

> Investigation of the effect of class patterns on adolescent behavior in a midwestern town of about 6,200.

1141. Institute for Religious and Social Studies. Jewish Theological Seminary of America. DILEMMAS OF YOUTH: IN AMERICA TODAY. Edited by R[obert] M[orrison] MacIver. New York: Institute for Religious and Social Studies, distributed by Harper, 1961. 141 p.

> Interdisciplinary study examines postponement of adulthood, emotional problems of adolescence, use of leisure time, educational values, pressures for conformity, and anti-intellectual pressures.

MacIver, R[obert] M[orrison], ed. See Institute for Religious and Social Studies.

1142. Pettitt, George A. PRISONERS OF CULTURE. New York: Scribner, 1970. xii, 291 p.

> Observations on American youth, children of the "cultural dinosaur," characterized by rebellion, retreat from reality, anomie of job regimentation, and compulsory leisure. Bibliography (pp. 275-81).

1143. Rosenberg, Morris. SOCIETY AND THE ADOLESCENT SELF-IMAGE. Princeton, N.J.: Princeton University Press, 1965. xi, 326 p.

> A survey study of adolescents' self images which appear unaffected by the social status of their ethnic or religious groups.

1144. Sebald, Hans. ADOLESCENCE: A SOCIOLOGICAL ANALYSIS. New York: Appleton-Century-Crofts, 1968. xii, 537 p.

> Discussion of family, teenage subculture, minority youth, and social problem areas.

1145. Sherif, Muzafer, and Sherif, Carolyn. REFERENCE GROUPS; EXPLORATION INTO CONFORMITY AND DEVIATION OF ADOLESCENTS. New York: Harper & Row, Publishers, 1964. xiv, 370 p.

> Interdisciplinary research on the behavior of adolescents; similarities in group behavior of upper, middle, and lower-class groups. Bibliography (pp. 319-27).

1146. Smith, Ernest A. AMERICAN YOUTH CULTURE; GROUP LIFE IN TEENAGE SOCIETY. New York: Free Press of Glencoe, 1962. 264 p.

> Reviews earlier studies of youth culture and discusses institutions that bridge the gap between childhood and adulthood. Bibliography.

C. YOUTH MOVEMENT

1147. Altbach, Philip G., and Laufer, Robert S., eds. THE NEW PILGRIMS; YOUTH PROTEST IN TRANSITION. New York: David McKay, 1972. x, 326 p.

> Seventeen essays on American student activism and generational conflict.

1148. Brown, Michael. THE POLITICS AND THE ANTI-POLITICS OF THE YOUNG. Beverly Hills: Glencoe Press, 1969. 136 p.

> Examines the origins of youth militancy, the evolution of

demands for student power and Black power, and the total rejection of politics by the hippies.

1149. Flacks, Richard A. YOUTH AND SOCIAL CHANGE. Chicago: Markham, 1971. xi, 147 p.

Evolution of contemporary youth culture as an alternative life style.

1150. Foster, Julian, and Long, Durward, eds. PROTEST! STUDENT ACTIVISM IN AMERICA. New York: Morrow, 1970. xi, 596 p.

Collection of readings analyzes causes, issues, and nature of student rebellions. Bibliography.

1151. Keniston, Kenneth. THE UNCOMMITTED; ALIENATED YOUTH IN AMERICAN SOCIETY. New York: Harcourt, Brace and World, 1965. viii, 500 p.

Rejection of conventional American values and adult roles, especially occupational and familial roles; cultural and social factors which give rise to youth alienation. Bibliography.

1152. _____. YOUNG RADICALS; NOTES ON COMMITTED YOUTH. New York: Harcourt, Brace and World, 1968. xi, 368 p. Bibliography pp. 361-68.

1153. _____. YOUTH AND DISSENT; THE RISE OF A NEW OPPOSITION. New York: Harcourt Brace Jovanovich, 1971. xii, 403 p.

1154. Lystad, Mary. AS THEY SEE IT; CHANGING VALUES OF COLLEGE YOUTH. Cambridge, Mass.: Schenkman, 1973. xiv, 158 p.

Alienation from traditional values and changes in attitudes toward social institutions.

1155. Orum, Anthony M., ed. THE SEEDS OF POLITICS; YOUTH AND POLITICS IN AMERICA. Englewood Cliffs, N.J.: Prentice-Hall, 1972. x, 385 p.

The origins of youth protest in the United States are explored in twenty-three articles.

D. COUNTERCULTURE AND GENERATION GAP

1156. Cavan, Sherri. HIPPIES OF THE HAIGHT. St. Louis, Mo.: New Critics Press, 1972. 213 p.

Data collected between 1961 and 1966 are examined to discover what is sanctioned and what is censured in the Haight community.

1157. Klein, Alexander, ed. NATURAL ENEMIES? YOUTH AND THE CLASH OF GENERATIONS. Philadelphia: Lippincott, 1970. xli, 533 p.

Seventy-seven essays by social critics, social scientists, and movement leaders on contemporary American youth.

1158. Mead, Margaret. CULTURE AND COMMITMENT; A STUDY OF THE GENERATION GAP. Garden City, N.Y.: Doubleday, Natural History Press, 1970. xxvii, 113 p. (Published for the American Museum of Natural History.)

Analysis of today's youth faced with the wide range of alternatives of a "prefigurative" culture, shaped by worldwide conditions of the post World War II period.

1159. Roszak, Theodore. THE MAKING OF A COUNTER CULTURE; REFLECTIONS ON THE TECHNOCRATIC SOCIETY AND ITS YOUTHFUL OPPOSITION. Garden City, N.Y.: Doubleday, 1969. xiv, 303 p.

An analysis of technology as a form of totalitarianism with science replacing humanity.

1160. Yablonsky, Lewis. THE HIPPIE TRIP; A FIRST-HAND ACCOUNT OF THE BELIEFS AND BEHAVIORS OF HIPPIES IN AMERICA. New York: Pegasus, 1968. 368 p.

Based on records and analysis of Big Sur, the East Village, Haight-Ashbury, and hippie communes in northern California.

E. READERS

1161. Clark, Shirley M., and Clark, John P., eds. YOUTH IN MODERN SOCIETY. New York: Holt, Rinehart and Winston, 1972. 470 p.

Discusses rural, urban, black, Mexican-American youth; some selections on youth in other societies.

1162. Cottle, Thomas J. THE PROSPECT OF YOUTH: CONTEXTS FOR SOCIOLOGICAL INQUIRY. Boston: Little, Brown and Co., 1972. 445 p.

Introduction to the study of youth and adolescence through essays.

1163. Ginzberg, Eli, ed. VALUES AND IDEALS OF AMERICAN YOUTH. New York: Columbia University Press, 1962. xii, 335 p.

Papers presented by twenty-three participants in the White House Conference on Children and Youth.

1164. Gottlieb, David, ed. YOUTH IN CONTEMPORARY SOCIETY. Beverly Hills: Sage Publications, 1972. 384 p. Bibliography.

1165. Herman, Melvin, et al., eds. WORK, YOUTH, AND UNEMPLOYMENT. New York: Thomas Y. Crowell Co., 1968. x, 675 p.

1166. Manning, Peter K. YOUTH: DIVERGENT PERSPECTIVES. New York: Wiley, 1973. x, 230 p.

A reader focusing on white, middle-class, college youth. Bibliography (pp. 228-30).

1167. Manning, Peter K., and Truzzi, Marcello, eds. YOUTH AND SOCIOL-OGY. Englewood Cliffs, N.J.: Prentice-Hall, 1972. xii, 398 p. Bibliography pp. 397-98.

1168. Silverstein, Harry. THE SOCIOLOGY OF YOUTH: EVOLUTION AND REVOLUTION. New York: Macmillan, 1973. vii, 472 p.

Thirty-four readings from historical and contemporary works of sociology and social psychology.

* * *

See also Chapter 17, Sections F and J; and Chapter 20, Sections A, C, and D.

Chapter 17

EDUCATION

Chapter 17

EDUCATION

A. REFERENCE WORKS AND BIBLIOGRAPHIES

1169. Cordasco, Francesco, et al. THE EQUALITY OF EDUCATIONAL OP-
PORTUNITY: A BIBLIOGRAPHY OF SELECTED REFERENCES. Totowa,
N.J.: Rowman and Littlefield, 1973. xiii, 139 p.

1170. ENCYCLOPEDIA OF EDUCATION. Lee C. Deighton, editor-in-chief.
10 vols. New York: Macmillan, 1971. 6,154 p.

> Supplemented by an annual publication, EDUCATION YEAR-
> BOOK, 1972-73--.

1171. ENCYCLOPEDIA OF EDUCATIONAL RESEARCH. 4th ed. New York:
Macmillan, 1969. 1522 p.

> Earlier editions appeared in 1941, 1950, and 1960. Articles
> are followed by bibliographies.

1172. Travers, Robert W. SECOND HANDBOOK OF RESEARCH ON TEACH-
ING. Chicago: Rand McNally, 1973. 1400 p.

> A project of the American Educational Research Association,
> the HANDBOOK first appeared in 1963 under the editorship
> of Nathaniel Gage.

1173. Weinberg, Meyer, ed. EDUCATION OF THE MINORITY CHILD: A
COMPREHENSIVE BIBLIOGRAPHY OF 10,000 SELECTED ENTRIES.
Chicago: Integrated Education Association, 1970. 530 p.

B. SOCIOLOGY OF EDUCATION

1174. Cave, William M., and Chesler, Mark A. SOCIOLOGY OF EDUCA-
TION: AN ANTHOLOGY OF ISSUES AND PROBLEMS. New York:

Macmillan, 1974. viii, 552 p.

Articles on education as a reflection of social structure and on the management of conflict in schools.

1175. Havighurst, Robert J., and Neugarten, Bernice L. SOCIETY AND EDUCATION. 3rd ed. Boston: Allyn & Bacon, 1968. xiii, 538 p.

Discusses social mobility and the school and college as selecting agencies; the process of socialization; and the role of the school in the community and the wider society. Bibliography (pp. 509-32).

1176. Pavalko, Ronald M., ed. SOCIOLOGY OF EDUCATION; A BOOK OF READINGS. Itasca, Ill.: F.E. Peacock, 1968. x, 604 p.

Selected articles from scholarly journals.

1177. Sieber, Sam D., and Wilder, David E., eds. THE SCHOOL IN SOCIETY; STUDIES IN THE SOCIOLOGY OF EDUCATION. New York: Free Press, 1973. vii, 440 p.

C. AMERICAN EDUCATION: CRISIS AND CHANGE

1178. Berg, Ivar. EDUCATION AND JOBS: THE GREAT TRAINING ROBBERY. New York: Praeger, 1970. 200 p.

Critical evaluation of the relationship between education and economic advancement.

1179. Coleman, James S., et al. EQUALITY OF EDUCATIONAL OPPORTUNITY. Washington, D.C.: Department of Health, Education, and Welfare, Office of Education, 1966. Part 1, vi, 737 p.; part 2 (Supplemental Appendix), vii, 548 p.

A national survey of nearly 600,000 students in grades one, three, six, nine, and twelve and their teachers and administrators, providing data on the segregation of racial and ethnic groups. A publication of the National Center for Educational Statistics, the survey is accompanied by a supplemental appendix which contains correlation tables.

1180. Corwin, Ronald G. EDUCATION IN CRISIS; A SOCIOLOGICAL ANALYSIS OF SCHOOLS AND UNIVERSITIES IN TRANSITION. New York: Wiley, 1974. xii, 380 p.

Discusses poverty, racism, student activism, teacher militancy, future of public education, and educational reform.

1181. Ferriss, Abbott L. INDICATORS OF TRENDS IN AMERICAN EDUCA-
TION. New York: Russell Sage Foundation, 1969. xviii, 454 p.

Time series data on education. Bibliography.

1182. Goodman, Paul. COMPULSORY MIS-EDUCATION AND THE COMMU-
NITY OF SCHOLARS. New York: Random House, Vintage, 1966.
339 p.

Two essays of critical appraisal of the American educational
system.

1183. Jencks, Christopher, et al. INEQUALITY; A REASSESSMENT OF THE
EFFECT OF FAMILY AND SCHOOLING IN AMERICA. New York:
Basic Books, 1972. xii, 399 p. Bibliography.

1184. Rickover, Hyman G. AMERICAN EDUCATION, A NATIONAL FAILURE;
THE PROBLEM OF OUR SCHOOLS AND WHAT WE CAN LEARN FROM
ENGLAND. New York: E.P. Dutton, 1963. viii, 502 p.

1185. Riesman, David. CONSTRAINT AND VARIETY IN AMERICAN EDUCA-
TION. Rev. ed. Lincoln: University of Nebraska Press, 1958. 137 p.

1186. Silberman, Charles E. CRISIS IN THE CLASSROOM; THE REMAKING
OF AMERICAN EDUCATION. New York: Random House, 1970.
553 p.

Schools tend to make children docile; remedy lies in informal
education modeled on recent English experiments.

D. SCHOOL ADMINISTRATION

1187. Anderson, James G. BUREAUCRACY IN EDUCATION. Baltimore: The
Johns Hopkins University Press, 1968. 217 p.

High level of bureaucratization was associated with students
of low socioeconomic status and teachers of lower competence.
Bibliography.

1188. Gross, Neal. WHO RUNS OUR SCHOOLS? New York: Wiley, 1958.
195 p.

Roles and behavior of school superintendents and school board
members.

1189. Gross, Neal, and Herriott, Robert E. STAFF LEADERSHIP IN PUBLIC
SCHOOLS: A SOCIOLOGICAL INQUIRY. New York: Wiley, 1965.
xi, 247 p.

Data from the 1960–61 National Principalship Study; evalua-
tions of seventy-five principals were made by 1,303 of their
teachers.

1190. Gross, Neal, et al. EXPLORATIONS IN ROLE ANALYSIS; STUDIES
OF THE SCHOOL SUPERINTENDENCY ROLE. New York: Wiley, 1958.
xiv, 379 p.

1191. Herriott, Robert E., and St. John, Nancy Hoyt. SOCIAL CLASS AND
THE URBAN SCHOOL; THE IMPACT OF PUPIL BACKGROUND ON
TEACHERS AND PRINCIPALS. New York: Wiley, 1966. xvi, 289 p.

Data from the 1960 national survey of the roles of the principal
in 501 public schools in forty-one American cities.

1192. McCarty, Donald J., and Ramsey, Charles E. THE SCHOOL MAN-
AGERS; POWER AND CONFLICT IN AMERICAN PUBLIC EDUCATION.
Westport, Conn.: Greenwood, 1971. xxii, 281 p.

Relationship between school boards, superintendents, and
community power structure in fifty-one communities classified
as: dominated, factional, pluralistic, and inert. Bibliography.

1193. Seeman, Melvin. SOCIAL STATUS AND LEADERSHIP; THE CASE OF
THE SCHOOL EXECUTIVE. Educational Research Monograph, no. 35.
Columbus: Bureau of Educational Research and Service, Ohio State
University, 1960. xiv, 156 p.

Information obtained from school administrations in twenty-six
Ohio communities.

E. SCHOOL TEACHING

1194. Bennett, William S., Jr., and Falk, R. Frank. NEW CAREERS AND
URBAN SCHOOLS; A SOCIOLOGICAL STUDY OF TEACHER AND
TEACHER AIDE ROLES. New York: Holt, Rinehart and Winston, 1970.
xi, 220 p. Bibliography.

1195. Corwin, Ronald G. MILITANT PROFESSIONALISM; A STUDY OF
ORGANIZATIONAL CONFLICT IN HIGH SCHOOLS. New York:
Appleton-Century-Crofts, 1970. 397 p.

Based on interviews with nearly 2,000 teachers in twenty-
four midwestern high schools from 1963 to 1965. Militance
among teachers is viewed as a response to anachronistic administrative styles.

1196. _____. REFORM AND ORGANIZATIONAL SURVIVAL; THE TEACHER

CORPS AS AN INSTRUMENT OF EDUCATIONAL CHANGE. New York: Wiley-Interscience, 1973. xxv, 469 p.

An appraisal of the Teacher Corps Program which strengthened educational opportunities in low-income areas. Bibliography (pp. 439-55).

1197. Gracey, Harry L. CURRICULUM OR CRAFTSMANSHIP: ELEMENTARY SCHOOL TEACHERS IN A BUREAUCRATIC SYSTEM. Chicago: University of Chicago Press, 1972. x, 208 p. Bibliography.

1198. McPherson, Gertrude H. SMALL TOWN TEACHER. Cambridge, Mass.: Harvard University Press, 1972. xii, 247 p.

Participant observation of the role-set of an elementary teacher in a traditional small town school in New England. Bibliography.

F. SCHOOLS AND STUDENTS

1199. Cervantes, Lucius F. THE DROPOUT: CAUSES AND CURES. Ann Arbor: University of Michigan Press, 1965. vii, 244 p.

Study of 300 predominantly white youths from blue collar areas of six large cities.

1200. Conant, James B. THE AMERICAN HIGH SCHOOL TODAY: A FIRST REPORT TO INTERESTED CITIZENS. New York: McGraw-Hill, 1959. xiii, 140 p.

Comparative analysis of American secondary education with proposals for the reorganization of school systems.

1201. Dentler, Robert A., and Warshauer, Mary Ellen. BIG CITY DROPOUTS AND ILLITERATES. New York: Praeger, 1968. xiii, 140 p. (For the Center for Urban Education.)

Using forty-nine indicators, this study provides an analysis of illiteracy and withdrawal from high school in 131 large cities. Bibliography (pp. 137-40).

1202. Fichter, Joseph H. PAROCHIAL SCHOOL: A SOCIOLOGICAL STUDY. Notre Dame, Ind.: University of Notre Dame Press, 1958. xii, 494 p.

Study of 3,632 pupils of a parochial school and of 181 Catholic pupils of a public school and their parents.

1203. Greeley, Andrew M., and Rossi, Peter H. THE EDUCATION OF

CATHOLIC AMERICANS. Chicago: Aldine, 1966. xxii, 368 p.

Interview responses of 2,000 Catholic adults educated in denominational or public schools. Authors identify positive relationship between Catholic schooling and achievement in college and occupation.

1204. Havighurst, Robert J., et al. GROWING UP IN RIVER CITY. New York: Wiley, 1962. 189 p.

A group of 487 sixth-grade students in 1951-52 was tested and evaluated, and then followed until 1960. Bibliography.

1205. McDill, Edward L., and Rigsby, Leo C. STRUCTURE AND PROCESS IN SECONDARY SCHOOLS: THE ACADEMIC IMPACT OF EDUCATION-AL CLIMATES. Baltimore: The Johns Hopkins University Press, 1973. xiv, 201 p.

Study of academic and social dimensions of school climate, based on 1964-65 survey of 20,000 high school students, teachers, and principals. Bibliography.

1206. Stinchcombe, Arthur L. REBELLION IN A HIGH SCHOOL. Chicago: Quadrangle, 1965. xi, 240 p.

Analysis of adolescent misbehavior. Bibliography.

1207. Turner, Ralph H. THE SOCIAL CONTEXT OF AMBITION; A STUDY OF HIGH-SCHOOL SENIORS IN LOS ANGELES. San Francisco: Chandler, 1964. xv, 269 p.

G. URBAN EDUCATION

1208. Cronin, Joseph M. THE CONTROL OF URBAN SCHOOLS; PERSPECTIVE ON THE POWER OF EDUCATIONAL REFORMERS. New York: Free Press, 1973. xxv, 262 p.

Analysis of school boards in the fourteen largest U.S. cities and discussion of current reform proposals.

1209. Dentler, Robert A., et al., eds. THE URBAN R'S; RACE RELATIONS AS THE PROBLEM IN URBAN EDUCATION. New York: Praeger, 1967. xii, 304 p. (For the Center for Urban Education.)

Eighteen papers dealing with intergroup relations in New York City schools.

1210. Havighurst, Robert J., and Levine, Daniel U. EDUCATION IN METRO-

POLITAN AREAS. 2nd ed. Boston: Allyn & Bacon, 1971. xi, 350 p. Bibliography.

1211. Roberts, Joan I. SCENE OF THE BATTLE; GROUP BEHAVIOR IN THE URBAN CLASSROOMS. Garden City, N.Y.: Doubleday, 1970. 441 p.

Study sponsored by Project TRUE at Hunter College. Bibliography.

1212. Sexton, Patricia Cayo. EDUCATION AND INCOME; INEQUALITIES OF OPPORTUNITY IN OUR PUBLIC SCHOOLS. New York: Viking, 1961. 298 p.

A study of elementary and high schools in a large midwestern city.

1213. Street, David, ed. INNOVATION IN MASS EDUCATION. New York: Wiley-Interscience, 1969. 342 p.

A sociological critique of the status quo in urban schools with suggestions for possible innovations. Bibliography.

H. INTEGRATION

1214. Crain, Robert L. THE POLITICS OF SCHOOL DESEGREGATION; COMPARATIVE CASE STUDIES OF COMMUNITY STRUCTURE AND POLICY-MAKING. National Opinion Research Center Monograph in Social Research, no. 14. Garden City, N.Y.: Doubleday, Anchor, 1969. 415 p.

Review of data from eight northern and seven southern cities in which school desegregation was a central issue from 1959 to 1965.

1215. Mack, Raymond W., ed. OUR CHILDREN'S BURDEN; STUDIES OF DESEGREGATION IN NINE AMERICAN COMMUNITIES. New York: Random House, 1968. 473 p.

Reports on desegregation, from small Mississippi towns to Los Angeles and Chicago. The concluding chapter discusses variations in desegregation as a function of community size. Bibliography.

1216. Rogers, David. 110 LIVINGSTON STREET; POLITICS AND BUREAUCRACY IN THE NEW YORK CITY SCHOOL SYSTEM. New York: Random House, 1968. 584 p.

A five-year case study focusing on the failure of school desegregation in New York City.

1217. Stember, Charles Herbert. EDUCATION AND ATTITUDE CHANGE; THE
EFFECT OF SCHOOLING ON PREJUDICE AGAINST MINORITY GROUPS.
New York: Institute of Human Relations Press, 1961. xvii, 182 p.

Analysis of data covering a twenty-year period suggests that
formal education reduces the impact of false stereotypes.

1218. Tumin, Melvin M. DESEGREGATION: RESISTANCE AND READINESS.
Princeton, N.J.: Princeton University Press, 1958. xvii, 270 p.

Based on interviews; formal education, exposure to mass media,
and occupational status were positively related to readiness
for desegregation.

1219. Weinberg, Meyer. DESEGREGATION RESEARCH: AN APPRAISAL. 2nd
ed. Bloomington, Ind.: Phi Delta Kappa, 1970. 460 p.

A project of the Phi Delta Kappa Commission on education,
human rights, and responsibilities. Bibliography.

1220. Wilson, Alan B. THE CONSEQUENCES OF SEGREGATION: ACADEMIC
ACHIEVEMENT IN A NORTHERN COMMUNITY. Berkeley: Survey
Research Center, University of California, 1969. viii, 92 p.

Questionnaires, completed by 4,077 students in eleven public
junior and senior high schools in the San Francisco-Oakland
area in spring 1965, reveal that class differences rather than
racial differences affect educational achievement. Bibliography.

1221. Zimmer, Basil G., and Hawley, Amos H. METROPOLITAN AREA
SCHOOLS; RESISTANCE TO DISTRICT REORGANIZATION. Beverly
Hills: Sage Publications, 1968. 317 p. Bibliography.

I. COLLEGES AND UNIVERSITIES

1222. Astin, Alexander W. THE COLLEGE ENVIRONMENT. Washington,
D.C.: American Council on Education, 1968. xi, 187 p.

Responses to an Inventory of College Activities by 60,505
students who had completed the freshman year in the spring
of 1962 in 246 accredited colleges and universities. Bibliography.

1223. Astin, Alexander W., and Panos, Robert J. THE EDUCATIONAL AND
VOCATIONAL DEVELOPMENT OF COLLEGE STUDENTS. Washington,
D.C.: American Council on Education, 1969. xii, 211 p.

Survey of 127,000 freshmen in 246 colleges and universities in the fall of 1961, with follow-up studies in 1962 and 1965; student achievement is little affected by college environment of "quality and excellence." Bibliography.

1224. Becker, Howard S., et al. MAKING THE GRADE: THE ACADEMIC SIDE OF COLLEGE LIFE. New York: Wiley, 1968. 150 p.

Based on fieldwork at the University of Kansas from 1959 to 1960. Bibliography.

1225. Clark, Burton R. THE DISTINCTIVE COLLEGE: ANTIOCH, REED AND SWARTHMORE. Chicago: Aldine, 1970. 280 p.

Case studies of three innovative, private, liberal arts colleges.

1226. Crossland, Fred E. MINORITY ACCESS TO COLLEGE; A FORD FOUN-DATION REPORT. New York: Schocken Books, 1971. 139 p.

Report on access of minority groups, such as Blacks, Mexican-Americans, Puerto Ricans, and American Indians to higher education. Bibliography.

1227. Fashing, Joseph, and Deutsch, Steven E. ACADEMICS IN RETREAT; THE POLITICS OF EDUCATIONAL INNOVATION. Albuquerque: University of New Mexico Press, 1971. 325 p.

Examination of curricular development in six west coast colleges. Bibliography.

1228. Feldman, Kenneth A., and Newcomb, Theodore M. THE IMPACT OF COLLEGE ON STUDENTS. Vol. 1: ANALYSIS OF FOUR DECADES OF RESEARCH; vol. 2: SUMMARY TABLES. San Francisco: Jossey-Bass, 1969. Vol. 1, 474 p.; vol. 2, 171 p.

Review of research from mid-1920s to mid-1960s.

1229. Greeley, Andrew M. THE CHANGING CATHOLIC COLLEGE. National Opinion Research Center Monograph in Social Research, no. 13. Chicago: Aldine, 1967. xiii, 226 p.

A 1965 interview study of changes in thirty Roman Catholic colleges and universities. Bibliography.

1230. _____. FROM BACKWATER TO MAINSTREAM; A PROFILE OF CATHO-LIC HIGHER EDUCATION. New York: McGraw-Hill, 1969. viii, 184 p.

Sponsored by the Carnegie Commission on Higher Education.

1231. Jencks, Christopher, and Riesman, David. THE ACADEMIC REVOLU-
TION. Garden City, N.Y.: Doubleday, 1968. xvii, 580 p.

> The bureaucratization of American society is reflected in
> higher education and transformation of a wide range of col-
> leges into vocational training institutions. Bibliography.

1232. Kaysen, Carl, ed. CONTENT AND CONTEXT: ESSAYS ON COLLEGE
EDUCATION. New York: McGraw-Hill, 1973. xviii, 565 p.

> Carnegie Commission on Higher Education research study;
> chapters by Neil Smelser, Norman Birnbaum, Everett C.
> Hughes, James S. Coleman, and others.

1233. Parsons, Talcott, and Platt, Gerald M. THE AMERICAN UNIVERSITY.
Cambridge, Mass.: Harvard University Press, 1973. xi, 463 p.

> Interpretation of selected aspects of the American academic
> system, undergraduate college, and professional school.

1234. Riesman, David, and Stadtman, Verne A., eds. ACADEMIC TRANSFOR-
MATION; SEVENTEEN INSTITUTIONS UNDER PRESSURE. New York:
McGraw-Hill, 1973. xx, 489 p.

> A collection of essays on institutional changes in the late
> 1960s written for the Carnegie Commission on Higher Education.

1235. Riesman, David, et al. ACADEMIC VALUES AND MASS EDUCATION;
THE EARLY YEARS OF OAKLAND AND MONTEITH. Garden City,
N.Y.: Doubleday, 1970. 332 p.

> Describes attempts to provide stimulating educational programs
> for undergraduates. Bibliography.

J. STUDENTS IN HIGHER EDUCATION

1236. Bolton, Charles D., and Kammeyer, Kenneth C. W. THE UNIVERSITY
STUDENT; A STUDY OF STUDENT BEHAVIOR AND VALUES. New
Haven: College and University Press, 1967. 286 p.

> Study of student subcultures and informal social interaction
> based on questionnaires from about 200 students.

1237. Edwards, Harry. BLACK STUDENTS. New York: Free Press, 1970.
[22], 234 p. Bibliography.

1238. Gossman, Charles S., et al. MIGRATION OF COLLEGE AND UNIVER-
SITY STUDENTS IN THE UNITED STATES. Seattle: University of

Washington Press, 1968. xvii, 180 p.

> Data were derived from the U.S. Office of Education surveys of student migration between 1930 and 1963; a factor analysis of migration rates.

1239. Lee, Alfred McClung. FRATERNITIES WITHOUT BROTHERHOOD; A STUDY OF PREJUDICE ON THE AMERICAN CAMPUS. Boston: Beacon Press, [c.1955]. xii, 159 p.

1240. Newcomb, Theodore M., and Wilson, Everett K., eds. COLLEGE PEER GROUPS; PROBLEMS AND PROSPECTS FOR RESEARCH. National Opinion Research Center Monograph in Social Research, no. 8. Chicago: Aldine, 1966. 303 p.

1241. Scott, William A. VALUES AND ORGANIZATIONS; A STUDY OF FRATERNITIES AND SORORITIES. Chicago: Rand McNally, 1965. 290 p. Bibliography.

1242. Spaeth, Joe E., and Greeley, Andrew M. RECENT ALUMNI AND HIGHER EDUCATION; A SURVEY OF COLLEGE GRADUATES. New York: McGraw-Hill, 1970. xiv, 199 p.

> Carnegie Commission on Higher Education research study. Bibliography.

1243. Wallace, Walter L. STUDENT CULTURE; SOCIAL STRUCTURE AND CONTINUITY IN A LIBERAL ARTS COLLEGE. National Opinion Research Center Monograph in Social Research, no. 9. Chicago: Aldine, 1966. xxi, 236 p.

> Attempts to determine how values that characterize a college campus are transmitted to incoming freshmen.

1244. Willie, Charles V., and McCord, Arline S. BLACK STUDENTS AT WHITE COLLEGES. New York: Praeger, 1972. 136 p.

> The Black student's social life, housing, and relationship with teachers at four campuses.

1245. Yamamoto, Kaoru. THE COLLEGE STUDENT AND HIS CULTURE; AN ANALYSIS. Boston: Houghton Mifflin Co., 1968. xii, 493 p.

K. GRADUATE AND PROFESSIONAL EDUCATION

1246. Becker, Howard S., et al. BOYS IN WHITE; STUDENT CULTURE IN MEDICAL SCHOOL. Chicago: University of Chicago Press, 1961. 456 p.

Participant observation of medical students at the University of Kansas.

1247. Berelson, Bernard [R.] GRADUATE EDUCATION IN THE UNITED STATES. New York: McGraw-Hill, 1960. 346 p.

Based mainly on questionnaires from graduate deans and graduate faculty. Bibliography.

1248. Davis, James A. GREAT ASPIRATIONS; THE GRADUATE SCHOOL PLANS OF AMERICA'S COLLEGE SENIORS. National Opinion Research Center Monograph in Social Research, no. 1. Chicago: Aldine, 1964. xxvi, 319 p.

Draws upon NORC (National Opinion Research Center) data for almost 34,000 June 1961 graduates of 135 American colleges and universities.

1249. Hughes, Everett C., et al. EDUCATION FOR THE PROFESSIONS OF MEDICINE, LAW, THEOLOGY AND SOCIAL WORK. New York: McGraw-Hill, 1974. 273 p.

Carnegie Commission on Higher Education research study.

1250. Merton, Robert K., et al., eds. THE STUDENT PHYSICIAN; INTRODUCTORY STUDIES IN THE SOCIOLOGY OF MEDICAL EDUCATION. Cambridge, Mass.: Harvard University Press, 1957. 360 p.

1251. Sibley, Elbridge. THE EDUCATION OF SOCIOLOGISTS IN THE UNITED STATES. New York: Russell Sage Foundation, 1963. 218 p.

L. FACULTY

1252. Anderson, Charles H., and Murray, John D., eds. THE PROFESSORS; WORK AND LIFE STYLES AMONG ACADEMICIANS. Cambridge, Mass.: Schenkman, 1971. 350 p.

Twenty-two previously published selections discuss significant aspects of academic life--work, leisure, alienation, work as community, and work as political responsibility.

1253. Caplow, Theodore, and McGee, Reece. THE ACADEMIC MARKETPLACE. Garden City, N.Y.: Doubleday, Anchor, 1965. 226 p.

Strategies used in making academic appointments.

1254. Daniels, Arlene K., et al. ACADEMICS ON THE LINE: THE FACULTY STRIKE AT SAN FRANCISCO STATE. San Francisco: Jossey-Bass, 1970.

269 p.

> Nineteen articles on the strike at San Francisco State College from November 1968 to March 1969.

1255. Hagstrom, Warren O. THE SCIENTIFIC COMMUNITY. New York: Basic Books, 1965. x, 304 p.

> Interviews with seventy-six scientists, most of them in four leading universities.

1256. Lazarsfeld, Paul F., and Thielens, Wagner Jr. THE ACADEMIC MIND. New York: Free Press, 1958. xiii, 460 p.

> Study of the effects of McCarthyism on teachers in the social sciences; based on interviews with 2,451 teachers from a sample of 165 undergraduate colleges.

1257. McGee, Reece. ACADEMIC JANUS: THE PRIVATE COLLEGE AND ITS FACULTY. San Francisco: Jossey-Bass, 1971. 264 p.

> A study of the labor market behavior of faculty members at eleven midwestern liberal arts colleges. Bibliography.

1258. Marshall, Howard D. THE MOBILITY OF COLLEGE FACULTIES. New York: Pageant Press, 1964. 152 p.

1259. Nisbet, Robert [A.] THE DEGRADATION OF THE ACADEMIC DOGMA: THE UNIVERSITY IN AMERICA, 1945-1970. New York: Basic Books, 1971. 252 p.

1260. Rieff, Philip. FELLOW TEACHERS. New York: Harper & Row, Publishers, 1973. 243 p.

> Discussion of mass education, higher learning, and cultural liberation. Bibliographic references.

1261. Scimecca, Joseph, and Damiano, Roland. CRISIS AT ST. JOHN'S; STRIKE AND REVOLUTION ON THE CATHOLIC CAMPUS. New York: Random House, 1968. ix, 213 p.

> Two faculty members who participated in the 1966 faculty strike discuss broader issues of parochial higher education.

M. ADMINISTRATION

1262. Baldridge, J. Victor, ed. ACADEMIC GOVERNANCE; RESEARCH ON INSTITUTIONAL POLITICS AND DECISION MAKING. Berkeley:

McCutchan, 1971. vii, 579 p. Bibliography.

1263. _____ . POWER AND CONFLICT IN THE UNIVERSITY; RESEARCH IN
THE SOCIOLOGY OF COMPLEX ORGANIZATIONS. New York: Wiley,
1971. 238 p.

Case study of New York University as a political model of
decision making. Bibliography.

1264. Bennis, Warren [G.], with Biederman, Patricia W. THE LEANING IVORY
TOWER. San Francisco: Jossey-Bass, 1973. xiii, 154 p.

The problems of university administration, especially those at
the University of Buffalo in the years of the crises culminating
in the Kent State confrontation in May 1970.

1265. Blau, Peter M[ichael]. THE ORGANIZATION OF ACADEMIC WORK.
New York: Wiley-Interscience, 1973. xvii, 310 p.

Uses data from 115 American universities and colleges to
explore the effects of administrative structure on achievement.

1266. Cohen, Michael D., and March, James G. LEADERSHIP AND AMBIGU-
ITY: THE AMERICAN COLLEGE PRESIDENT. New York: McGraw-Hill,
1974. 270 p.

A general report prepared for the Carnegie Commission on
Higher Education; based on a stratified sample of forty-two
universities and colleges in which presidents and officers were
interviewed. Presidency is seen as an academically parochial
office, reactive rather than anticipatory, in an atmosphere of
ambiguity, shifting power, and a diffuse process of decision
making.

1267. Demerath, Nicholas J., et al. POWER, PRESIDENTS, AND PROFESSORS.
New York: Basic Books, 1967. viii, 275 p.

The nature and effect of administrative succession at a university; observations of the university presidency; and the power
hierarchies in certain academic departments.

1268. Gross, Edward, and Grambsch, Paul V. UNIVERSITY GOALS AND
ACADEMIC POWER. Washington, D.C.: American Council on Education, 1968. xi, 164 p.

An abridged version of a 1967 report for the Department of
Health, Education and Welfare, based on a mail questionnaire
sent in 1964 to over 15,000 academic administrators and faculty members in sixty-eight nondenominational American universities.

1269. Wallerstein, Immanuel. UNIVERSITY IN TURMOIL: THE POLITICS OF CHANGE. New York: Atheneum Press, 1969. 147 p.

> An institutional analysis of American universities and of social movements and pressures for the democratization of administration.

* * *

See also Chapter 20, Sections A and D.

Chapter 18

MASS CULTURE

Chapter 18

MASS CULTURE

A. REFERENCE WORKS AND BIBLIOGRAPHIES

1270. Allswang, John M., and Bova, Patrick. NORC SOCIAL RESEARCH, 1941-1964: AN INVENTORY OF STUDIES AND PUBLICATIONS IN SOCIAL RESEARCH. Chicago: National Opinion Research Center, 1964. vi, 80 p.

> Lists and annotates studies through June 1964, and includes publications.

1271. Danielson, Wayne A., and Wilhoit, G.C., Jr. A COMPUTERIZED BIBLIOGRAPHY OF MASS COMMUNICATION RESEARCH, 1944-1964. New York: Magazine Publishers Association, 1967. 399 p.

> Key-word-in-context index to articles appearing in forty-eight social science journals from 1944 to 1964.

1272. Gallup, George Horace. THE GALLUP POLL; PUBLIC OPINION 1935-1971. 3 vols. New York: Random House, 1972. xliv, 2388 p.

> Supplemented by reports appearing in the GALLUP OPINION INDEX (see item 232).

1273. Hansen, Donald A., and Parsons, J.H. MASS COMMUNICATION: A RESEARCH BIBLIOGRAPHY. Berkeley: Glendessary, 1968. 144 p.

> Lists 3,000 books, articles, and reports from 1945 on, concerning the media, their programs, content, audiences, and social effects.

1274. National Opinion Research Center. Library. BIBLIOGRAPHY OF PUBLICATIONS, 1941-1960: SUPPLEMENT, 1961 - DECEMBER 1970. Chicago: 1971. 146 p.

> Lists publications since 1961 and indicates the study numbers.

1275. Pool, Ithiel de Sola, et al., eds. HANDBOOK OF COMMUNICATION. Chicago: Rand McNally, 1973. 1011 p.

>An interdisciplinary review of communications and their operations in different social settings.

B. LANGUAGE

1276. Fishman, Joshua A., et al. LANGUAGE LOYALTY IN THE UNITED STATES; THE MAINTENANCE AND PERPETUATION OF NON-ENGLISH MOTHER TONGUES BY AMERICAN ETHNIC AND RELIGIOUS GROUPS. The Hague, Netherlands: Mouton, 1966. 478 p.

>Study of the 11 percent of the population who have a non-English mother tongue, with in-depth study of six groups. Bibliography.

1277. Labov, William. LANGUAGE IN THE INNER CITY: STUDIES IN THE BLACK ENGLISH VERNACULAR. Conduct and Communication Series. Philadelphia: University of Pennsylvania Press, 1972. xxiv, 412 p.

1278. _____ . THE SOCIAL STRATIFICATION OF ENGLISH IN NEW YORK CITY. Washington, D.C.: Center for Applied Linguistics, 1966. 655 p.

>Analysis of linguistic and social factors which determine variations and changes in speech patterns. Bibliography.

1279. Mueller, Claus. THE POLITICS OF COMMUNICATION; A STUDY IN THE POLITICAL SOCIOLOGY OF LANGUAGE, SOCIALIZATION, AND LEGITIMATION. New York: Oxford University Press, 1973. x, 226 p.

>A study of linguistic manipulation in the United States and some European countries. Language codes and concepts are manipulated by the power structure to control political attitudes. Bibliography.

C. COMMUNICATION, PUBLIC OPINION, AND MEDIA

1280. Berelson, Bernard [R.], and Janowitz, Morris, eds. READER IN PUBLIC OPINION AND COMMUNICATION. 2nd ed. Glencoe, Ill.: Free Press, 1966. ix, 788 p.

>One quarter of the papers are by sociologists. Collection deals with theory, formation, and impact of public opinion, audiences, and effects of communications.

1281. DeFleur, Melvin L., and Larsen, Otto N. THE FLOW OF INFORMA-
TION; AN EXPERIMENT IN MASS COMMUNICATION. New York:
Harper & Brothers, 1958. 301 p.

Account of "Project Revere," the message diffusion studies
of the Washington Public Opinion Laboratory. Leaflets were
dropped over towns and responses to these were examined to
determine the speed of diffusion of information and the chan-
nels through which it took place.

1282. Dexter, Lewis A., and White, David Manning, eds. PEOPLE, SOCI-
ETY AND MASS COMMUNICATIONS. New York: Free Press of
Glencoe, 1964. xii, 595 p.

Thirty articles from specialized journals.

1283. Ellis, Albert. THE FOLKLORE OF SEX. New York: Boni, 1951.
313 p.

Content analysis of the products of the mass media (best sellers,
magazines, movies, plays and musicals, newspapers, songs,
radio and TV programs) on January 1, 1950, in order to
reveal current ideas and attitudes about sex.

1284. Greenberg, Bradley S., and Parker, Edwin B., eds. THE KENNEDY
ASSASSINATION AND THE AMERICAN PUBLIC; SOCIAL COMMUNI-
CATION IN CRISIS. Stanford: Stanford University Press, 1965.
xvi, 392 p.

Twenty-six papers describe the reporting of the event and
present research findings about public reaction.

1285. Janowitz, Morris. THE COMMUNITY PRESS IN AN URBAN SETTING;
THE SOCIAL ELEMENTS OF URBANISM. 2nd ed. Chicago: University of Chicago Press, 1967. xxiii, 275 p.

Survey of the urban community press of Chicago as one of
the social mechanisms through which the individual is integrated into the urban social structure.

1286. Klapper, Joseph T. THE EFFECTS OF MASS COMMUNICATION.
Foundations of Communications Research, vol. 3. Glencoe, Ill.:
Free Press, 1960. 302 p.

Reviews literature on mass communication and discusses areas
and problems of future research. Bibliography.

1287. Lazarsfeld, Paul F., and Field, Henry. THE PEOPLE LOOK AT RADIO.
Chapel Hill: University of North Carolina Press, 1946. ix, 158 p.

National survey in November 1945 examines attitudes toward

advertising and discusses functions of the radio.

1288. Lazarsfeld, Paul F., and Kendall, Patricia L. RADIO LISTENING IN AMERICA; THE PEOPLE LOOK AT RADIO - AGAIN. New York: Prentice-Hall, 1948. v, 178 p.

> Reports and interprets a National Opinion Research Center survey made in 1947 on behalf of the radio industry.

1289. Merton, Robert K., et al. MASS PERSUASION; THE SOCIAL PSYCHOLOGY OF A WAR BOND DRIVE. New York: Harper & Brothers, 1946. xiii, 210 p.

> Research on the content of propaganda; use of appeals, rhetorical devices, and emotive language.

1290. Rosenberg, Bernard, and White, David Manning, eds. MASS CULTURE REVISITED. New York: Van Nostrand-Reinhold, 1971. xii, 473 p.

> Examination of mass media and their social impact.

1291. _____. MASS CULTURE: THE POPULAR ARTS IN AMERICA. Glencoe, Ill.: Free Press, 1957. 561 p.

1292. Schiller, Herbert I. MASS COMMUNICATIONS AND AMERICAN EMPIRE. New York: A.M. Kelley, 1969. Reprint. Boston: Beacon Press, 1971. 170 p.

> Argues that the American radio and television system is manipulated by the military-industrial complex to serve its global interests and the needs of the domestic market. Bibliography.

1293. Schramm, Wilbur, and Roberts, Donald F. THE PROCESS AND EFFECTS OF MASS COMMUNICATIONS. Rev. ed. Urbana: University of Illinois Press, 1971. ix, 997 p. Bibliography pp. 967-79.

1294. Wells, Alan, ed. MASS MEDIA AND SOCIETY. Palo Alto, Calif.: National Press Books, 1972. vii, 408 p.

> Fifty-two selections on the structure of media industry, media regulators, advertising, and audience.

D. TELEVISION

1295. Bogart, Leo. THE AGE OF TELEVISION; A STUDY OF VIEWING HABITS AND THE IMPACT OF TELEVISION ON AMERICAN LIFE. 3rd ed. New York: Frederick Ungar Publishing Co., 1972. xliv, 515 p.

A review and interpretation of a number of academic, commercial, and governmental research studies of television. Bibliography.

1296. Cantor, Muriel G. THE HOLLYWOOD TV PRODUCER: HIS WORK AND HIS AUDIENCE. New York: Basic Books, 1971. 256 p.

Interviews with fifty-nine producers of TV film series in 1967-68, and twenty-four producers of children's TV series in 1970. Three types are identified: film makers, writers-producers, and old-line producers. Older producers are often in conflict with the network bureaucracy. Bibliography.

1297. Glick, Ira O., and Levy, Sidney J. LIVING WITH TELEVISION. Chicago: Aldine, 1962. 262 p.

Report based on sixty-nine studies of viewer reactions to shows, personalities, and commercials.

1298. Lang, Kurt, and Lang, Gladys E. POLITICS AND TELEVISION. Chicago: Quadrangle, 1968. 315 p.

Research essays on the influence of broadcasting upon election results.

1299. Mendelsohn, Harold, and Crespi, Irving. POLLS, TELEVISION, AND THE NEW POLITICS. Scranton, Pa.: Chandler, 1970. xii, 329 p. Bibliography.

1300. Schramm, Wilbur, et al. TELEVISION IN THE LIVES OF OUR CHILDREN. Stanford: Stanford University Press, 1961. 342 p.

Survey data from a number of communities in the United States and Canada. The viewing patterns of children are related to norms they assimilate from their families. Bibliography.

1301. Winick, Charles, et al. CHILDREN'S TELEVISION COMMERCIALS; A CONTENT ANALYSIS. New York: Praeger, 1973. xiv, 156 p.

Data from 264 child-oriented TV commercials, representing 136 products. Bibliography.

E. ART, MUSIC, AND DANCE

1302. Albrecht, Milton C., et al. THE SOCIOLOGY OF ART AND LITERATURE: A READER. New York: Praeger, 1970. 752 p.

Collection of articles and excerpts from books selected to

emphasize art as an institution and the ways in which society affects the arts.

1303. Braun, D. Duane. TOWARD A THEORY OF POPULAR CULTURE: THE SOCIOLOGY AND HISTORY OF AMERICAN MUSIC AND DANCE, 1920-1968. Ann Arbor, Mich.: Ann Arbor Publishers, 1969. 165 p.

Study of new styles in music and dance expression. Bibliography.

1304. Denisoff, R. Serge, and Peterson, Richard A., eds. THE SOUNDS OF SOCIAL CHANGE: STUDIES IN POPULAR CULTURE. Chicago: Rand McNally, 1972. xi, 332 p.

Study of music as protest and in social movements; changing musical tastes and the music industry.

1305. Faulkner, Robert R. HOLLYWOOD STUDIO MUSICIANS, THEIR WORK AND CAREERS IN THE RECORDING INDUSTRY. Chicago: Aldine-Atherton, 1971. 218 p.

Studio workplace as an assembly line for the production of films. Bibliography.

1306. Gans, Herbert J. POPULAR CULTURE AND HIGH CULTURE. New York: Basic Books, 1974. 192 p.

Criticism of cultural elitism and examination of cultural preferences. The author argues that America has multiple taste cultures which express the different aesthetic standards of different segments of the public.

1307. Lewis, George H., ed. SIDE SADDLE ON THE GOLDEN CALF: SOCIAL STRUCTURE AND POPULAR CULTURE IN AMERICA. Pacific Palisades, Calif.: Goodyear, 1972. xix, 388 p. Bibliography.

1308. Nanry, Charles, ed. AMERICAN MUSIC: FROM STORYVILLE TO WOODSTOCK. New Brunswick, N.J.: E.P. Dutton, Transaction Books, 1972. xiv, 290 p.

Five papers presented at a conference on jazz and sociology held in 1970 at Rutgers University, and eight articles which appeared between 1947 and 1970.

1309. Rosenberg, Bernard, and Fliegel, Norris. THE VANGUARD ARTIST, PORTRAIT AND SELF-PORTRAIT. Chicago: Quadrangle, 1965. xi, 366 p.

From a sample of fifty New York City artists, twenty-nine participated in a series of focused but unstructured interviews;

characteristics of successful American artists and exploration
of their social and economic milieu.

F. LEISURE AND RECREATION

1310. Cavan, Sherri. LIQUOR LICENSE: AN ETHNOGRAPHY OF BAR
BEHAVIOR. Chicago: Aldine, 1966. 246 p.

Through participant observation and interviewing, data were
gathered from 1962 to 1965 in about 100 drinking establish-
ments in San Francisco.

1311. Frank, Lawrence K., et al. TRENDS IN AMERICAN LIVING AND
OUTDOOR RECREATION. Report to the Outdoor Recreation Resources
Review Commission. Washington, D.C.: Government Printing Office,
1962. xiv, 257 p.

1312. Hartman, William E., et al. NUDIST SOCIETY: AN AUTHORITATIVE,
COMPLETE STUDY OF NUDISM IN AMERICA. New York: Crown,
1970. 432 p.

Popular account of nudism by two sociologists and a nudist,
supported by information from nudist camp visits and 2,000
questionnaire respondents.

1313. Kaplan, Max. LEISURE IN AMERICA: A SOCIAL INQUIRY. New
York: Wiley, 1960. 350 p.

Ideal typology of leisure and a sixfold classification of leisure
activities.

1314. Kaplan, Max, and Bosserman, Philip, eds. TECHNOLOGY, HUMAN
VALUES, AND LEISURE. Nashville, Tenn.: Abingdon Press, 1971.
256 p. Bibliography.

1315. Polsky, Ned. HUSTLERS, BEATS, AND OTHERS. Chicago: Aldine,
1967. 218 p.

A treatise on poolroom culture and the lore and organization
of hustling.

1316. Smigel, Erwin O., ed. WORK AND LEISURE; A CONTEMPORARY
SOCIAL PROBLEM. New Haven: College and University Press, 1963.
208 p. Bibliography.

G. SPORTS

1317. Edwards, Harry. THE REVOLT OF THE BLACK ATHLETE. New York: Free Press, 1969. xx, 202 p. Bibliography.

1318. _____. SOCIOLOGY OF SPORT. Homewood, Ill.: Dorsey Press, 1973. xi, 395 p. Bibliography.

1319. Loy, John W., Jr., and Kenyon, Gerald S., eds. SPORT, CULTURE AND SOCIETY; A READER ON THE SOCIOLOGY OF SPORT. New York: Macmillan, 1969. xii, 464 p.

    Thirty-five articles discuss various aspects of American sport. Bibliography.

1320. Sage, George H., ed. SPORT AND AMERICAN SOCIETY, SELECTED READINGS. Reading, Mass.: Addison-Wesley, 1970. x, 422 p.

    Thirty-two articles from scholarly and popular journals, grouped into six sections: the heritage of sport in America; sport and the school; sport and social status; race and sport; women and sport; and sport and society. Bibliography.

1321. Talamini, John T., and Page, Charles H., eds. THE WAY WE PLAY: HOW SPORT AND SOCIETY MEET, CLASH AND AFFECT THE LIVES OF THEIR PARTICIPANTS. New York: Little, Brown and Co., 1973. x, 493 p. Bibliography pp. 473-88.

H. SOCIAL CONVENTIONS AND RITUALS

1322. Barnett, James H. THE AMERICAN CHRISTMAS; A STUDY IN NATIONAL CULTURE. New York: Macmillan, 1954. 173 p.

    Based on data from histories, newspapers, business statistics, popular stories, observations, and interviews.

1323. Bowman, LeRoy. THE AMERICAN FUNERAL; A STUDY IN GUILT, EXTRAVAGANCE, AND SUBLIMITY. Washington, D.C.: Public Affairs Press, 1959. 181 p.

    Explores the behavior and motivation of funeral directors and clients in a wide range of community contexts, through direct observation, interviews, questionnaires, and organizational documents.

1324. Cussler, Margaret, and DeGive, Mary L. TWIXT THE CUP AND THE LIP; PSYCHOLOGICAL AND SOCIO-CULTURAL FACTORS AFFECTING

FOOD HABITS. New York: Twayne, 1952. 262 p.

Based on a series of studies in 1940–41; analysis of food
selection patterns in three southern rural communities.

1325. Roach, Mary Ellen, and Eicher, Joanne B., eds. DRESS, ADORNMENT
AND THE SOCIAL ORDER. New York: Wiley, 1965. xv, 429 p.

Fifty-three selections on dress and its origins, functions, and
diversity in cultural patterns; annotated bibliography of 529
items.

1326. Warner, W. Lloyd. THE LIVING AND THE DEAD; A STUDY OF THE
SYMBOLIC LIFE OF AMERICANS. Yankee City Series, vol. 5. New
Haven: Yale University Press, 1959. xii, 528 p.

The last volume in the Yankee City series focuses on ceremo-
nial activities such as Memorial Day, rituals, and Catholic
and Protestant symbolism. Bibliography.

Chapter 19

FORMAL ORGANIZATIONS AND POLITICAL SYSTEMS

Chapter 19

FORMAL ORGANIZATIONS

AND POLITICAL SYSTEMS

A. REFERENCE WORKS AND BIBLIOGRAPHIES

1327. Hawley, Willis D., and Svara, James H. THE STUDY OF COMMU-
NITY POWER: A BIBLIOGRAPHIC REVIEW. Santa Barbara, Calif.:
American Bibliographical Center/Clio Press, 1972. viii, 123 p.

> A listing, in four broad categories, of books, articles, and
> doctoral dissertations on community power. Most entries are
> annotated and references to books include citations to critical
> reviews.

1328. Lang, Kurt. MILITARY INSTITUTIONS AND THE SOCIOLOGY OF
WAR; A REVIEW OF THE LITERATURE WITH ANNOTATED BIBLIOGRA-
PHY. Beverly Hills: Sage Publications, 1972. 337 p.

> International in scope. Five chapters survey the literature;
> annotated bibliography (pp. 159-337).

1329. Leif, Irving P. COMMUNITY POWER AND DECISION-MAKING:
AN INTERNATIONAL HANDBOOK. Metuchen, N.J.: Scarecrow,
1974. vi, 170 p.

> An annotated listing of 1,196 books, journal articles, doctoral
> dissertations, masters' theses, and papers presented at scholarly
> meetings. The majority of the studies are American, but
> research in languages other than English is included.

1330. Little, Roger N., ed. HANDBOOK OF MILITARY INSTITUTIONS.
Beverly Hills: Sage Publications, 1971. 607 p.

> Essays which reflect the recent work of the Inter-University
> Seminar on Armed Forces and Society. General bibliography
> and twenty-two pages of manpower statistics.

1331. March, James G., ed. HANDBOOK OF ORGANIZATIONS. Chicago:
Rand McNally, 1965. xvi, 1247 p.

Surveys the field of organizational studies.

1332. Russett, Bruce, and Stepan, Alfred, eds. MILITARY FORCE AND AMERICAN SOCIETY. New York: Harper & Row, Publishers, 1973. 371 p.

Five articles, followed by selected and annotated bibliography (pp. 196–371).

B. FORMAL ORGANIZATIONS

1333. Azumi, Koya, and Hage, Jerald. ORGANIZATIONAL SYSTEMS: A TEXT READER IN THE SOCIOLOGY OF ORGANIZATIONS. Lexington, Mass.: D.C. Heath, 1972. xviii, 582 p. Bibliography pp. 523–72.

1334. Blau, Peter M[ichael]. ON THE NATURE OF ORGANIZATIONS. New York: Columbia University Press, 1974. 400 p.

A collection of papers, written over a twenty-year period, concerning theory and research on formal organizations.

1335. Blau, Peter M[ichael], and Schoenherr, Richard A. THE STRUCTURE OF ORGANIZATIONS. New York: Basic Books, 1971. xix, 445 p.

Determines how given structural factors are influenced by various conditions both within and outside of the organization.

1336. Blau, Peter M[ichael], and Scott, W. Richard. FORMAL ORGANIZATIONS: A COMPARATIVE APPROACH. San Francisco: Chandler, 1962. 312 p.

Study of formal organizations based on analysis and comparison of empirical research (not cross-cultural); 800-item bibliography.

1337. Etzioni, Amitai. A SOCIOLOGICAL READER ON COMPLEX ORGANIZATIONS. 2nd ed. New York: Holt, Rinehart and Winston, 1969. xiv, 576 p.

Thirty-nine selections, many from journals, or excerpted from books.

1338. Grusky, Oscar, and Miller, George A., eds. THE SOCIOLOGY OF ORGANIZATIONS; BASIC STUDIES. New York: Free Press, 1970. x, 592 p.

1339. Hall, Richard H. ORGANIZATIONS: STRUCTURE AND PROCESS. Englewood Cliffs, N.J.: Prentice-Hall, 1972. xiii, 354 p.

Review of pertinent theory and research about organizations which stresses technology and environment.

1340. Heydebrand, Wolf V., ed. COMPARATIVE ORGANIZATIONS: THE RESULTS OF EMPIRICAL RESEARCH. Englewood Cliffs, N.J.: Prentice-Hall, 1973. xi, 571 p.

Thirty studies, theoretical and empirical.

1341. Warner, W. Lloyd, et al., eds. LARGE SCALE ORGANIZATIONS. The Emergent American Society, vol. 1. New Haven: Yale University Press, 1967. xvii, 667 p.

Describes some of the major parameters of organizations such as size, complexity, and bureaucratization, and their inter-relations.

1342. Whyte, William Hollingsworth, Jr. THE ORGANIZATION MAN. Garden City, N.Y.: Doubleday, 1957. 471 p.

Examines ideology, training, neuroses, and testing of organization men.

1343. Wilensky, Harold L. ORGANIZATIONAL INTELLIGENCE: KNOWL-EDGE AND POLICY IN GOVERNMENT AND INDUSTRY. New York: Basic Books, 1967. xiv, 226 p.

Macrosociology concerned with the collection, processing, and transmission of knowledge.

C. CORPORATION AND INDUSTRY

1344. Barber, Richard J. THE AMERICAN CORPORATION: ITS POWER, ITS MONEY, ITS POLITICS. New York: E.P. Dutton, 1970. viii, 309 p.

Recent growth of corporations; relationships between industry and research; and the internationalization of large business organizations.

1345. Baritz, Loren. THE SERVANTS OF POWER: A HISTORY OF THE USE OF SOCIAL SCIENCE IN AMERICAN INDUSTRY. 2nd ed. New York: Wiley, 1960. 273 p.

History of the use of social sciences in American industry, especially industrial psychology and sociology. Industrial social scientists have generally displayed commitment to management's goals.

1346. Faunce, William A. PROBLEMS OF AN INDUSTRIAL SOCIETY. New York: McGraw-Hill, 1968. xiv, 189 p.

Automation, alienation, and social control in hierarchic work organizations.

1347. Galbraith, John Kenneth. THE NEW INDUSTRIAL STATE. 2nd rev. ed. Boston: Houghton Mifflin Co., 1971. xxii, 423 p.

1348. Gross, Edward. INDUSTRY AND SOCIAL LIFE. Dubuque, Iowa: W.C. Brown, 1965. xii, 172 p.

A review of literature on community, organizations, management, work group motivation, and productivity.

1349. Moore, Wilbert E. THE CONDUCT OF THE CORPORATION. New York: Random House, 1962. 292 p.

Presents the modern large business corporation as a study in power.

D. BUREAUCRACY

1350. Argyris, Chris. INTERPERSONAL COMPETENCE AND ORGANIZATIONAL EFFECTIVENESS. Homewood, Ill.: Dorsey Press, 1962. xii, 274 p.

An analysis of a group of executives in a large division of a large corporation.

1351. Blau, Peter Michael. THE DYNAMICS OF BUREAUCRACY; A STUDY OF INTERPERSONAL RELATIONSHIPS IN TWO GOVERNMENT AGENCIES. 2nd ed. Chicago: University of Chicago Press, 1963. 322 p.

An expanded edition of a case study of lower level civil service employees in two agencies; first published in 1955.

1352. Cohen, Harry. THE DEMONICS OF BUREAUCRACY: PROBLEMS OF CHANGE IN A GOVERNMENT AGENCY. Ames: Iowa State University Press, 1965. xvi, 276 p.

Modeled after Blau's DYNAMICS OF BUREAUCRACY (see item 1351). Study from 1956 to 1959 of a public employment agency in a large urban area serving the clothing industry.

1353. Eells, Richard. THE GOVERNMENT OF CORPORATIONS. New York: Free Press of Glencoe, 1962. 338 p.

Examines corporate power and control of the corporation as a private state.

1354. Francis, Roy G., and Stone, Robert C. SERVICE AND PROCEDURE IN BUREAUCRACY, A CASE STUDY. Minneapolis: University of Minnesota Press, 1956. vi, 201 p.

A case study of a staff of ninety-six persons in a local office of the Louisiana Division of Employment and Security.

1355. Gouldner, Alvin W. PATTERNS OF INDUSTRIAL BUREAUCRACY: A CASE STUDY OF MODERN FACTORY ADMINISTRATION. Glencoe, Ill.: Free Press, 1954. 282 p.

A case study of the process of bureaucratization in a gypsum plant and mine.

1356. Lawrence, Paul R., and Lorsch, Jay W. ORGANIZATION AND EN-VIRONMENT; MANAGING DIFFERENTIATION AND INTEGRATION. Boston: Division of Research, Graduate School of Business Administration, Harvard University, 1967. xv, 279 p.

A "contingency theory" of organizations derived from the study of ten firms.

1357. Likert, Rensis. NEW PATTERNS OF MANAGEMENT. New York: McGraw-Hill, 1961. ix, 279 p.

Summary of studies done at the University of Michigan's Institute for Social Research since 1947. Examines communication, leadership, group processes in business corporations, labor unions, and voluntary associations.

1358. Young, Donald R., and Moore, Wilbert E. TRUSTEESHIP AND THE MANAGEMENT OF FOUNDATIONS. New York: Russell Sage Foundation, 1969. viii, 158 p.

Raises the question of private wealth versus public interest.

E. MILITARY LIFE

1359. Coates, Charles H., and Pellegrin, Roland J. MILITARY SOCIOLOGY: A STUDY OF AMERICAN MILITARY INSTITUTIONS AND MILITARY LIFE. University Park, Md.: Social Science Press, 1965. x, 424 p.

Includes historical material, detailed organizational charts, and tabular data.

1360. Gowman, Alan G. THE WAR BLIND IN AMERICAN SOCIAL STRUC-TURE. New York: American Foundation for the Blind, 1957. 237 p.

Examination of the process of resocialization in America;
statuses and roles assigned to the war blind.

1361. Havighurst, Robert J., et al. THE AMERICAN VETERAN BACK HOME:
A STUDY OF VETERAN ADJUSTMENT. New York: Longmans, Green
and Co., 1951. vii, 271 p.

Case studies of veteran readjustment to small town life.

1362. Hickman, Martin B., comp. THE MILITARY AND AMERICAN SOCIETY.
Beverly Hills: Glencoe Press, 1971. 167 p.

The military-industrial complex, the role of ROTC (Reserve
Officer Training Corps) on the college campus.

1363. Janowitz, Morris. THE PROFESSIONAL SOLDIER, A SOCIAL AND
POLITICAL PORTRAIT. Glencoe, Ill.: Free Press, 1960. xiv, 464 p.

1364. _____, ed. THE NEW MILITARY; CHANGING PATTERNS OF ORGA-
NIZATION. New York: Russell Sage Foundation, 1964. 369 p.

Essays on the adaptation of the American military to the needs
of the modern age, with its change in emphasis from warfare
to constabulary functions.

1365. Little, Roger N., ed. SELECTIVE SERVICE AND AMERICAN SOCIETY.
New York: Russell Sage Foundation, 1969. xvi, 220 p.

Seven essays on manpower procurement; discusses two case
studies of local boards, the Negro and the draft, and occupational mobility within the military service.

1366. Moskos, Charles C., Jr. THE AMERICAN ENLISTED MAN; THE RANK
AND FILE IN TODAY'S MILITARY. New York: Russell Sage Foundation, 1970. x, 274 p.

Discussion of race relations and tensions arising from social
patterns of middle-class and working-class youth.

1367. _____, ed. PUBLIC OPINION AND THE MILITARY ESTABLISHMENT.
Beverly Hills: Sage Publications, 1971. xvi, 294 p.

1368. Stouffer, Samuel A., et al. THE AMERICAN SOLDIER. Vol. 1:
ADJUSTMENT DURING ARMY LIFE; vol. 2: COMBAT AND ITS
AFTERMATH. Studies in Social Psychology in World War II, vols.
1 and 2. Princeton, N.J.: Princeton University Press, 1949. Vol. 1,
599 p.; vol. 2, 675 p. (Prepared for the Social Science Research
Council.)

F. VOLUNTARY ASSOCIATIONS

1369. Babchuk, Nicholas, and Gordon, C. Wayne. THE VOLUNTARY
ASSOCIATION IN THE SLUM. University of Nebraska, New Series,
no. 27. Lincoln: University of Nebraska, 1962. 144 p.

> The effects of personal influence on recruitment and participa-
> tion in voluntary organizations.

1370. Glaser, William A., and Sills, David L., eds. THE GOVERNMENT
OF ASSOCIATIONS; SELECTIONS FROM THE BEHAVIORAL SCIENCES.
Totowa, N.J.: Bedminster Press, 1966. xvi, 264 p.

1371. Hausknecht, Murray. THE JOINERS; A SOCIOLOGICAL DESCRIPTION
OF VOLUNTARY ASSOCIATION MEMBERSHIP IN THE UNITED STATES.
Totowa, N.J.: Bedminster Press, 1962. 141 p.

> Data from a National Opinion Research Center study of 1955
> and an American Institute of Public Opinion survey of 1954.

1372. Kiger, Joseph C. AMERICAN LEARNED SOCIETIES. Washington,
D.C.: Public Affairs Press, 1963. 291 p.

> Sketches the origins, structure, organization, and vital statis-
> tics of sixty learned societies. Twenty-nine pages of reference
> notes and a sixteen-page bibliography.

1373. Zald, Mayer N. ORGANIZATIONAL CHANGE: THE POLITICAL
ECONOMY OF THE YMCA. Chicago: University of Chicago Press,
1970. xvii, 260 p.

> Case study of the Chicago YMCA from 1961 to 1967; data
> were derived from interviews and observation of board and
> cabinet meetings.

G. COMMUNITY POWER STRUCTURE AND POLITICS

1374. Aiken, Michael, and Mott, Paul E., eds. THE STRUCTURE OF COM-
MUNITY POWER. New York: Random House, 1970. xi, 540 p.

> Comprehensive collection of substantive articles that helped
> establish the field of community power, along with several
> original contributions. Bibliography.

1375. Alford, Robert R., with Scoble, Harry M. BUREAUCRACY AND PAR-
TICIPATION: POLITICAL CULTURES IN FOUR WISCONSIN CITIES.
Chicago: Rand McNally, 1969. xv, 244 p.

Tests the hypothesis that bureaucratization and participation are a function of the size and economic development of the community.

1376. Bonjean, Charles M., et al., eds. COMMUNITY POLITICS; A BE-HAVIORAL APPROACH. New York: Free Press, 1971. xi, 403 p.

Interdisciplinary approach; articles by twenty-three political scientists and thirteen sociologists on local governments, participation in community politics, elite and power structures, local political leadership, and urban policy.

1377. Clark, Terry N., ed. COMMUNITY STRUCTURE AND DECISION MAKING: COMPARATIVE ANALYSES. San Francisco: Chandler, 1968. x, 498 p.

Analysis of community decision making which synthesizes findings from community power research by political scientists and sociologists.

1378. Crain, Robert L., et al. THE POLITICS OF COMMUNITY CONFLICT: THE FLUORIDATION DECISION. Indianapolis: Bobbs-Merrill, 1969. xix, 269 p.

A sociologist, social psychologist, and political scientist studied fluoridation in 700 cities to investigate the community decision-making process.

1379. Crenson, Matthew A. THE UN-POLITICS OF AIR POLLUTION; A STUDY OF NON-DECISION-MAKING IN THE CITIES. Baltimore: The Johns Hopkins University Press, 1971. viii, 227 p.

Political factors affecting air pollution control in Gary and East Chicago, Indiana.

1380. Greer, Scott A. METROPOLITICS: A STUDY OF POLITICAL CULTURE. New York: Wiley, 1963. xiii, 207 p.

Problems of communicating complex issues to the electorate. Based on a survey in St. Louis County, Missouri, after the 1959 defeat of a referendum.

1381. Hunter, Floyd. COMMUNITY POWER STRUCTURE: A STUDY OF DECISION MAKERS. Chapel Hill: University of North Carolina Press, 1953. xiv, 297 p.

A study of the power structure of a southern city of 500,000 people, based on interviews with forty individuals reputed to be holders of power in that community. Bibliography (pp. 273-87).

1382. Mills, C. Wright. POWER, POLITICS AND PEOPLE; THE COLLECTED ESSAYS OF C. WRIGHT MILLS. Edited by Irving L. Horowitz. New York: Oxford University Press, 1963. 657 p. Bibliography.

1383. Mills, C. Wright, with Schneider, Helen. THE NEW MEN OF POWER, AMERICA'S LABOR LEADERS. New York: Harcourt, Brace & World, 1948. 323 p.

    A collective portrait of 500 national, state, and city leaders.

1384. Presthus, Robert V., and Blankenship, L. Vaughn. MEN AT THE TOP; A STUDY IN COMMUNITY POWER. New York: Oxford University Press, 1964. x, 485 p.

    This study of two small communities in upper New York state tests the pluralist hypothesis about the structure of community power and the elitist pyramidal decision-making model.

1385. Schaffer, Albert, and Schaffer, Ruth C. WOODRUFF, A STUDY OF COMMUNITY DECISION MAKING. Chapel Hill: University of North Carolina Press, 1970. 325 p.

    Examination of social power, community decision making, and community development over a period of thirty years.

1386. Williams, Oliver P., and Adrian, Charles. FOUR CITIES: A STUDY IN COMPARATIVE POLICY MAKING. Philadelphia: University of Pennsylvania Press, 1963. 334 p.

    Analysis of community decision making and typology of local government in four midwestern communities.

H. IDEOLOGY

1387. Bell, Daniel. THE END OF IDEOLOGY: ON THE EXHAUSTION OF POLITICAL IDEAS IN THE FIFTIES. 3rd rev. ed. New York: Collier, 1965. 474 p.

    A collection of essays, written from an anti-ideological perspective; criticism of the "romantic" components in the concepts of mass society and power elite. First published in 1960.

1388. Dolbeare, Kenneth M., and Dolbeare, Patricia. AMERICAN IDEOLOGIES; THE COMPETING POLITICAL BELIEFS OF THE 1970S. Chicago: Markham, 1971. 251 p.

    Examination of seven political ideologies. Bibliography.

1389. Huber, Joan, and Form, William H. INCOME AND IDEOLOGY: AN ANALYSIS OF THE AMERICAN POLITICAL FORMULA. New York: Free Press, 1973. xiv, 226 p.

> Belief systems of the poor, middle income, and wealthy regarding causes of poverty, significance of money, equality of opportunity, and the political and governmental process. Bibliography (pp. 194-216).

1390. Lane, Robert E. POLITICAL IDEOLOGY: WHY THE AMERICAN COMMON MAN BELIEVES WHAT HE DOES. New York: Free Press of Glencoe, 1962. xi, 509 p.

1391. McPherson, William. IDEOLOGY AND CHANGE: RADICALISM AND FUNDAMENTALISM IN AMERICA. Palo Alto, Calif.: National Press Books, 1973. 301 p.

> A monograph and a reader on ideologies of extremism in America; on radicalism versus fundamentalism.

1392. Sutton, Francis X., et al. THE AMERICAN BUSINESS CREED. 2nd ed. New York: Schocken Books, 1962. 414 p.

> Joint work of three economists and a sociologist on the analysis of the ideology of American business; based on pamphlets, ads, public statements, and other materials from business firms.

I. THE LEFT

1393. Fischer, George, ed. THE REVIVAL OF AMERICAN SOCIALISM; SELECTED PAPERS OF THE SOCIALIST SCHOLARS CONFERENCE. New York: Oxford University Press, 1971. xvi, 330 p.

> Sixteen essays on a new social movement in American life.

1394. Glazer, Nathan. THE SOCIAL BASIS OF AMERICAN COMMUNISM. New York: Harcourt, Brace and World, 1961. 244 p.

> History of the American Communist Party between 1920 and 1950; examines class, racial, and ethnic backgrounds of party members.

1395. Harrington, Michael. TOWARD A DEMOCRATIC LEFT; A RADICAL PROGRAM FOR A NEW MAJORITY. New York: Macmillan, 1968. vi, 314 p.

1396. Howe, Irving, and Coser, Lewis [A.] THE AMERICAN COMMUNIST PARTY, A CRITICAL HISTORY. 2nd ed. New York: Praeger, 1962. 612 p.

1397. Yorburg, Betty. UTOPIA AND REALITY: A COLLECTIVE PORTRAIT
OF AMERICAN SOCIALISTS. New York: Columbia University Press,
1969. x, 198 p.

Based on tape recorded interviews with thirty-four former and
present leaders of the American Socialist Party.

J. THE RIGHT

1398. Bell, Daniel, ed. THE RADICAL RIGHT. Garden City, N.Y.:
Doubleday, 1964. xi, 468 p.

Expanded version of THE NEW AMERICAN RIGHT (New York:
Criterion Books, 1955). Essays by Richard Hofstadter, David
Riesman, Nathan Glazer, Talcott Parsons, and Seymour M.
Lipset.

1399. Broyles, J. Allen. THE JOHN BIRCH SOCIETY: ANATOMY OF A
PROTEST. Boston: Beacon Press, 1964. 169 p.

1400. Epstein, Benjamin R., and Forster, Arnold. THE RADICAL RIGHT:
REPORT ON THE JOHN BIRCH SOCIETY AND ITS ALLIES. New
York: Random House, 1967. xi, 239 p.

1401. Lipset, Seymour Martin, and Raab, Earl. THE POLITICS OF UNREA-
SON: RIGHT WING EXTREMISM IN AMERICA, 1790-1970. New
York: Harper & Row, Publishers, 1970. xxiv, 547 p.

Movements analyzed in this study: Know-Nothings, Anti-
Masons, KKK (Ku Klux Klan), the American Protective Association, the Coughlinites, McCarthyists, Birchers, and Wallace-
ites are all characterized by anti-Catholic, anti-Semitic, and/
or anti-Negro sentiment.

1402. McEvoy, James. RADICALS OR CONSERVATIVES? THE CONTEM-
PORARY AMERICAN RIGHT. Chicago: Rand McNally, 1971. xix,
167 p.

Examination of right wing political movements which supported
Goldwater in 1964 and Wallace in 1968.

1403. Rose, Arnold M[arshall]. LIBEL AND ACADEMIC FREEDOM; A LAWSUIT
AGAINST POLITICAL EXTREMISTS. Minneapolis: University of Minnesota Press, 1968. ix, 287 p.

Discussion of issues surrounding a 1963 suit against a Minnesota right wing extremist group known as Christian Research.

1404. Shils, Edward. THE TORMENT OF SECRECY; THE BACKGROUND AND CONSEQUENCES OF AMERICAN SECURITY POLICIES. Glencoe, Ill.: Free Press, 1956. 238 p.

> Examination of the early 1950s, when a tide of hysteria brought Joseph McCarthy to prominence.

K. VOTING

1405. Berelson, Bernard R., et al. VOTING; A STUDY OF OPINION FORMATION IN A PRESIDENTIAL CAMPAIGN. Chicago: University of Chicago Press, 1954. xix, 395 p.

> A study by the Columbia University Bureau of Applied Social Research of the 1948 presidential election in Elmira, New York.

Campbell, Angus, et al. See Michigan. University.

1406. Hamilton, Richard F. CLASS AND POLITICS IN THE UNITED STATES. New York: Wiley, 1972. xiv, 589 p.

> Analysis of election studies from 1952, 1956, and 1964; rejects pluralist and mass society theories and argues in favor of "group politics" theory--transmittal of political attitudes by social groups with stable political traditions.

1407. Kornhauser, Arthur William, et al. WHEN LABOR VOTES, A STUDY OF AUTO WORKERS. New York: University Books, 1956. 352 p.

> Analysis of the voting of the Detroit members of the United Auto Workers in the 1952 presidential election.

1408. McPhee, William N., and Glaser, William A., eds. PUBLIC OPINION AND CONGRESSIONAL ELECTIONS. New York: Free Press of Glencoe, 1962. x, 326 p.

> Twelve studies of problems connected with voting behavior; data derived from opinion surveys in Colorado, Washington, Minnesota, and Iowa during the 1950 congressional campaign.

1409. MacRae, Duncan, [Jr.], with Goldner, Fred H. DIMENSIONS OF CONGRESSIONAL VOTING; A STATISTICAL STUDY OF THE HOUSE OF REPRESENTATIVES IN THE EIGHTY-FIRST CONGRESS. University of California Publications in Sociology and Social Institutions, vol. 1, no. 3. Berkeley: University of California Press, 1958. v, 203-390 p.

1410. Michigan. University. Survey Research Center. Institute for

Social Research. THE AMERICAN VOTER. By Angus Campbell, et al. New York: Wiley, [1960]. viii, 573 p.

Draws primarily on presidential election surveys done in 1952 and 1956 at the Survey Research Center.

1411. _____. ELECTIONS AND THE POLITICAL ORDER. By Angus Campbell, et al. New York: Wiley, [1966]. ix, 385 p.

1412. Polsby, Nelson W., and Wildavsky, Aaron B. PRESIDENTIAL ELECTIONS; STRATEGIES OF AMERICAN ELECTORAL POLITICS. 3rd ed. New York: Scribner, 1971. xvii, 332 p. Bibliography.

* * *

See also Chapter 7, Section I; and Chapter 13, Section G.

Chapter 20

COLLECTIVE BEHAVIOR

Chapter 20

COLLECTIVE BEHAVIOR

A. BIBLIOGRAPHIES

1413. Altbach, Philip G., and Kelly, David H. AMERICAN STUDENTS; A SELECTED BIBLIOGRAPHY ON STUDENT ACTIVISM AND RELATED TOPICS. Lexington, Mass.: D.C. Heath, Lexington Books, 1973. xiv, 537 p.

1414. Keniston, Kenneth. RADICALS AND MILITANTS; AN ANNOTATED BIBLIOGRAPHY OF EMPIRICAL RESEARCH ON CAMPUS UNREST. Lexington, Mass.: D.C. Heath, Lexington Books, 1973. 415 p.

Three hundred and four abstracts of literature on activism, campus unrest, and youth revolt.

B. SOCIAL MOVEMENTS

1415. Ash, Roberta. SOCIAL MOVEMENTS IN AMERICA. Chicago: Markham, 1972. viii, 274 p.

Historical analysis of social movements from the colonial era to the cold war.

1416. Aya, Roderick, and Miller, Norman, eds. THE NEW AMERICAN REVOLUTION. New York: Free Press, 1971. x, 342 p.

Eight essays examine radical movements, white and Black, of the 1960s.

1417. Berger, Peter L., and Neuhaus, Richard J. MOVEMENT AND REVOLUTION: A CONVERSATION ON AMERICAN RADICALISM. Garden City, N.Y.: Doubleday, 1970. 240 p.

Expression of concern about American involvement in Vietnam and other related issues.

1418. Brown, Michael, and Goldin, Amy. COLLECTIVE BEHAVIOR: A REVIEW AND REINTERPRETATION OF THE LITERATURE. Pacific Palisades, Calif.: Goodyear, 1973. xvii, 349 p. Bibliography pp. 322-38.

1419. Cameron, William Bruce. MODERN SOCIAL MOVEMENTS; A SOCIO-LOGICAL OUTLINE. New York: Random House, 1966. viii, 183 p. Bibliography.

1420. Evans, Robert R., ed. SOCIAL MOVEMENTS: A READER AND SOURCEBOOK. Chicago: Rand McNally, 1973. xvi, 605 p.

1421. Gusfield, Joseph R. PROTEST, REFORM AND REVOLT: A READER IN SOCIAL MOVEMENTS AND COLLECTIVE ACTION. New York: Wiley, 1970. xiv, 576 p.

1422. _____. SYMBOLIC CRUSADE: STATUS POLITICS AND THE AMERI-CAN TEMPERANCE MOVEMENT. Urbana: University of Illinois Press, 1963. viii, 198 p.

   Analysis of the rise and decline of status groups, reflected in the political conflict over drinking habits.

1423. Horowitz, Irving Louis. THE STRUGGLE IS THE MESSAGE; THE ORGANIZATION AND IDEOLOGY OF THE ANTI-WAR MOVEMENT. Berkeley: Glendessary Press, 1970. xii, 175 p.

   Analyzes the relationship between the contemporary antiwar movement and mass violence. Bibliography (pp. 169-71).

1424. Howard, John R. THE CUTTING EDGE: SOCIAL MOVEMENTS AND SOCIAL CHANGE IN AMERICA. Philadelphia: Lippincott, 1974. lx, 276 p.

   Social movements developed by Blacks, women, youth, and homosexuals are discussed along with the hippie movement, communes, and new religions.

1425. Humphreys, Laud. OUT OF THE CLOSET: THE SOCIOLOGY OF HOMOSEXUAL LIBERATION. Englewood Cliffs, N.J.: Prentice-Hall, 1972. 176 p.

   Examines the homophile movement in America.

1426. Lang, Kurt, and Lang, Gladys E. COLLECTIVE DYNAMICS. New York: Thomas Y. Crowell Co., 1961. 563 p.

1427. Roberts, Ronald E., and Kloss, Robert M. SOCIAL MOVEMENTS.

St. Louis, Mo.: C.V. Mosby, 1974. 225 p.

1428. Rush, Gary B., and Denisoff, R. Serge, eds. SOCIAL AND POLITICAL MOVEMENTS. New York: Appleton-Century-Crofts, 1971. xiii, 520 p.

> Readings discuss social movements as ideological organizations which present solutions to social problems. Bibliography (pp. 497-513).

1429. Stolz, Matthew F., comp. POLITICS OF THE NEW LEFT. Beverly Hills: Glencoe Press, 1971. xiii, 190 p.

> Eighteen selections deal with the New Left activism. Bibliography.

1430. Turner, Ralph H., and Killian, Lewis M. COLLECTIVE BEHAVIOR. 2nd ed. Englewood Cliffs, N.J.: Prentice-Hall, 1972. vii, 435 p.

1431. Useem, Michael. CONSCRIPTION, PROTEST, AND SOCIAL CONFLICT; THE LIFE AND DEATH OF A DRAFT RESISTANCE MOVEMENT. New York: Wiley, 1973. xx, 329 p.

1432. Wittner, Lawrence S. REBELS AGAINST WAR; THE AMERICAN PEACE MOVEMENT, 1941-1960. New York: Columbia University Press, 1969. xi, 339 p.

> Popularity of pacifism in the 1930s, its decline during war years, and resurgence in the sixties; forty-two-page bibliography.

C. COMMUNES AND COMMUNAL MOVEMENTS

1433. Fairfield, Richard. COMMUNES U.S.A.; A PERSONAL TOUR. Baltimore: Penguin Books, 1972. x, 400 p.

> Taped interviews by the publisher of the ALTERNATIVES JOURNAL (formerly THE MODERN UTOPIAN). Bibliography (pp. 386-400).

1434. Hedgepeth, William, and Stock, Dennis. ALTERNATIVE; COMMUNAL LIFE IN NEW AMERICA. New York: Macmillan, 1970. 191 p.

1435. Houriet, Robert. GETTING BACK TOGETHER. New York: Coward, McCann & Geoghegan, [1971]. xxxv, 412 p.

> Describes religious, urban, rural, and countercultural communal movements.

1436. Infield, Henrik F. THE AMERICAN INTENTIONAL COMMUNITIES: STUDY ON THE SOCIOLOGY OF COOPERATION. Glen Gardner, N.J.: Community Press, 1955. 118 p.

A shortened version of case studies of three rural communities (Campanella, Macedonia, and Gould Farm) originally published in COOPERATIVE LIVING, a periodical published from 1949 to 1957 by the Group Farming Research Institute, Poughkeepsie, New York.

1437. Kanter, Rosabeth M. COMMITMENT AND COMMUNITY; COMMUNES AND UTOPIAS IN SOCIOLOGICAL PERSPECTIVE. Cambridge, Mass.: Harvard University Press, 1972. x, 303 p.

Analyzes the structure of nineteen utopian communities and examines modern communes. Bibliography.

1438. Melville, Keith. COMMUNES IN THE COUNTER CULTURE; ORIGINS, THEORIES, STYLES OF LIFE. New York: Morrow, 1972. 256 p.

Based on participant observation and analysis of current litera-ture. Discussion of utopian experiments, the student movement in the 1960s, activists, and Yippies.

1439. Roberts, Ronald E. THE NEW COMMUNES, COMING TOGETHER IN AMERICA. Englewood Cliffs, N.J.: Prentice-Hall, 1971. 144 p.

Describes some of the utopian and communalist movements active in the United States in 1970.

1440. Zablocki, Benjamin. THE JOYFUL COMMUNITY: AN ACCOUNT OF THE BRUDERHOF, A COMMUNAL MOVEMENT NOW IN ITS THIRD GENERATION. Baltimore: Penguin Books, 1971. 362 p.

Based on three-and-a-half months of participant observation in 1965 at Woodcrest, the Bruderhof's largest colony. This fundamental Anabaptist community was founded in Germany in 1920 and it migrated to the United States in 1954.

D. STUDENT PROTEST AND CAMPUS CONFLICT

1441. Bell, Daniel, and Kristol, Irving, eds. CONFRONTATION; THE STUDENT REBELLION AND THE UNIVERSITIES. New York: Basic Books, 1969. xii, 191 p.

Reportage and interpretation of the student rebellion at Berke-ley, Columbia, and Cornell, and the Black Studies movement at San Francisco State.

1442. Heirich, Max. THE SPIRAL OF CONFLICT: BERKELEY, 1964. New York: Columbia University Press, 1971. 502 p.

> Examines the Free Speech movement during 1964–65. Bibliography.

1443. Horowitz, Irving Louis, and Friedland, William H. THE KNOWL-EDGE FACTORY; STUDENT POWER AND ACADEMIC POLITICS IN AMERICA. Chicago: Aldine, 1970. 354 p.

> Study of civil rights, anti-Vietnam War, and student movements on campuses between 1960 and 1970; case studies of Cornell and Stanford. Bibliography.

1444. Lipset, Seymour Martin, and Schaflander, Gerald M. PASSION AND POLITICS: STUDENT ACTIVISM IN AMERICA. Boston: Little, Brown and Co., 1971. xxiii, 440 p.

> Part I, by Lipset, consists of seven chapters under the general title, The Dimensions of Student Involvement. Part II, by Schaflander, is entitled, Passion, Pot and Politics, and consists of four chapters. Bibliography.

1445. Lipset, Seymour Martin, and Wolin, Sheldon S., eds. THE BERKELEY STUDENT REVOLT: FACTS AND INTERPRETATIONS. Garden City, N.Y.: Doubleday, Anchor, 1965. xiv, 585 p.

1446. McEvoy, James, and Miller, Abraham, eds. BLACK POWER AND STUDENT REBELLION: CONFLICT ON THE AMERICAN CAMPUS. Belmont, Calif.: Wadsworth, 1969. 440 p.

> Case studies of rebellions at San Francisco State, Columbia, University of Chicago, Duke, Stanford, and Berkeley. Bibliography.

1447. Wallerstein, Immanuel, and Starr, Paul, eds. THE UNIVERSITY CRISIS READER. Vol. 1: THE LIBERAL UNIVERSITY UNDER ATTACK; vol. 2: CONFRONTATION AND COUNTERATTACK. New York: Random House, 1971. Vol. 1, 558 p.; vol. 2, 575 p.

> Documents, including position papers, manifestos, lists of demands, official replies, statements and comments related to student protest in the 1960s.

E. RIOTS AND VIOLENCE

1448. Besag, Frank P., and Cook, Philip. THE ANATOMY OF A RIOT: BUFFALO, 1967. Rev. ed. Buffalo, N.Y.: University Press, [1970]. 225 p.

1449. Boesel, David, and Rossi, Peter H., eds. CITIES UNDER SIEGE: AN ANATOMY OF THE GHETTO RIOTS, 1964–68. New York: Basic Books, 1971. 436 p.

> Emphasizes the role of political factors in the interpretation of recent Black rioting.

1450. Cohen, Nathan, ed. THE LOS ANGELES RIOTS; A SOCIO-PSYCHOLOGICAL STUDY. New York: Praeger, 1970. 742 p.

> Survey of a study of the 1965 Watts riot based on 2,000 personal interviews. Bibliography.

1451. Feagin, Joe R., and Hahn, Harlan. GHETTO REVOLTS: THE POLITICS OF VIOLENCE IN AMERICAN CITIES. New York: Macmillan, 1973. 338 p.

1452. Fogelson, Robert M. VIOLENCE AS PROTEST; A STUDY OF RIOTS AND GHETTOS. Garden City, N.Y.: Doubleday, 1971. 265 p.

> Analysis of the 1960s riots as a protest against genuine grievances in the Black ghettos. Bibliography.

1453. Gordon, Leonard, comp. A CITY IN RACIAL CRISIS; THE CASE OF DETROIT PRE- AND POST- THE 1967 RIOT. Dubuque, Iowa: W.C. Brown, 1971. xvii, 167 p.

> Documentation of social forces operating in the 1960s; discussion of racial conflict and accommodation.

1454. Harris, Dale B., and Sample, John A., eds. VIOLENCE IN CONTEMPORARY AMERICAN SOCIETY. University Park: Pennsylvania State University Press, 1969. 261 p.

> Collection of multidisciplinary papers presented at Pennsylvania State University in 1967 at a seminar on violence.

1455. Janowitz, Morris. SOCIAL CONTROL OF ESCALATED RIOTS. Chicago: Center for Policy Study, 1968. 44 p.

1456. Masotti, Louis H., and Bowen, Don R., eds. RIOTS AND REBELLION; CIVIL VIOLENCE IN THE URBAN COMMUNITY. Beverly Hills: Sage Publications, 1968. 459 p.

> A collection of twenty-six articles on civil violence in urban ghettos. Bibliography.

1457. Oppenheimer, Martin. THE URBAN GUERRILLA. Chicago: Quadrangle, 1969. 188 p.

Examines social movements in American cities--violent
political protest, terrorism, sabotage, and the causes of mass
alienation, with historical and comparative observations.

1458. Pinkney, Alphonso. THE AMERICAN WAY OF VIOLENCE. New
York: Random House, Vintage, 1972. 235 p.

Argues that the American value system rewards acts of violence
while placing property values above human ones and that the
United States is one of the most violent societies ever to
exist. Bibliography.

1459. Short, James F., Jr., and Wolfgang, Marvin E., eds. COLLECTIVE
VIOLENCE. Chicago: Aldine-Atherton, 1972. viii, 387 p.

Twenty-seven papers from the September 1970 issue of the
ANNALS of the American Academy of Political and Social
Sciences and from a special symposium on violence of the
American Anthropological Association in November 1969.

1460. Singer, Benjamin D., et al. BLACK RIOTERS; A STUDY OF SOCIAL
FACTORS AND COMMUNICATION IN THE DETROIT RIOT. Lexington,
Mass.: D.C. Heath, 1970. ix, 117 p.

Study of the July 1967 riot in Detroit, based on interviews
with 499 Blacks. Bibliography.

1461. Skolnick, Jerome H., ed. THE POLITICS OF PROTEST; A REPORT. New
York: Simon and Schuster, 1969. xxvii, 419 p. Bibliography.
(Prepared for the National Commission on the Causes and Prevention
of Violence.)

1462. United States National Advisory Commission on Civil Disorders. REPORT
OF THE COMMISSION. New York: Bantam Books, 1968. 609 p.

1463. Walker, Daniel. RIGHTS IN CONFLICT: CONVENTION WEEK IN
CHICAGO, AUGUST 25-29, 1968; A REPORT. New York: E.P.
Dutton, 1968. xx, 362 p.

A documented report of the events in Chicago during the
Democratic National Convention, as submitted to the National
Commission on the Causes and Prevention of Violence at the
end of 1968.

F. DISASTER STUDIES

1464. Baker, George W., and Chapman, Dwight W., eds. MAN AND

SOCIETY IN DISASTER. New York: Basic Books, 1962. 442 p.

Fourteen original contributions sponsored by the Disaster Research Group, National Academy of Sciences, and National Research Council. Bibliography.

1465. Clifford, Roy A. THE RIO GRANDE FLOOD; A COMPARATIVE STUDY OF BORDER COMMUNITIES IN DISASTER. Washington, D.C.: National Academy of Sciences, National Research Council, 1956. xv, 145 p.

Analysis of data from two different social systems—Texan and Mexican—exposed to the 1954 Rio Grande flood; study of influence of value orientation and social structure.

1466. Dynes, Russell R. ORGANIZED BEHAVIOR IN DISASTER. Lexington, Mass.: D.C. Heath, 1970. 235 p.

A publication of the Disaster Research Center at Ohio State University. Bibliography (pp. 227-35).

1467. Form, William H., and Nosow, Sigmund. COMMUNITY IN DISASTER. New York: Harper & Brothers, 1958. xiii, 273 p.

Analyzes the behavior of rescuers and victims in Flint, Michigan, after the 1953 tornado.

1468. Moore, Harry Estill. TORNADOES OVER TEXAS; A STUDY OF WACO AND SAN ANGELO IN DISASTER. Austin: University of Texas Press, [1958]. xxiii, 334 p. (Research Publication in Mental Health for the Hogg Foundation.)

Economic cost, the role of communication media, family adjustments, and race differences are considered.

* * *

See also Chapter 11, Section F; and Chapter 16, Section C.

Chapter 21

DEVIANCE

Chapter 21
DEVIANCE

A. BIBLIOGRAPHIES

1469. Bahr, Howard M., ed. DISAFFILIATED MAN; ESSAYS AND BIBLIOG-
RAPHY ON SKID ROW, VAGRANCY AND OUTSIDERS. Toronto:
University of Toronto Press, 1970. xiv, 428 p.

Five essays and 300 pages of annotated bibliography.

1470. Farberow, Norman L. BIBLIOGRAPHY ON SUICIDE AND SUICIDE
PREVENTION, 1897-1957, 1958-1967. Chevy Chase, Md.: National
Institute of Mental Health, 1969. vii, 203 p.

Lists 2,202 books and papers published from 1897 to 1957;
1,267 more were published from 1958 to 1967.

1471. INTERNATIONAL BIBLIOGRAPHY OF STUDIES ON ALCOHOL. Edited
by Mark Keller. Vol. 1: REFERENCES 1901-1950, prepared by Sarah
S. Jordy, 1966. Vol. 2: INDEXES TO VOLUME 1, 1901-1950:
PART 1: SUBJECTS, prepared by Vera Efron; PART 2: AUTHORS,
prepared by Sarah S. Jordy, 1968. New Brunswick, N.J.: Rutgers
Center of Alcohol Studies. Vol. 1, xxxxvi, 631 p.; vol. 2, xi,
134 p.

Supplemented by bibliographic lists published in the QUARTER-
LY JOURNAL OF STUDIES ON ALCOHOL (see item 216);
further cumulative volumes are in preparation.

1472. Menditto, Joseph. DRUGS OF ADDICTION AND NON-ADDICTION,
THEIR USE AND ABUSE; A COMPREHENSIVE BIBLIOGRAPHY, 1960-
1969. Troy, N.Y.: Whitston Publishing Co., 1970. 315 p.

Supplemented by an annual publication to be cumulated quin-
quennially, DRUG ABUSE BIBLIOGRAPHY, compiled by Jean
C. Advena (Troy, N.Y.: Whitston Publishing Co., 1970).

1473. Meyer, Alan S., ed. SOCIAL AND PSYCHOLOGICAL FACTORS IN

OPIATE ADDICTION: A REVIEW OF RESEARCH FINDINGS TOGETHER WITH AN ANNOTATED BIBLIOGRAPHY. New York: Bureau of Applied Social Research, Columbia University, 1952. ix, 170 p.

1474. Parker, William. HOMOSEXUALITY: A SELECTIVE BIBLIOGRAPHY OF OVER 3,000 ITEMS. Metuchen, N.J.: Scarecrow Press, 1971. viii, 323 p.

> More than 3,000 English language references to scientific, popular nonfiction and religious material, newspaper articles, chapters in books, and judicial decisions and citations.

1475. Seiden, Richard H. SUICIDE AMONG YOUTH; A REVIEW OF THE LITERATURE, 1900-1967. Chevy Chase, Md.: National Institute of Mental Health, 1969. iv, 62 p. (Sold by Government Printing Office.)

1476. Weinberg, Martin S., and Bell, Alan B. HOMOSEXUALITY; AN ANNOTATED BIBLIOGRAPHY. New York: Harper & Row, Publishers, 1972. 550 p.

> A publication of the Indiana Institute for Sex Research.

B. DEVIANT BEHAVIOR

1477. Becker, Howard S. OUTSIDERS; STUDIES IN THE SOCIOLOGY OF DEVIANCE. New York: Free Press of Glencoe, 1963. 179 p.

> Discusses the social context in which deviance occurs; stresses the definition of deviance by others rather than the deviant act itself. Bibliography.

1478. Bell, Robert R. SOCIAL DEVIANCE; A SUBSTANTIVE ANALYSIS. Homewood, Ill.: Dorsey Press, 1971. xi, 482 p.

> Examines contemporary patterns of sexual and deviant behavior and the emergence of feminist and student subcultures.

1479. Clinard, Marshall B[arron]. SOCIOLOGY OF DEVIANT BEHAVIOR. 4th ed. New York: Holt, Rinehart and Winston, 1974. xiv, 685 p.

1480. _____, ed. ANOMIE AND DEVIANT BEHAVIOR: A DISCUSSION AND CRITIQUE. New York: Free Press of Glencoe, 1964. xii, 324 p.

> Series of papers presented at the 1962 Annual Meeting of the American Sociological Association, criticizing Merton's concept of anomie.

1481. Erikson, Kai T. WAYWARD PURITANS; A STUDY IN THE SOCIOL-
OGY OF DEVIANCE. New York: Wiley, 1966. xv, 228 p.

Theoretical framework for understanding deviant behavior
illustrated by examination of three crises in the seventeenth-
century Massachusetts Bay Colony. Bibliography.

1482. Hewitt, John P. SOCIAL STRATIFICATION AND DEVIANT BEHAVIOR.
New York: Random House, 1970. viii, 176 p.

A self-esteem theory is developed to link social inequality
and deviance.

1483. Jessor, Richard, et al. SOCIETY, PERSONALITY, AND DEVIANT
BEHAVIOR; A STUDY OF A TRI-ETHNIC COMMUNITY. New York:
Holt, Rinehart and Winston, 1968. 500 p.

An interdisciplinary field research investigation of drinking
problems and other deviant behavior in a small Anglo-Spanish-
Indian community in southern Colorado.

1484. Matza, David. BECOMING DEVIANT. Englewood Cliffs, N.J.:
Prentice-Hall, 1969. ix, 203 p.

Deals with the phenomenological and social psychological
aspects of deviance and focuses on the inner life of the
deviant person.

1485. Sagarin, Edward. ODD MAN IN: SOCIETIES OF DEVIANTS IN
AMERICA. Chicago: Quadrangle, 1969. 287 p.

Survey of literature and interviews with officers and members
of such groups as Alcoholics Anonymous, Gamblers Anonymous,
Synanon, and Mattachine Society.

1486. Schur, Edwin M. CRIMES WITHOUT VICTIMS. Englewood Cliffs,
N.J.: Prentice-Hall, 1965. ix, 180 p.

Analysis of abortion, homosexuality, and drug addiction as
victimless crimes.

1487. _____. LABELING DEVIANT BEHAVIOR, ITS SOCIOLOGICAL IMPLI-
CATION. New York: Harper & Row, Publishers, 1971. x, 177 p.

C. READERS

1488. Becker, Howard S. THE OTHER SIDE; PERSPECTIVES ON DEVIANCE.
New York: Free Press of Glencoe, 1964. 297 p.

Articles selected from SOCIAL PROBLEMS (see item 131).

1489. Dinitz, Simon, et al. DEVIANCE: STUDIES IN THE PROCESS OF STIGMATIZATION AND SOCIETAL REACTION. New York: Oxford University Press, 1969. 575 p.

Fifty-eight readings present traditional problems (organized crime, drug abuse, homosexuality, suicide) as well as more recent ones (abortion, pornography, urban violence).

1490. Douglas, Jack D., ed. OBSERVATIONS OF DEVIANCE. New York: Random House, 1970. viii, 340 p.

Case reports by participant observers capture the thoughts and feelings of deviants.

1491. Lefton, Mark, et al. APPROACHES TO DEVIANCE; THEORIES, CON-CEPTS, AND RESEARCH FINDINGS. New York: Appleton-Century-Crofts, 1968. x, 391 p.

1492. McCaghy, Charles H., et al., eds. IN THEIR OWN BEHALF; VOICES FROM THE MARGIN. New York: Appleton-Century-Crofts, 1968. ix, 230 p.

Selections of writings by individuals whose behavior has been defined as deviant. Bibliography.

1493. Rainwater, Lee, ed. SOCIAL PROBLEMS AND PUBLIC POLICY: DE-VIANCE AND LIBERTY: A SURVEY OF MODERN PERSPECTIVES ON DEVIANT BEHAVIOR. Chicago: Aldine, 1974. 437 p.

Thirty-nine articles on substantive and problematic issues.

1494. Rubington, Earl, and Weinberg, Martin S., comp. DEVIANCE, THE INTERACTIONIST PERSPECTIVE; TEXT AND READINGS IN THE SO-CIOLOGY OF DEVIANCE. New York: Macmillan, 1968. x, 422 p.

D. ALCOHOLISM

1495. Cahalan, Don, et al. AMERICAN DRINKING PRACTICES; A NATION-AL STUDY OF DRINKING BEHAVIOR AND ATTITUDES. Monograph no. 6. New Brunswick, N.J.: Publications Division, Rutgers Center of Alcohol Studies, distributed by College and University Press, New Haven, 1969. xxvi, 260 p.

Information was obtained in 1964-65 from 2,746 interviews, representing a national probability sample of the population over twenty-one. Bibliography.

1496. Gellman, Irving Peter. THE SOBER ALCOHOLIC; AN ORGANIZA-
TIONAL ANALYSIS OF ALCOHOLICS ANONYMOUS. New Haven:
College and University Press, 1964. 206 p.

> Through participant observation the author concentrated on a
> single Alcoholics Anonymous local and analyzes Alcoholics
> Anonymous as a social movement.

1497. Maddox, George L., ed. THE DOMESTICATED DRUG: DRINKING
AMONG COLLEGIANS. New Haven: College and University Press,
1970. 479 p.

> Collection of twenty-one articles with bibliographic references
> to the literature from 1938 to 1968.

1498. Maddox, George L., and McCall, Bevode C. DRINKING AMONG
TEENAGERS: A SOCIOLOGICAL INTERPRETATION OF ALCOHOL
USE BY HIGH SCHOOL STUDENTS. New Brunswick, N.J.: Publications Division, Rutgers Center of Alcohol Studies, distributed by College
and University Press, New Haven, 1964. xvi, 127 p.

> Discusses a 1955 study of Michigan high school students.

1499. Plaut, Thomas F.A., ed. ALCOHOL PROBLEMS: A REPORT TO THE
NATION BY THE COOPERATIVE COMMISSION ON THE STUDY OF
ALCOHOLISM. New York: Oxford University Press, 1967. xvi,
200 p.

1500. Snyder, Charles R. ALCOHOL AND THE JEWS; A CULTURAL STUDY
OF DRINKING AND SOBRIETY. Monographs of the Yale Center of
Alcohol Studies, no. 1. Glencoe, Ill.: Free Press, 1958. 226 p.

> Based on data from interviews with a sample of seventy-three
> New Haven Jewish men and from questionnaires to a sample
> of 644 male Jewish college students. Bibliography.

1501. Straus, Robert, and Bacon, Sheldon D. DRINKING IN COLLEGE.
New Haven: Yale University Press, 1953. vii, 221 p.

> A questionnaire survey of 15,747 college students from twenty-
> seven colleges conducted from 1949 to 1951.

1502. Trice, Harrison M. ALCOHOLISM IN AMERICA. New York: McGraw-
Hill, 1966. xi, 140 p.

> Alcoholism, as a symptom of personal behavior, is the result
> of numerous factors, some unique to American society.

1503. Trice, Harrison M., and Roman, Paul M. SPIRITS AND DEMONS AT
WORK: ALCOHOL AND OTHER DRUGS ON THE JOB. Ithaca,

N.Y.: New York State School of Industrial and Labor Relations, Cornell University, 1972. ix, 268 p.

E. SKID ROW

1504. Bahr, Howard M. SKID ROW; AN INTRODUCTION TO DISAFFILIA-TION. New York: Oxford University Press, 1973. x, 335 p.

Study of the inhabitants of skid row in several cities and problems of their rehabilitation: aging, mental illness, and psychological alienation.

1505. Bahr, Howard M., and Caplow, Theodore. OLD MEN, DRUNK AND SOBER. New York: New York University Press, 1974. 407 p.

Results of the first six years (1963–68) of the Columbia Bow-ery Project conducted by the Bureau of Applied Research.

1506. Blumberg, Leonard, et al. SKID ROW AND ITS ALTERNATIVES; RESEARCH AND RECOMMENDATIONS FROM PHILADELPHIA. Phila-delphia: Temple University Press, 1973. xxv, 309 p.

Reports on a decade of work at Philadelphia's Diagnostic and Rehabilitation Center. Bibliography (pp. 289-97).

1507. Bogue, Donald J. SKID ROW IN AMERICAN CITIES. Chicago: Community and Family Study Center, University of Chicago, 1963. xiv, 521 p.

Chicago's skid row is the main focus of this study.

1508. Spradley, James P. YOU OWE YOURSELF A DRUNK: AN ETHNOG-RAPHY OF URBAN NOMADS. Boston: Little, Brown and Co., 1970. 301 p.

Skid row men in Seattle, their encounters with law enforce-ment officers, and the repeated arrests and jailings which perpetuate rather than control deviance.

1509. Wallace, Samuel E. SKID ROW AS A WAY OF LIFE. Totowa, N.J.: Bedminster Press, 1965. vii, 202 p. Bibliography (pp. 207-14).

1510. Wiseman, Jacqueline P. STATIONS OF THE LOST; THE TREATMENT OF SKID ROW ALCOHOLICS. Englewood Cliffs, N.J.: Prentice-Hall, 1970. xxi, 346 p.

Insiders' views on various stages of progress between skid row and correctional and rehabilitation agencies. Discusses the myth of rehabilitation.

F. DRUGS

1511. Blum, Richard H., et al. SOCIETY AND DRUGS; SOCIAL AND CULTURAL OBSERVATIONS. San Francisco: Jossey-Bass, 1969. xvi, 400 p.

   An inquiry into the social and psychological factors associated with the use of psychoactive drugs.

1512. _____. STUDENTS AND DRUGS; COLLEGE AND HIGH SCHOOL OBSERVATIONS. San Francisco: Jossey-Bass, 1969. xix, 399 p.

   Reports findings from over 1300 student interviews at five western colleges and universities and from 5,500 student questionnaires from four California high schools. Bibliography.

1513. _____. UTOPIATES; THE USE AND USERS OF LSD-25. New York: Atherton Press, 1964. xvi, 303 p.

1514. Carey, James T. THE COLLEGE DRUG SCENE. Englewood Cliffs, N.J.: Prentice-Hall, 1968. ix, 210 p.

1515. Chein, Isidor, et al. THE ROAD TO H: NARCOTICS, DELINQUENCY, AND SOCIAL POLICY. New York: Basic Books, 1964. xii, 482 p.

   Reports on studies in New York City to determine the frequency of narcotics use and its social and psychological context.

1516. Duster, Troy. THE LEGISLATION OF MORALITY: LAW, DRUGS, AND MORAL JUDGMENT. New York: Free Press, 1970. x, 274 p.

   Data from the California Rehabilitation Center about drug addiction and the stigmatization of the addict.

1517. Goode, Erich. DRUGS IN AMERICAN SOCIETY. New York: Knopf, 1972. ix, 260 p.

   Relates features of drug use to society's definitions and illegalization process. Bibliography.

1518. _____. THE MARIJUANA SMOKERS. New York: Basic Books, 1970. x, 340 p.

   Interviews with 204 marijuana users are used to illustrate a proposed "recreational" and a "subcultural" model of use.

1519. _____, ed. MARIJUANA. New York: Atherton Press, 1969. xii, 197 p.

Twenty-four papers discuss controversies concerning the use
of marijuana, its physiological effects, and legislation.

1520. Johnson, Bruce D. MARIJUANA USERS AND DRUG SUBCULTURES.
New York: Wiley, 1973. xv, 290 p.

Based on interview data from 3,500 students and their friends
from twenty-one colleges in the New York City area; urges
liberalization of drug laws.

1521. Lindesmith, Alfred R. THE ADDICT AND THE LAW. Bloomington:
Indiana University Press, 1965. xiii, 337 p.

A critique of Bureau of Narcotic policies and procedures;
recommends a medical treatment approach.

1522. O'Donnell, John A. NARCOTIC ADDICTS IN KENTUCKY. Chevy
Chase, Md.: National Institute of Mental Health, 1969. xi, 297 p.

Research on a sample of 266 rural white Anglo-Saxon drug
addicts hospitalized in Lexington, Kentucky.

1523. O'Donnell, John A., and Ball, John C., eds. NARCOTIC ADDIC-
TION. New York: Harper & Row, Publishers 1966. viii, 248 p.
Bibliography.

1524. Yablonsky, Lewis. THE TUNNEL BACK: SYNANON. New York:
Macmillan, 1965. xi, 403 p.

Treatment of drug addicts in a community of former drug
addicts.

G. SEXUAL DEVIANCE

1525. Gagnon, John H., and Simon, William, eds. SEXUAL DEVIANCE.
New York: Harper & Row, Publishers, 1967. viii, 310 p.

Discusses female prostitution and male and female homosexuality.

1526. Gebhard, Paul H., et al. SEX OFFENDERS; AN ANALYSIS OF
TYPES. New York: Harper & Row, Publishers, 1965. xxiv, 923 p.

Research from the Institute for Sex Research at Indiana University. Bibliography (pp. 877-82).

1527. Greenwald, Harold. THE CALL GIRL: A SOCIAL AND PSYCHO-
ANALYTIC STUDY. New York: Ballantine Books, 1958. 245 p.

Authored by a social psychologist, an exploratory study based on interviews of twenty women and the psychoanalysis of six women.

1528. _____. THE ELEGANT PROSTITUTE; A SOCIAL AND PSYCHOANA- LYTIC STUDY. New York: Walker and Co., 1970. xxii, 305 p.

A revised edition, with new material, of THE CALL GIRL (see item 1527). Bibliography.

1529. Humphreys, Laud. TEAROOM TRADE; IMPERSONAL SEX IN PUBLIC PLACES. Chicago: Aldine, 1970. xix, 180 p.

A study of male homosexual behavior in metropolitan public restrooms.

1530. Oliver, Bernard J., Jr. SEXUAL DEVIATION IN AMERICAN SOCIETY; A SOCIAL-PSYCHOLOGICAL STUDY OF SEXUAL NONCONFORMITY. New Haven: College and University Press, 1968. 256 p.

Data on 202 sex offenders classified by type of offense. Bibliography.

1531. Williams, Colin J., and Weinberg, Martin S. HOMOSEXUALS AND THE MILITARY; A STUDY OF LESS THAN HONORABLE DISCHARGE. New York: Harper & Row, Publishers, 1971. xii, 221 p. Bibliography.

1532. Winick, Charles, and Kinsie, Paul M. THE LIVELY COMMERCE; PROSTITUTION IN THE UNITED STATES. Chicago: Quadrangle, 1971. ix, 320 p.

Based on 2,000 interviews conducted across the country over the past ten years, and on the files of the American Social Health Association.

H. SUICIDE

1533. Dublin, Louis I. SUICIDE; A SOCIOLOGICAL AND STATISTICAL STUDY. New York: Ronald Press, 1963. viii, 240 p.

This book brings up to date TO BE OR NOT TO BE; A STUDY OF SUICIDE, by Louis Dublin and Bessie Bunzel (New York: A. Smith and R. Haas, 1933).

1534. Farberow, Norman L., and Shneidman, Edwin S. THE CRY FOR HELP. New York: McGraw-Hill, Blakiston Division, 1961. xvi, 398 p.

Comprehensive study of a large number of suicides and attempted suicides in Los Angeles County. Bibliography.

1535. Gibbs, Jack P., and Martin, Walter T. STATUS INTEGRATION AND
SUICIDE; A SOCIOLOGICAL STUDY. Eugene: University of Oregon
Books, 1964. xvii, 225 p.

Authors used census data to obtain patterns that represent
categories of individuals with comparatively high or low status
integration.

1536. Henry, Andrew F., and Short, James F., Jr. SUICIDE AND HOMI-
CIDE; SOME ECONOMIC, SOCIOLOGICAL AND PSYCHOLOGICAL
ASPECTS OF AGGRESSION. New York: Free Press of Glencoe,
1954. 214 p. Bibliography.

1537. Jacobs, Jerry. ADOLESCENT SUICIDE. New York: Wiley-Interscience, 1971. xi, 147 p.

Based on interviews with fifty suicide attempters in Los
Angeles County General Hospital in 1964–65. Bibliography.

1538. Maris, Ronald W. SOCIAL FORCES IN URBAN SUICIDE. Homewood,
III.: Dorsey Press, 1969. xiv, 214 p.

Provides an overview of work on suicide, and an investigation
of the death certificates of 2,153 completed suicides in Cook
County, Illinois.

* * *

See also Chapter 4, Section H.

Chapter 22

CRIME AND DELINQUENCY

Chapter 22

CRIME AND DELINQUENCY

A. REFERENCE WORKS AND BIBLIOGRAPHIES

1539. Chambliss, William J., and Seidman, Robert B. SOCIOLOGY OF THE LAW; A RESEARCH BIBLIOGRAPHY. Berkeley: Glendessary, 1970. viii, 113 p.

1540. Glaser, Daniel, ed. HANDBOOK OF CRIMINOLOGY. Chicago: Rand McNally, 1974. 1180 p.

Thirty-one chapters concerned with explanations for crime and delinquency, law enforcement and adjudication, corrections, and prevention of crime and delinquency. Bibliography.

1541. Prostano, Emanuel T., and Piccirillo, Martin L. LAW ENFORCEMENT: A SELECTIVE BIBLIOGRAPHY. Littleton, Colo.: Libraries Unlimited, 1974. 203 p.

1542. Tompkins, Dorothy C. BAIL IN THE UNITED STATES; A BIBLIOGRA-PHY. Berkeley: Institute of Governmental Studies, University of California, 1964. vii, 49 p.

1543. _____. JUVENILE GANGS AND STREET GROUPS; A BIBLIOGRAPHY. Berkeley: Institute of Governmental Studies, University of California, 1966. viii, 88 p.

1544. _____. THE PRISON AND THE PRISONER; A BIBLIOGRAPHY. Public Policies Bibliographies, no. 1. Berkeley: Institute of Governmental Studies, University of California, 1972. 156 p.

1545. _____. WHITE COLLAR CRIME; A BIBLIOGRAPHY. Berkeley: Institute of Governmental Studies, University of California, 1967. vii, 85 p.

1546. United States Federal Bureau of Investigation. UNIFORM CRIME REPORTS/CRIME IN THE UNITED STATES. Washington, D.C.: Government Printing Office, 1930--. Annual.

1547. Wolfgang, Marvin E., and Ferracuti, Franco. THE SUBCULTURE OF VIOLENCE; TOWARDS AN INTEGRATED THEORY IN CRIMINOLOGY. London: Tavistock, 1967. iii-xxiii, 387 p.

> Theoretical discussion and an overview of sociological literature on violence; bibliography of about 1,000 items.

Part 1: Crime

B. TEXTS AND READERS

1548. Bloch, Herbert A., and Geis, Gilbert. MAN, CRIME AND SOCIETY. 2nd ed. New York: Random House, 1970. xxii, 642 p. Bibliography pp. 497-537.

1549. Blumberg, Abraham S., ed. CURRENT PERSPECTIVES ON CRIMINAL BEHAVIOR; ORIGINAL ESSAYS ON CRIMINOLOGY. New York: Random House, 1974. 368 p.

> Original essays by Richard Quinney, Milton L. Barron, Gilbert Geis, Edward Sagarin, William J. Goode, Marvin E. Wolfgang, Abraham Blumberg, and others survey the important issues of criminology. Annotated bibliography.

1550. Clinard, Marshall B[arron], and Quinney, Richard. CRIMINAL BEHAVIOR SYSTEMS; A TYPOLOGY. 2nd ed. New York: Holt, Rinehart and Winston, 1973. xi, 274 p.

> Distinguishes nine types of criminal behavior: violent personal, occasional property, public order, conventional, political, occupational, organized, professional, and corporate.

1551. Cressey, Donald R., and Ward, David A., eds. DELINQUENCY, CRIME, AND SOCIAL PROCESS. New York: Harper & Row, Publishers, 1969. xv, 1151 p.

1552. Glaser, Daniel, ed. CRIME IN THE CITY. New York: Harper & Row, Publishers, 1970. ix, 308 p.

1553. Haskell, Martin R., and Yablonsky, Lewis. CRIME AND DELINQUENCY. Chicago: Rand McNally, 1970. x, 517 p.

> Discusses the crime problem in general, patterns of criminality, and the treatment and control of juvenile delinquency.

1554. Johnson, Elmer D. CRIME, CORRECTION, AND SOCIETY. 3rd ed. Homewood, Ill.: Dorsey Press, 1974. 671 p.

1555. Reckless, Walter C. THE CRIME PROBLEM. 5th ed. New York: Appleton-Century-Crofts, 1973. xiv, 718 p.

> Discusses crime causation and punishment, abnormal sex offenders, and the criminality of women.

1556. Schur, Edwin M. OUR CRIMINAL SOCIETY; THE SOCIAL AND LEGAL SOURCES OF CRIME IN AMERICA. Englewood Cliffs, N.J.: Prentice-Hall, 1969. ix, 244 p.

> Surveys twenty-five years of sociology as it relates to crime in America.

1557. Sutherland, Edwin H. THE SUTHERLAND PAPERS. Edited by Albert [Kircidel] Cohen, et al. Bloomington: Indiana University Press, 1956. vi, 330 p.

> A collection of Sutherland's writings, spanning twenty-five years, topically arranged.

1558. Sutherland, Edwin H., and Cressey, Donald R. CRIMINOLOGY. 9th ed. Philadelphia: Lippincott, 1974. ix, 659 p.

> Crime and delinquency are related to differential association and social organization; discusses control of crime, punishment, and treatment.

C. WHITE COLLAR CRIME

1559. Clinard, Marshall Barron. THE BLACK MARKET; A STUDY OF WHITE COLLAR CRIME. New York: Rinehart, [1952]. xvii, 392 p.

> A case study of the American black market in World War II as a form of white collar crime. Bibliography.

1560. Cressey, Donald R. OTHER PEOPLE'S MONEY; A STUDY IN THE SOCIAL PSYCHOLOGY OF EMBEZZLEMENT. Belmont, Calif.: Wadsworth, 1971. 191 p.

> Based on interviews with 133 prison inmates at Joliet, Terre Haute, and Chino, and on examination of 200 cases collected earlier by E.H. Sutherland. Bibliography.

1561. Geis, Gilbert, ed. WHITE-COLLAR CRIMINAL; THE OFFENDER IN BUSINESS AND THE PROFESSIONS. New York: Atherton Press,

1968. xii, 448 p.

Thirty-two previously published articles selected from legal and sociological journals and some popular magazines. Bibliography.

1562. Smigel, Erwin O., and Ross, H. Laurence. CRIMES AGAINST BUREAU-CRACY. New York: Van Nostrand, 1970. vii, 142 p.

Seven articles, with an introduction by the editors, defining concepts and reviewing the literature.

1563. Sutherland, Edwin H. WHITE COLLAR CRIME. New York: Dryden Press, 1949. Reprint. New York: Holt, Rinehart and Winston, 1961. 272 p.

Unlawful activities of corporations, corporate owners, and executives.

D. ORGANIZED CRIME

1564. Albini, Joseph L. THE AMERICAN MAFIA; GENESIS OF A LEGEND. New York: Appleton-Century-Crofts, 1971. xi, 354 p.

Argues that syndicated crime cannot be explained as the creation of a foreign criminal organization. Reports on pre-Italian, mostly Irish examples of syndicate crime in America; eighteen-page bibliography.

1565. Conklin, John E., ed. THE CRIME ESTABLISHMENT: ORGANIZED CRIME AND AMERICAN SOCIETY. Englewood Cliffs, N.J.: Prentice-Hall, 1973. 181 p.

Analysis of the economic and political system under which organized crime operates.

1566. Cressey, Donald R. THEFT OF THE NATION; THE STRUCTURE AND OPERATIONS OF ORGANIZED CRIME IN AMERICA. New York: Harper & Row, Publishers, 1969. xii, 367 p.

1567. Gardiner, John A. THE POLITICS OF CORRUPTION; ORGANIZED CRIME IN AN AMERICAN CITY. New York: Russell Sage Foundation, 1970. xi, 129 p.

An intensive case study of an eastern industrial city of 100,000 based on data from interviews with key political personnel; explores the relationship between organized crime and government.

1568. Herman, Robert D., ed. GAMBLING. New York: Harper & Row, Publishers, 1967. viii, 264 p.

> Twenty selections in four sections: forms of gambling, the gambling enterprise, gambling as pathology, and gambling, crime, and public policy.

1569. Kefauver, Estes. CRIME IN AMERICA. Garden City, N.Y.: Doubleday, 1951. xvi, 333 p.

> Based on testimony and reports to the Special Committee to Investigate Crime in Interstate Commerce from May 1950 to May 1951.

E. CRIMES AGAINST PERSON AND PROPERTY

1570. Amir, Menachem. PATTERNS IN FORCIBLE RAPE. Chicago: University of Chicago Press, 1971. ix, 394 p.

> Study of 646 forcible rapes in Philadelphia. Bibliography.

1571. Cameron, Mary Owen. THE BOOSTER AND THE SNITCH: DEPARTMENT STORE SHOPLIFTING. New York: Free Press of Glencoe, 1964. 202 p.

1572. Conklin, John E. ROBBERY, AND THE CRIMINAL JUSTICE SYSTEM. Philadelphia: Lippincott, 1972. xvi, 208 p.

> Robbery as a total behavior system -- trends in robbery rates, types of offenders, use of force, and response of police.

1573. Sutherland, Edwin H. THE PROFESSIONAL THIEF. Chicago: University of Chicago Press, 1937. 256 p.

F. ADMINISTRATION OF JUSTICE

1574. Blumberg, Abraham S. CRIMINAL JUSTICE. Chicago: Quadrangle, 1967. xiv, 206 p.

> A penetrating analysis of criminal courts; the roles of the lawyer and the judge; and the adversary system.

1575. Chambliss, William J. CRIME AND THE LEGAL PROCESS. New York: McGraw-Hill, 1968. xii, 447 p.

> Twenty-five articles reporting empirical studies of the legal system, grouped under three headings: emergence of legal norms, administration of criminal law, and impact of legal

sanctions.

1576. Douglas, Jack D., ed. CRIME AND JUSTICE IN AMERICAN SOCI-
ETY. Indianapolis: Bobbs-Merrill, 1971. xxi, 297 p.

Eight articles examine the failure of the system of criminal
justice to achieve real justice and discuss the need for revo-
lutionary changes.

1577. Freed, Daniel J., and Wald, Patricia M. BAIL IN THE UNITED
STATES, 1964. Washington, D.C.: National Conference on Bail
and Criminal Justice, 1964. viii, 116 p. Bibliography.

1578. Glaser, Daniel. ADULT CRIME AND SOCIAL POLICY. Englewood
Cliffs, N.J.: Prentice-Hall, 1972. viii, 128 p. Bibliography.

1579. Grupp, Stanley E., ed. THEORIES OF PUNISHMENT. Bloomington:
Indiana University Press, 1972. vi, 401 p.

1580. Hills, Stuart L. CRIME, POWER, AND MORALITY: THE CRIMINAL
LAW PROCESS IN THE UNITED STATES. Scranton, Pa.: Chandler,
1971. xi, 215 p.

Discusses formulation of criminal law, sanctions, and the
public image of crime; marijuana use, organized crime, and
white collar crime receive special attention.

1581. Newman, Donald J. CONVICTION; THE DETERMINATION OF
GUILT OR INNOCENCE WITHOUT TRIAL. Boston: Little, Brown
and Co., 1966. xxvii, 259 p.

Study for the American Bar Foundation of factors affecting
negative pleas and related policy issues in Michigan, Wisconsin, and Kansas.

1582. Quinney, Richard. CRIMINAL JUSTICE IN AMERICA; A CRITICAL
UNDERSTANDING. Boston: Little, Brown and Co., 1974. 464 p.

The nature and operation of the criminal law is seen as a
function of power relationships in the society. Readings in
primary legal systems--police, courts, and prisons; criticism
and future of criminal justice.

1583. _____. THE SOCIAL REALITY OF CRIME. Boston: Little, Brown
and Co., 1970. x, 339 p.

Suggests a conflict approach to the formulation and administration of the criminal law; criminal definitions are formulated
and applied by those segments of society that have the power

to control the enforcement and administration of justice.

1584. Schur, Edwin M. LAW AND SOCIETY; A SOCIOLOGICAL VIEW. New York: Random House, 1968. x, 239 p.

Summarizes recent empirical research on the American legal system--courts, judges, juries, police behavior, and practice of law.

1585. Turk, Austin T. CRIMINALITY AND LEGAL ORDER. Chicago: Rand McNally, 1969. xiv, 184 p.

Argues that criminal status is an ascribed rather than an achieved status; criminologists should reappraise the operations of the legal order and its power.

1586. United States President's Commission on Law Enforcement. THE CHAL-LENGE OF CRIME IN A FREE SOCIETY. Washington, D.C.: Government Printing Office, 1967. xi, 340 p.

An attempt by political and legal leaders to evaluate crime and its control, and to make policy suggestions regarding official reporting of crime, prevention, rehabilitation, and administration of justice.

G. POLICE

1587. Bordua, David J., ed. THE POLICE: SIX SOCIOLOGICAL ESSAYS. New York: Wiley, 1967. xv, 258 p.

Sociological analyses of police behavior in the detection of crime, and the discrepancies between ideal practices of police academies and orientations of patrolmen after field experience.

1588. Niederhoffer, Arthur. BEHIND THE SHIELD; THE POLICE IN URBAN SOCIETY. Garden City, N.Y.: Doubleday, 1969. 263 p.

1589. Niederhoffer, Arthur, and Blumberg, Abraham S., eds. THE AMBIVA-LENT FORCE. Waltham, Mass.: Ginn, 1970. viii, 360 p. Bibliography.

1590. Reiss, Albert J., Jr. THE POLICE AND THE PUBLIC. New Haven: Yale University Press, 1971. xv, 228 p.

1591. Skolnick, Jerome H. JUSTICE WITHOUT TRIAL; LAW ENFORCEMENT IN DEMOCRATIC SOCIETY. New York: Wiley, 1966. xi, 279 p.

Participant observation of police department action in a
California city of 400,000. Includes discussion of the concept of legality.

1592. Stark, Rodney. POLICE RIOTS; COLLECTIVE VIOLENCE AND LAW
ENFORCEMENT. Belmont, Calif.: Wadsworth, 1972. 250 p.

Documents the causes and prevalence of police violence using
surveys, police investigations, and personal interviews.

H. PRISONS

1593. Brodsky, Stanley L., and Eggleston, Norman E., eds. MILITARY
PRISON; THEORY, RESEARCH, AND PRACTICE. Carbondale: Southern
Illinois University Press, 1970. 205 p.

Systematic examination of military correctional institutions
by clinical psychologists, educators, psychiatrists, social
workers, and sociologists who have served in those institutions.
Bibliography.

1594. Carter, Robert M., et al., eds. CORRECTIONAL INSTITUTIONS.
Philadelphia: Lippincott, 1972. xxii, 554 p.

An anthology on correctional and penal institutions, institutional and community programs, and policies.

Cloward, Richard A., et al. See Conference Group on Correctional
Organization.

1595. Conference Group on Correctional Organization. THEORETICAL STUDIES
IN SOCIAL ORGANIZATION OF THE PRISON. By Richard A.
Cloward, et al. New York: Social Science Research Council, 1960.
vi, 146 p.

Six essays on prison inmate social structures and the social
organization of treatment-oriented and custodial prisons.

1596. Giallombardo, Rose. SOCIETY OF WOMEN: A STUDY OF A WOMEN'S
PRISON. New York: Wiley, 1966. ix, 244 p.

Variations in inmate social relations and culture reflect inmate
populations; preprison identities affect prison social structure.
Bibliography.

1597. Hazelrigg, Lawrence E., ed. PRISON WITHIN SOCIETY; A READER
IN PENOLOGY. Garden City, N.Y.: Doubleday, 1968. xiv,
536 p.

1598. Heffernan, Esther. MAKING IT IN PRISON: THE SQUARE, THE COOL AND THE LIFE. New York: Wiley-Interscience, 1972. xvi, 231 p.

> Study of a women's prison. Bibliography.

1599. Hopper, Columbus B. SEX IN PRISON: THE MISSISSIPPI EXPERIMENT WITH CONJUGAL VISITING. Baton Rouge: Louisiana State University Press, 1969. 160 p.

> Describes an experiment at the Mississippi State Prison at Parchmont, with a population of 2,223.

1600. Minton, Robert J., Jr., ed. INSIDE: PRISON AMERICAN STYLE. New York: Random House, 1971. xvii, 325 p.

> A collection of the writings of a number of prisoners and ex-prisoners from the California system.

1601. Sykes, Gresham M. THE SOCIETY OF CAPTIVES; A STUDY OF A MAXIMUM SECURITY PRISON. Princeton, N.J.: Princeton University Press, 1958. 144 p.

> An analysis of a maximum security prison in New Jersey.

1602. Truzzi, Marcello, and Petersen, David M., eds. CRIMINAL LIFE; VIEWS FROM THE INSIDE. Englewood Cliffs, N.J.: Prentice-Hall, 1972. 228 p.

1603. Wright, Erik O. THE POLITICS OF PUNISHMENT; A CRITICAL ANALYSIS OF PRISONS IN AMERICA. New York: Harper & Row, Publishers, 1973. viii, 349 p.

> Internal operation of American prisons: rehabilitation as manipulation, totalitarianism, and lawlessness of the prison system and prisoners' resistance to it.

I. PROBATION AND PAROLE

1604. Arnold, William R. JUVENILES ON PAROLE; A SOCIOLOGICAL PERSPECTIVE. New York: Random House, 1970. 177 p.

> A systematic analysis of the social world of juvenile males on parole.

1605. Carter, Robert M., and Wilkins, Leslie T., eds. PROBATION AND PAROLE; SELECTED READINGS. New York: Wiley, 1970. xv, 693 p.

Fifty-nine selections grouped under six headings: probation, parole, supervision, legal aspects, research and prediction, and personnel.

1606. Dressler, David. PRACTICE AND THEORY OF PROBATION AND PAROLE. 2nd ed. New York: Columbia University Press, 1969. 347 p.

Probation and parole should be regarded as social work with attention to casework, group work, community organization, and community center programs.

1607. Glaser, Daniel. THE EFFECTIVENESS OF A PRISON AND PAROLE SYSTEM. Abr. ed. Indianapolis: Bobbs-Merrill, 1969. xii, 345 p.

Four-year study of the federal correctional system.

1608. Kassebaum, Gene, et al. PRISON TREATMENT AND PAROLE SURVIV-AL: AN EMPIRICAL ASSESSMENT. New York: Wiley, 1971. xi, 380 p.

This study of nearly 1,000 men released from a medium security men's prison in California found that participation in various types of group counseling had no measurable impact on parole outcome.

Part 2: Juvenile Delinquency

J. TEXTS AND READERS

1609. Cavan, Ruth S. JUVENILE DELINQUENCY; DEVELOPMENT, TREAT-MENT, CONTROL. 2nd ed. Philadelphia: Lippincott, 1969. xvi, 555 p.

1610. _____, ed. READINGS IN JUVENILE DELINQUENCY. 2nd ed. Philadelphia: Lippincott, 1969. x, 499 p.

Forty selections on current issues.

1611. Garabedian, Peter G., and Gibbons, Don C., eds. BECOMING DELINQUENT; YOUNG OFFENDERS AND THE CORRECTIONAL PROCESS. Chicago: Aldine, 1970. viii, 304 p.

1612. Giallombardo, Rose, ed. JUVENILE DELINQUENCY; A BOOK OF READINGS. 2nd ed. New York: Wiley, 1972. x, 613 p.

Collection of readings on juvenile delinquency: theories of

delinquency, the gang, legal processing of delinquency, treatment, and prevention.

1613. Knudten, Richard D., and Schafer, Stephen, eds. JUVENILE DELIN-QUENCY: A READER. New York: Random House, 1970. xi, 386 p.

1614. Reed, John P., and Baali, Fuad, eds. FACES OF DELINQUENCY: AN INTRODUCTION. Englewood Cliffs, N.J.: Prentice-Hall, 1972. xii, 420 p.

1615. Schafer, Stephen, and Knudten, Richard D. JUVENILE DELINQUENCY: AN INTRODUCTION. New York: Random House, 1970. xviii, 394 p.

1616. Teele, James E., ed. JUVENILE DELINQUENCY; A READER. Itasca, Ill.: F.E. Peacock, 1970. ix, 461 p.

Forty-six selections.

1617. Vaz, Edmund W., ed. MIDDLE-CLASS JUVENILE DELINQUENCY. New York: Harper & Row, Publishers, 1967. vi, 289 p.

Articles suggest that the sources of middle class delinquency are in the youth culture.

K. STUDIES AND MONOGRAPHS ON DELINQUENCY

1618. Ferdinand, Theodore N. TYPOLOGIES OF DELINQUENCY; A CRITICAL ANALYSIS. New York: Random House, 1966. x, 246 p.

Develops three typologies: social (six types), psychological (three major types, nine subtypes), and synthetic.

1619. Gibbons, Don C. DELINQUENT BEHAVIOR. Englewood Cliffs, N.J.: Prentice-Hall, 1970. ix, 276 p.

Defends the sociological approach to delinquent behavior; discusses working class delinquency, hidden delinquency, and problems in labeling delinquents.

1620. Glueck, Sheldon. PREDICTING DELINQUENCY AND CRIME. Cambridge, Mass.: Harvard University Press, 1959. xxii, 283 p.

Synthesis of sixty prediction tables; links relationships within family to future delinquent behavior.

1621. Glueck, Sheldon, and Glueck, Eleanor T. DELINQUENTS AND

NONDELINQUENTS IN PERSPECTIVE. Cambridge, Mass.: Harvard University Press, 1968. xx, 268 p.

A follow-up study to UNRAVELING JUVENILE DELINQUENCY (see item 1622).

1622. _____. UNRAVELING JUVENILE DELINQUENCY. Cambridge, Mass.: Harvard University Press, 1950. xv, 399 p. (For the Commonwealth Fund.)

Study of causation to determine a basis for crime prevention programs and effective therapy. Research was conducted from 1939 to 1949.

1623. Gold, Martin. DELINQUENT BEHAVIOR IN AN AMERICAN CITY. Monterey, Calif.: Brooks/Cole Publishing Co., 1970. viii, 150 p.

Study of 2,500 delinquent acts committed by 522 Flint, Michigan, youths in the early 1960s. Bibliography.

1624. _____. STATUS FORCES IN DELINQUENT BOYS. Ann Arbor: Intercenter Program on Children, Youth, and Family Life, Institute for Social Research, University of Michigan, 1963. xv, 229 p.

The second in the series of monographs from the Flint, Michigan, Youth Study; concerned with the manner in which status problems provoke delinquent behavior. Bibliography.

1625. Hirschi, Travis. CAUSES OF DELINQUENCY. Berkeley: University of California Press, 1969. 309 p.

Social control theory of delinquency articulated with survey research data. Bibliography.

1626. Lander, Bernard. TOWARDS AN UNDERSTANDING OF JUVENILE DELINQUENCY; A STUDY OF 8,464 CASES OF JUVENILE DELINQUENCY IN BALTIMORE. New York: Columbia University Press, 1954. xv, 143 p.

Analyzes the variations in the delinquency rate by census tracts in relation to seven variables.

1627. Martin, John M., and Fitzpatrick, Joseph P. DELINQUENT BEHAVIOR: A REDEFINITION OF THE PROBLEM. New York: Random House, 1965. xii, 210 p.

Survey and critical appraisal of theories used to explain delinquent behavior.

1628. Matza, David. DELINQUENCY AND DRIFT. New York: Wiley,

1964. x, 199 p.

Discussion of the subculture of delinquency in the legal
context and of delinquency as an infraction rather than an
action; a critique of positivistic determinism.

1629. Rosenberg, Bernard, and Silverstein, Harry. THE VARIETIES OF DELIN-
QUENT EXPERIENCE. Waltham, Mass.: Blaisdell, 1969. 165 p.

A study of three block samples of 112 young people in New
York, Chicago, and Washington, D.C., slums, using unstructured interviews.

1630. Shaw, Clifford R., and McKay, Henry D. JUVENILE DELINQUENCY
AND URBAN AREAS; A STUDY OF RATES OF DELINQUENCY IN
RELATION TO DIFFERENTIAL CHARACTERISTICS OF LOCAL COM-
MUNITIES IN AMERICAN CITIES. Rev. ed. Chicago: University
of Chicago Press, 1969. liv, 394 p.

1631. Spergel, Irving. RACKETVILLE, SLUMTOWN, HAULBURG; AN EX-
PLORATORY STUDY OF DELINQUENT SUBCULTURES. Chicago:
University of Chicago Press, 1964. xxiv, 211 p.

1632. Sterne, Richard S. DELINQUENT CONDUCT AND BROKEN HOMES,
A STUDY OF 1,050 BOYS. New Haven: College and University
Press, 1964. 144 p.

A study of delinquent white boys living in Trenton, New
Jersey, with 326 from broken homes and 724 from unbroken
homes, supports the conclusion that broken and unbroken
homes do not significantly affect delinquent behavior. Bibliography.

1633. Vedder, Clyde B., and Somerville, Dora B. THE DELINQUENT GIRL.
Springfield, Ill.: Charles C Thomas, 1970. xi, 166 p.

Discusses types of delinquent: runaway, incorrigible, sex-
delinquent, probation violator, and truant.

1634. Wolfgang, Marvin E., et al. DELINQUENCY IN A BIRTH COHORT.
Chicago: University of Chicago Press, 1972. x, 327 p.

An examination of the relationship between social characteristics and patterns of delinquency, based on the study of adolescence of almost all of the 9,945 boys born in Philadelphia
in 1945.

L. GANGS

1635. Cloward, Richard A., and Ohlin, Lloyd E. DELINQUENCY AND OPPOR-
TUNITY; A THEORY OF DELINQUENT GANGS. Glencoe, Ill.:
Free Press, 1960. 220 p.

> Utilizes Merton's theory of anomie and presents a typology
> of delinquent subcultures, based on differential opportunity
> in' neighborhoods--the criminal, conflict, and retreatist gangs.

1636. Cohen, Albert Kircidel. DELINQUENT BOYS: THE CULTURE OF THE
GANG. Glencoe, Ill.: Free Press, 1955. 202 p.

> General theory of subcultures and investigation of relationship
> between delinquency and social class.

1637. Klein, Malcolm W. STREET GANGS AND STREET WORKERS. Englewood Cliffs, N.J.: Prentice-Hall, 1971. xiii, 338 p.

> Action research; ethics and policy of experiments; and impor-
> tance of delinquency control.

1638. _____, ed. JUVENILE GANGS IN CONTEXT: THEORY AND
RESEARCH, AND ACTION. Englewood Cliffs, N.J.: Prentice-Hall,
1967. xi, 210 p. Bibliography.

1639. Short, James F., Jr., and Strodtbeck, Fred L. GROUP PROCESS
AND GANG DELINQUENCY. Chicago: University of Chicago Press,
1965. xv, 294 p.

> Discusses a 1958 study comparing six groups of boys, lower
> and middle class, white and Black, gang and non-gang.

1640. Thrasher, Frederick M. THE GANG; A STUDY OF 1,313 GANGS
IN CHICAGO. Abr. ed. Chicago: University of Chicago Press,
1963. lviii, 388 p.

> Study first published in 1927 of gangs as products of city
> slums. New introduction by James Short.

1641. Yablonsky, Lewis. THE VIOLENT GANG. New York: Macmillan,
1962. 264 p.

> An account of a Manhattan gang during its eight months'
> existence in the 1950s.

M. JUVENILE COURTS AND SOCIAL POLICY

1642. Cicourel, Aaron Victor. THE SOCIAL ORGANIZATION OF JUVENILE JUSTICE. New York: Wiley, 1967. xi, 345 p.

1643. Emerson, Robert M. JUDGING DELINQUENTS; CONTEXT AND PROCESS IN JUVENILE COURT. Chicago: Aldine, 1969. xiv, 293 p.

> Case study of a juvenile court in a large northern city. Bibliography.

1644. Kassebaum, Gene. DELINQUENCY AND SOCIAL POLICY. Englewood, Cliffs, N.J.: Prentice-Hall, 1974. 192 p.

> Relates juvenile delinquency to racial, generational, class, and social conflicts; evaluates agencies and laws that define and implement juvenile justice.

1645. Rosenheim, Margaret Keeney, ed. JUSTICE FOR THE CHILD; THE JUVENILE COURT IN TRANSITION. New York: Free Press of Glencoe, 1962. 240 p.

> Ten papers which focus on the legitimate functions of the court and its role in balancing the administration of justice with rehabilitation. Bibliography.

1646. Schur, Edwin M. RADICAL NONINTERVENTION; RETHINKING THE DELINQUENCY PROBLEM. Englewood Cliffs, N.J.: Prentice-Hall, 1973. x, 180 p.

> Proposes the elimination of court jurisdiction over conduct illegal only for children.

N. CONTROL AND PREVENTION OF DELINQUENCY

1647. Ahlstrom, Winton M., and Havighurst, Robert J. FOUR HUNDRED LOSERS: DELINQUENT BOYS IN HIGH SCHOOL. San Francisco: Jossey-Bass, 1971. 246 p.

> Describes the failure of a specially designed high school program to reverse patterns of delinquency and school failure in Kansas City seventh grade boys.

1648. McCord, William, and McCord, Joan. ORIGINS OF CRIME: A NEW EVALUATION OF THE CAMBRIDGE-SOMERVILLE YOUTH STUDY. New York: Columbia University Press, 1959. 219 p.

Origins, causes, and control of delinquency in a sample of
325 boys.

1649. MacIver, Robert M[orrison]. THE PREVENTION AND CONTROL OF
DELINQUENCY. New York: Atherton Press, 1966. vi, 215 p.

Evaluation of a six-year study of New York City agencies
concerned with juvenile delinquency. Discusses delinquency
causation.

1650. Powers, Edwin, and Witmer, Helen. AN EXPERIMENT IN THE PREVEN-
TION OF DELINQUENCY: THE CAMBRIDGE-SOMERVILLE YOUTH
STUDY. New York: Columbia University Press, 1951. xliii, 649 p.

Six hundred fifty boys studied over a four-year period in two
groups--the treatment group and the control group.

1651. Reckless, Walter C., and Dinitz, Simon. THE PREVENTION OF
JUVENILE DELINQUENCY; AN EXPERIMENT. Columbus: Ohio State
University Press, 1972. xvii, 253 p.

Based on a 1970 report of the Ohio State University Research
Foundation to the National Institute of Mental Health.

1652. Stratton, John R., and Terry, Robert M., eds. PREVENTION OF
DELINQUENCY; PROBLEMS AND PROGRAMS. New York: Macmillan, 1968. xi, 334 p.

Selection of thirty-one articles which discuss programs and
prevention orientations.

1653. Wheeler, Stanton, ed. CONTROLLING DELINQUENTS. New York:
Wiley, 1968. xx, 332 p.

Collection of research reports on social agencies involved in
controlling juvenile delinquency.

1654. Wheeler, Stanton, and Cottrell, Leonard S., Jr. JUVENILE DELIN-
QUENCY; ITS PREVENTION AND CONTROL. New York: Russell
Sage Foundation, 1966. vii, 54 p.

O. CORRECTION AND REHABILITATION

1655. Amos, William E., and Manella, Raymond L., eds. DELINQUENT
CHILDREN IN JUVENILE CORRECTIONAL INSTITUTIONS; STATE
ADMINISTERED RECEPTION AND DIAGNOSTIC CENTERS. Spring-
field, Ill.: Charles C Thomas, 1969. xiii, 159 p.

1656. Empey, LaMar T., and Erickson, Maynard L. THE PROVO EXPERI-
MENT; EVALUATING COMMUNITY CONTROL OF DELINQUENCY.
Lexington, Mass.: D.C. Heath, Lexington Books, 1972. xvii, 321 p.
Bibliography.

1657. Empey, LaMar T., and Lubeck, Steven G. THE SILVER LAKE EX-
PERIMENT; TESTING DELINQUENCY THEORY AND COMMUNITY
INTERVENTION. Chicago: Aldine, 1971. x, 354 p.

1658. Empey, LaMar T., et al. EXPLAINING DELINQUENCY: CONSTRUC-
TION, TEST, AND REFORMULATION OF A SOCIOLOGICAL THEORY.
Lexington, Mass.: D.C. Heath, Lexington Books, 1971. xv, 223 p.

    Etiology of delinquency, with empirical data about delinquent
    and nondelinquent males in Los Angeles and Utah.

1659. Giallombardo, Rose. THE SOCIAL WORLD OF IMPRISONED GIRLS:
A COMPARATIVE STUDY OF INSTITUTIONS FOR JUVENILE DELIN-
QUENCY. New York: Wiley, 1974. viii, 317 p.

1660. McCorkle, Lloyd W., et al. THE HIGHFIELDS STORY; AN EXPERI-
MENTAL TREATMENT PROJECT FOR YOUTHFUL OFFENDERS. New
York: Holt, 1958. 182 p.

    Data from an experimental New Jersey program providing a
    permissive and therapeutic environment.

1661. Stephenson, Richard M., and Scarpitti, Frank R. GROUP INTERAC-
TION AS THERAPY: THE USE OF THE SMALL GROUP IN CORREC-
TIONS. Westport, Conn.: Greenwood Press, 1974. xiii, 235 p.

    Describes the Essexfields program in New Jersey and compares
    it with other rehabilitative approaches. Bibliography (pp.
    223-28).

1662. Street, David, et al. ORGANIZATION FOR TREATMENT: A COM-
PARATIVE STUDY OF INSTITUTIONS FOR DELINQUENTS. New
York: Free Press, 1966. xx, 330 p. Bibliography.

1663. Weeks, H. Ashley, et al. YOUTHFUL OFFENDERS AT HIGHFIELDS;
AN EVALUATION OF THE EFFECTS OF THE SHORT-TERM TREATMENT
OF DELINQUENT BOYS. Ann Arbor: University of Michigan Press,
1959. 208 p.

* * *

See also Chapter 4, Section H.

Chapter 23

HEALTH AND SOCIAL SERVICES

Chapter 23

HEALTH AND SOCIAL SERVICES

A. REFERENCE WORKS AND BIBLIOGRAPHIES

1664. Birren, James E., ed. HANDBOOK OF AGING AND THE INDIVID-
UAL: PSYCHOLOGICAL AND BIOLOGICAL ASPECTS. Chicago:
University of Chicago Press, 1960. xii, 939 p.

Prepared under the sponsorship of the Inter-University Training
Institute on Social Gerontology.

1665. ENCYCLOPEDIA OF SOCIAL WORK. Robert Morris, editor-in-chief.
2 vols. New York: National Association of Social Workers, 1971.
1654 p.

The sixteenth issue of the yearbook of the National Association
of Social Workers.

1666. Freeman, Howard E., et al. HANDBOOK OF MEDICAL SOCIOLOGY.
2nd ed. Englewood Cliffs, N.J.: Prentice-Hall, 1972. 598 p.

1667. REFERENCE DATA ON SOCIOECONOMIC ISSUES OF HEALTH.
Chicago: American Medical Association, Center for Health Services
Research and Development, 1970--. Annual.

Compilation and analysis of data on the U.S. population,
morbidity, mortality, and health services delivery. Based
on the CURRENT POPULATION REPORTS issued by the U.S.
Census Bureau, on VITAL STATISTICS REPORTS, and on other
publications of the federal government and the American
Medical Association.

1668. REFERENCE DATA ON THE PROFILE OF MEDICAL PRACTICE. Chicago: American Medical Association, Center for Health Services Research
and Development, 1970--. Annual.

Data on physician manpower, income, expenses, and fees,

and on the utilization of physicians' services; also includes
brief articles on related issues.

1669. Shock, Nathan W. A CLASSIFIED BIBLIOGRAPHY OF GERONTOLOGY
AND GERIATRICS. Stanford: Stanford University Press, 1951. 599 p.

Continued by supplements covering the years 1949 to 1955
(1957, 525 p.) and the years 1956 to 1961 (1963, 624 p.);
kept up-to-date by a special bibliographic section in the
JOURNAL OF GERONTOLOGY (see item 208).

1670. Tibbitts, Clark, ed. HANDBOOK OF SOCIAL GERONTOLOGY:
SOCIETAL ASPECTS OF AGING. Chicago: University of Chicago
Press, 1960. xix, 770 p.

Sponsored by the Inter-University Training Institute in Social
Gerontology.

B. AGING AND RETIREMENT

1671. Albrecht, Ruth E., ed. AGING IN A CHANGING SOCIETY.
Gainesville: University of Florida Press, 1962. xii, 187 p.

Eleventh annual Southern Conference on Gerontology, held
at the University of Florida in 1962.

1672. Atchley, Robert C. THE SOCIAL FORCES IN LATER LIFE: AN INTRO-
DUCTION TO SOCIAL GERONTOLOGY. Belmont, Calif.: Wadsworth, 1972. 341 p.

An overview of the major conceptual and research issues;
bibliographies follow each chapter. General bibliography
(pp. 336-38).

1673. Blau, Zena Smith. OLD AGE IN A CHANGING SOCIETY. New
York: New Viewpoints, 1973. xiv, 285 p.

Problems of aging in a postindustrial society; recommends
self-governing communities, vocational training, and the end
of compulsory retirement.

1674. Britton, Joseph H., and Britton, Jean O. PERSONALITY CHANGES
IN AGING: A LONGITUDINAL STUDY OF COMMUNITY RESIDENTS.
New York: Springer Publishing, 1972. xiii, 222 p.

A social psychological study of the total aged population
residing and surviving in a central Pennsylvania village over
a nine-year period from 1956 to 1965. Bibliography.

1675. Burgess, Ernest W., ed. RETIREMENT VILLAGES. Ann Arbor: University of Michigan, Division of Gerontology, 1961. 156 p.

The result of research undertaken by the Conference on Retirement Villages under the aegis of the American Society of the Aged.

1676. Cumming, M. Elaine, and Henry, William E. GROWING OLD; THE PROCESS OF DISENGAGEMENT. New York: Basic Books, 1961. 293 p.

Sample of old people from some 8700 dwelling units in Kansas City illustrates authors' theory that the elderly voluntarily end or change relationships with other people. Bibliography.

1677. Johnson, Sheila K. IDLE HAVEN: COMMUNITY BUILDING AMONG THE WORKING-CLASS RETIRED. Berkeley: University of California Press, 1971. 208 p.

A case study of 200 retirees living in a mobile home community in the Oakland area.

1678. Lowenthal, Marjorie F. LIVES IN DISTRESS; THE PATHS OF THE ELDERLY TO THE PSYCHIATRIC WARD. New York: Basic Books, 1964. xx, 266 p.

1679. Lowenthal, Marjorie F., et al. AGING AND MENTAL DISORDER IN SAN FRANCISCO; A SOCIAL PSYCHIATRIC STUDY. Langley Porter Institute Studies of Aging. San Francisco: Jossey-Bass, 1967. xix, 341 p. Bibliography.

1680. McKinney, John C., and DeVyver, Frank T. AGING AND SOCIAL POLICY. New York: Appleton-Century-Crofts, 1966. viii, 338 p.

Papers from a symposium held at Duke University on March 25-26, 1965.

1681. Palmore, Erdman, ed. NORMAL AGING; REPORTS FROM THE DUKE LONGITUDINAL STUDY, 1955-1969. Durham, N.C.: Duke University Press, 1970. xxiv, 431 p.

Research project of the Duke University Center for the Study of Aging and Human Development.

1682. _____. NORMAL AGING II: REPORTS FROM THE DUKE LONGITUDINAL STUDY, 1970-1973. Durham, N.C.: Duke University Press, 1974. 368 p.

Updates and extends findings reported in the first volume (see item 1681), and presents the first reports in the series on the middle-aged persons studied.

1683. Riley, Matilda White, et al. AGING AND SOCIETY. Vol. 1: AN INVENTORY OF RESEARCH FINDINGS. New York: Russell Sage Foundation, 1968. xii, 636 p.

> Organizes research in social gerontology into four major areas: sociocultural contexts, the organism, the personality, and social roles.

1684. _____. AGING AND SOCIETY. Vol. 2: AGING AND THE PROFESSIONS. New York: Russell Sage Foundation, 1969. xvii, 410 p.

> Draws on the inventory in volume 1 and interprets it for several professional and related fields.

1685. _____. AGING AND SOCIETY. Vol. 3: A SOCIOLOGY OF AGE STRATIFICATION. New York: Russell Sage Foundation, 1972. xvii, 652 p.

1686. Rose, Arnold, and Peterson, Warren A., eds. OLDER PEOPLE AND THEIR SOCIAL WORLD; THE SUBCULTURE OF THE AGING. Philadelphia: F.A. Davis, 1965. xv, 391 p.

1687. Rosenberg, George S. THE WORKER GROWS OLD: POVERTY AND ISOLATION IN THE CITY. San Francisco: Jossey-Bass, 1970. xiv, 206 p.

> Based on data about 1,596 persons in Philadelphia; working class isolation is not related to the characteristics of the individual, but to the social composition of the neighborhood.

1688. Rosow, Irving. SOCIAL INTEGRATION OF THE AGED. New York: Free Press, 1967. xix, 354 p.

> Tests propositions about the nature of age grading, friendship, kin, and neighbor relations in working class, middle class, and upper class residential areas. Bibliography.

1689. Simpson, Ida Harper, and McKinney, John C., eds. SOCIAL ASPECTS OF AGING. Durham, N.C.: Duke University Press, 1966. vii, 341 p.

1690. Streib, Gordon F., and Schneider, Clement J., S.J. RETIREMENT IN AMERICAN SOCIETY; IMPACT AND PROCESS. Ithaca, N.Y.: Cornell University Press, 1971. 316 p.

> Based on the Cornell Study of Occupational Retirement, a longitudinal survey which interviewed workers aged sixty-three to sixty-five years in 1952-53, 1954, 1956, 1957, and 1958-59. Aging is seen as a process of differential disen-

gagement. Bibliography.

1691. Williams, Richard H., and Wirths, Claudine G. LIVES THROUGH THE YEARS; STYLES OF LIFE AND SUCCESSFUL AGING. New York: Atherton Press, 1965. xiii, 298 p.

Study of 168 residents of Kansas City between the ages of fifty and ninety, interviewed seven times over a period of about five years to observe the process of aging.

C. SICKNESS AND HEALTH CARE

1692. Alford, Robert R. HEALTH CARE POLITICS: IDEOLOGICAL AND INTEREST GROUP BARRIERS TO REFORM. Chicago: University of Chicago Press, 1974. 352 p.

Examines the health care system in New York City, and the political role played by the major investigative commissions from 1950 to 1970.

1693. Bullough, Bonnie, and Bullough, Vern L. POVERTY, ETHNIC IDENTITY AND HEALTH CARE. New York: Appleton-Century-Crofts, 1972. ix, 226 p.

Examines current health care inadequacies. Bibliography.

1694. Duff, Raymond S., and Hollingshead, August [de] B[elmont]. SICKNESS AND SOCIETY. New York: Harper & Row, Publishers, 1968. xiii, 390 p.

An intensive study of the impact of illness and hospitalization on 161 families using a large New England medical center.

1695. Kosa, John, et al., eds. POVERTY AND HEALTH: A SOCIOLOGICAL ANALYSIS. Cambridge, Mass.: Harvard University Press, 1969. xvi, 449 p.

1696. Sussman, Marvin B., ed. SOCIOLOGY AND REHABILITATION. Washington, D.C.: American Sociological Association, in cooperation with the Vocational Rehabilitation Administration, U.S. Department of Health, Education, and Welfare, 1966. 265 p.

Proceedings of the 1965 Carmel, California, conference on "Sociological Theory, Research in Rehabilitation."

1697. Sussman, Marvin B., et al. THE WALKING PATIENT: A STUDY IN OUTPATIENT CARE. Cleveland: Press of Western Reserve University, 1967. xiii, 260 p.

A study of the attitudes and beliefs of patients and staff con-

cerning logistics of the delivery of out-patient care in
Cleveland's University hospitals. Bibliography.

D. MENTAL HEALTH

1698. Brenner, M. Harvey. MENTAL ILLNESS AND THE ECONOMY. Cambridge, Mass.: Harvard University Press, 1973. xxiv, 287 p.

> Based on correlation of economic and institutional data, 1841–
> 1967, in New York State. Argues that instabilities in the
> economy are an important source of fluctuations in mental
> hospital admissions rates.

1699. Dohrenwend, Bruce P., and Dohrenwend, Barbara S. SOCIAL STATUS
AND PSYCHOLOGICAL DISORDER; A CAUSAL INQUIRY. New
York: Wiley-Interscience, 1969. xv, 207 p.

> Data from a study of the Washington Heights area in New
> York City are used to measure the relative power of environ-
> mental and genetic factors.

1700. Dunham, H. Warren. COMMUNITY AND SCHIZOPHRENIA; AN
EPIDEMIOLOGICAL ANALYSIS. Lafayette Clinic Monograph in Psychiatry, no. 1. Detroit: Wayne State University Press, 1965. xxv,
312 p.

> Studies incidence of schizophrenia in two Detroit communities
> and finds no evidence of a relationship between social class
> and schizophrenia.

1701. Farber, Bernard. MENTAL RETARDATION: ITS SOCIAL CONTEXT
AND SOCIAL CONSEQUENCES. Boston: Houghton Mifflin Co.,
1968. xi, 287 p.

> The solution to the problem of mental retardation is sought in
> the social structure since efficiency rather than personal de-
> velopment is the objective of our major social institutions.

1702. Hollingshead, August [de] B[elmont] , and Redlich, Frederick C.
SOCIAL CLASS AND MENTAL ILLNESS; A COMMUNITY STUDY.
New York: Wiley, 1958. ix, 442 p.

> A study of the frequency of mental illness in different social
> classes in New Haven, Connecticut, and the character of the
> psychiatric treatment received.

1703. Hurley, Rodger L. POVERTY AND MENTAL RETARDATION; A CAUS-
AL RELATIONSHIP. New York: Random House, 1969. xii, 301 p.

Mental retardation is related to social retardation and environmental deprivation. Inadequacy of I.Q. tests is generally
responsible for a misleading evaluation of the intellectual
potential of the poor.

1704. Langner, Thomas Simon, and Michael, Stanley T. LIFE STRESS AND
MENTAL HEALTH: THE MIDTOWN MANHATTAN STUDY. Vol. 2.
Thomas A. C. Rennie Series in Social Psychiatry, vol. 2. New York:
Free Press of Glencoe; London: Collier-Macmillan, [c.1963]. xxii,
517 p. Bibliography. (See also item 1710.)

1705. McLean, Alan A., ed. MENTAL HEALTH AND WORK ORGANIZA-
TIONS. Chicago: Rand McNally, 1970. 322 p.

Report of the Cornell Occupational Mental Health Conferences
of 1967–69; more than 400 bibliographic references.

1706. Martindale, Don [Albert], and Martindale, Edith. THE SOCIAL DIMEN-
SIONS OF MENTAL ILLNESS, ALCOHOLISM AND DRUG DEPENDENCE.
Westport, Conn.: Greenwood Press, 1971. xvi, 330 p. Bibliography.

1707. Mercer, Jane R. LABELING THE MENTALLY RETARDED. Berkeley:
University of California Press, 1973. 319 p.

Data derived from field surveys of three ethnic groups: Anglos,
Mexican-Americans, and Blacks in Riverdale, California.
Distinguishes between situational and comprehensive retardation.
Data support the proposition that mental retardation is essen-
tially an achieved status.

1708. Myers, Jerome K., and Bean, Lee L. A DECADE LATER; A FOLLOW-
UP OF SOCIAL CLASS AND MENTAL ILLNESS. New York: Wiley,
1968. xii, 250 p.

This follow-up survey (begun in 1960) of the New Haven
psychiatric patients surveyed first by Hollingshead and Redlich
(see item 1702) considers whether social class is at all a
relevant variable in mental illness.

1709. Myers, Jerome K., and Roberts, Bertram H. FAMILY AND CLASS
DYNAMICS IN MENTAL ILLNESS. New York: Wiley, 1959. 295 p.

Part of the larger ten-year Yale investigation, directed by
Hollingshead and Redlich (see item 1702). Bibliography.

1710. Srole, Leo, et al. MENTAL HEALTH IN THE METROPOLIS: THE
MIDTOWN MANHATTAN STUDY. Vol. 1. New York: McGraw-
Hill, 1962. v, 428 p.

Study of mental health and illness in Manhattan carried out

by anthropologists, psychologists, psychiatrists, social workers, and sociologists; uses a probability sample of 1,911 adults twenty to fifty-nine years of age. A total of 1,660 individuals were interviewed; 20 percent of adults were found psychiatrically impaired. (See also item 1704.)

E. HOSPITALS

1711. Belknap, Ivan, and Steinle, John G. THE COMMUNITY AND ITS HOSPITALS; A COMPARATIVE ANALYSIS. Syracuse, N.Y.: Syracuse University Press, 1963. 234 p.

An intensive study of hospital systems in two Texas communities of 150,000 and 120,000 people.

1712. Coser, Rose Laub. LIFE IN THE WARD. East Lansing: Michigan State University Press, 1962. xxxi, 182 p.

Patient adaptation to the hospital setting. Bibliography (pp. 169-77).

1713. Dunham, H. Warren, and Weinberg, S. Kirson. THE CULTURE OF THE STATE MENTAL HOSPITAL. Detroit: Wayne State University Press, 1960. 284 p.

Data were gathered at Columbus State Hospital in 1946 to analyze relations and structure within the hospital as they affect patients. Bibliography.

1714. Goffman, Erving. ASYLUMS: ESSAYS ON THE SOCIAL SITUATION OF MENTAL PATIENTS AND OTHER INMATES. Garden City, N.Y.: Doubleday, Anchor, 1961. 386 p.

Three-year study of ward behavior at the National Institute of Health Clinical Center and one year of semiparticipant observation at a 7,000-bed federal mental hospital. Bibliography.

1715. Heydebrand, Wolf V. HOSPITAL BUREAUCRACY: A COMPARATIVE STUDY OF ORGANIZATIONS. New York: Dunellen-University Press of Cambridge, 1974. 362 p.

Based on information collected in 1959 from 7,000 member hospitals of the American Hospital Association.

1716. Rosengren, William R., and Lefton, Mark. HOSPITALS AND PATIENTS. New York: Atherton Press, 1969. 225 p.

Study of the hospital as an organizational entity with focus on the patient.

1717. Rushing, William A. THE PSYCHIATRIC PROFESSIONS; POWER, CON-
FLICT, AND ADAPTATION IN A PSYCHIATRIC HOSPITAL STAFF.
Chapel Hill: University of North Carolina Press, 1964. xii, 267 p.

Reports on a study, by interview and observation, of the
professionals, other than psychiatrists, working in a university department of psychiatry.

1718. Strauss, Anselm L., et al. PSYCHIATRIC IDEOLOGIES AND INSTITU-
TIONS. New York: Free Press of Glencoe, 1964. xi, 418 p.

Examines the professional ideologies of staff members in a
large state hospital and in a small, private, teaching hospital.

F. MEDICAL SOCIOLOGY

1719. Coe, Rodney M. SOCIOLOGY OF MEDICINE. New York: McGraw-
Hill, 1970. viii, 388 p.

1720. Freidson, Eliot. PROFESSIONAL DOMINANCE: THE SOCIAL STRUC-
TURE OF MEDICAL CARE. New York: Atherton Press, 1970. 242 p.

Study of medical care settings; discussion of substantive issues
in medical sociology and professional practice.

1721. _____. PROFESSION OF MEDICINE; A STUDY OF THE SOCIOLOGY
OF APPLIED KNOWLEDGE. New York: Dodd, Mead, 1970. xxi,
409 p.

1722. Freidson, Eliot, and Lorber, Judith, eds. MEDICAL MEN AND THEIR
WORK: A SOCIOLOGICAL READER. Chicago: Aldine-Atherton,
1972. xiii, 482 p.

1723. Jaco, E. Gartly, ed. PATIENTS, PHYSICIANS AND ILLNESS; A
SOURCEBOOK IN BEHAVIORAL SCIENCE AND HEALTH. 2nd ed.
New York: Free Press, 1972. xiv, 413 p.

1724. Stevens, Rosemary. AMERICAN MEDICINE AND THE PUBLIC INTEREST.
New Haven: Yale University Press, 1971. xiii, 572 p.

A comprehensive survey of American medicine, the evolution
of specialization, and its supporting patterns of social organization. Bibliography.

G. WELFARE AND SOCIAL SERVICES

1725. Blackwell, Gordon W., and Gould, Raymond F. FUTURE CITIZENS
ALL. Chicago: American Public Welfare Association, 1952. xxix,
181 p.

> A nationwide study of 6,500 families with 19,000 children
> in the Aid to Dependent Children Program.

1726. Burgess, M. Elaine, and Price, Daniel O. AN AMERICAN DEPEN-
DENCY CHALLENGE. Chicago: American Public Welfare Association,
1963. 285 p.

> A follow-up survey to the 1950 study of recipients of Aid
> to Dependent Children. Bibliography.

1727. Kahn, Alfred J. STUDIES IN SOCIAL POLICY AND PLANNING.
New York: Russell Sage Foundation, 1969. x, 326 p.

> Examines government action on various social problems such
> as the war on poverty, juvenile delinquency, and income
> security.

1728. _____. THEORY AND PRACTICE OF SOCIAL PLANNING. New
York: Russell Sage Foundation, 1969. 348 p.

> Discusses social planning in America and provides a list of
> planning steps; defines planning as "policy formulation and
> realization."

1729. Kramer, Ralph M., and Specht, Harry. READINGS IN COMMUNITY
ORGANIZATION PRACTICE. Englewood Cliffs, N.J.: Prentice-
Hall, 1969. xiv, 458 p.

1730. Lubove, Roy. THE PROFESSIONAL ALTRUIST; THE EMERGENCE OF
SOCIAL WORK AS A CAREER, 1880-1930. Cambridge, Mass.: Harvard University Press, 1965. viii, 291 p.

1731. Marris, Peter, and Rein, Martin. DILEMMAS OF SOCIAL REFORM;
POVERTY AND COMMUNITY ACTION IN THE UNITED STATES.
New York: Atherton Press, 1967. vii, 248 p. Bibliography.

1732. Nagi, Saad Z. DISABILITY AND REHABILITATION: LEGAL, CLINI-
CAL, AND SELF-CONCEPTS AND MEASUREMENT. Columbus: Ohio
State University Press, 1970. 329 p.

> A large scale sociological study of the Social Security Admin-
> istration and its related programs.

1733. Piven, Frances Fox, and Cloward, Richard A. REGULATING THE POOR: THE FUNCTIONS OF PUBLIC WELFARE. New York: Pantheon Books, 1971. 389 p.

Explosion of the welfare rolls precipitates relief reforms.

1734. Wilensky, Harold L., and Lebeaux, Charles N. INDUSTRIAL SOCIETY AND SOCIAL WELFARE; THE IMPACT OF INDUSTRIALIZATION ON THE SUPPLY AND ORGANIZATION OF SOCIAL WELFARE SERVICES IN THE UNITED STATES. New York: Russell Sage Foundation, 1958. 401 p.

A sociologist and a social worker examine social welfare services in the context of changes brought about by urbanization and industrialization. Bibliography.

1735. Zald, Mayer N. SOCIAL WELFARE INSTITUTIONS; A SOCIOLOGICAL READER. New York: Wiley, 1965. xii, 671 p.

* * *

See also Chapter 12, Section F.

Chapter 24

SELECTED WORKS IN AMERICAN SOCIOLOGY

Chapter 24

SELECTED WORKS IN

AMERICAN SOCIOLOGY

This chapter lists selected works which deal with American sociology rather than with American society. History and theory of sociology, social thought, methodology, and comparative or cross-cultural studies are represented here, along with some works on social psychology and small group research.

1736. Abel, Theodore F. THE FOUNDATION OF SOCIOLOGICAL THEORY. New York: Random House, 1970. vii, 258 p.

1737. Bales, Robert F. INTERACTION PROCESS ANALYSIS; A METHOD FOR THE STUDY OF SMALL GROUPS. Cambridge, Mass.: Addison-Wesley, 1950. xi, 203 p.

1738. Barnes, Harry Elmer, ed. AN INTRODUCTION TO THE HISTORY OF SOCIOLOGY. Chicago: University of Chicago Press, 1948. 960 p.

1739. Barnes, Harry Elmer, et al., eds. CONTEMPORARY SOCIAL THEORY. New York: Appleton-Century-Crofts, 1940. 947 p.

1740. Becker, Howard P. THROUGH VALUES TO SOCIAL INTERPRETATION: ESSAYS ON SOCIAL CONTEXTS, ACTIONS, TYPES AND PROSPECTS. Durham, N.C.: Duke University Press, 1950. xviii, 341 p.

1741. Becker, Howard P., and Barnes, Harry Elmer. SOCIAL THOUGHT FROM LORE TO SCIENCE. 3rd ed., exp. and rev. 3 vols. New York: Dover Publications, 1961. xxxiv, 1178 p.

1742. Becker, Howard P., and Boskoff, Alvin, eds. MODERN SOCIOLOGICAL THEORY IN CONTINUITY AND CHANGE. New York: Dryden Press, 1957. xiii, 756 p. Bibliography.

1743. Becker, Howard S. SOCIOLOGICAL WORK; METHOD AND SUBSTANCE. Chicago: Aldine, 1970. 358 p. Bibliography.

1744. Bendix, Reinhard. EMBATTLED REASON: ESSAYS ON SOCIAL KNOWLEDGE. New York: Oxford University Press, 1970. xi, 395 p.

1745. Bendix, Reinhard, and Lipset, Seymour Martin, eds. CLASS, STATUS AND POWER; SOCIAL STRATIFICATION IN COMPARATIVE PERSPEC-TIVE. 2nd ed. New York: Free Press, 1966. xviii, 677 p.

1746. Berelson, Bernard [R.] CONTENT ANALYSIS IN COMMUNICATION RESEARCH. Glencoe, Ill.: Free Press, 1952. 220 p.

1747. Berelson, Bernard [R.], and Steiner, Gary. HUMAN BEHAVIOR; AN INVENTORY OF SCIENTIFIC FINDINGS. New York: Harcourt, Brace & World, 1964. xxiii, 712 p.

1748. Berger, Joseph, et al. SOCIOLOGICAL THEORIES IN PROGRESS. 2 vols. Boston: Houghton Mifflin Co. Vol. 1, 1966. xii, 306 p.; vol. 2, 1972. 397 p.

1749. Berger, Peter L. THE SACRED CANOPY: ELEMENTS OF A SOCIO-LOGICAL THEORY OF RELIGION. Garden City, N.Y.: Doubleday, 1967. vii, 230 p.

1750. Berger, Peter L., and Luckmann, Thomas. THE SOCIAL CONSTRUC-TION OF REALITY: A TREATISE IN THE SOCIOLOGY OF KNOWL-EDGE. Garden City, N.Y.: Doubleday, 1966. vii, 203 p.

1751. Bernard, Luther L., and Bernard, Jessie. ORIGINS OF AMERICAN SOCIOLOGY: THE SOCIAL SCIENCE MOVEMENT IN THE UNITED STATES. New York: Thomas Y. Crowell Co., 1943. xiv, 866 p.

1752. Birnbaum, Norman. THE CRISIS OF INDUSTRIAL SOCIETY. New York: Oxford University Press, 1969. xi, 185 p.

1753. _____. TOWARD A CRITICAL SOCIOLOGY. New York: Oxford University Press, 1971. 451 p.

1754. Blau, Peter M[ichael]. EXCHANGE AND POWER IN SOCIAL LIFE. New York: Wiley, 1964. xxiii, 352 p.

1755. Blumer, Herbert. SYMBOLIC INTERACTIONISM: PERSPECTIVE AND METHOD. Englewood Cliffs, N.J.: Prentice-Hall, 1969. x, 208 p.

1756. Bogardus, Emory S. THE DEVELOPMENT OF SOCIAL THOUGHT. 4th ed. New York: David McKay, 1960. 689 p.

1757. Bonjean, Charles M., et al. SOCIOLOGICAL MEASUREMENT: AN INVENTORY OF SCALES AND INDICES. San Francisco: Chandler, 1967. 580 p.

1758. Boskoff, Alvin. THEORY IN AMERICAN SOCIOLOGY: MAJOR SOURCES AND APPLICATIONS. New York: Thomas Y. Crowell Co., 1969. x, 374 p.

1759. Caplow, Theodore. PRINCIPLES OF ORGANIZATION. New York: Harcourt, Brace & World, 1964. xi, 383 p.

1760. _____. TWO AGAINST ONE: COALITIONS IN TRIADS. Englewood Cliffs, N.J.: Prentice-Hall, 1968. vii, 183 p. Bibliography pp. 168-76.

1761. Catton, William R., Jr. FROM ANIMISTIC TO NATURALISTIC SOCIOLOGY. New York: McGraw-Hill, 1966. xx, 364 p.

1762. Cooley, Charles H. HUMAN NATURE AND THE SOCIAL ORDER. New York: Scribner, 1902. viii, 413 p.

1763. _____. SOCIAL ORGANIZATION; A STUDY OF THE LARGER MIND. New York: Scribner, 1909. xvii, 426 p.

1764. Coser, Lewis A. MASTERS OF SOCIOLOGICAL THOUGHT; IDEAS IN HISTORICAL AND SOCIAL CONTEXT. New York: Harcourt Brace Jovanovich, 1971. xxi, 485 p.

1765. Coser, Lewis A., and Rosenberg, Bernard. SOCIOLOGICAL THEORY: A BOOK OF READINGS. 3rd ed. New York: Macmillan, 1969. xx, 748 p.

1766. Demerath, Nicholas J., and Peterson, Richard A., eds. SYSTEM, CHANGE, AND CONFLICT: A READER ON CONTEMPORARY SOCIOLOGICAL THEORY AND THE DEBATE OVER FUNCTIONALISM. New York: Free Press, 1967. viii, 533 p.

1767. Dubin, Robert, ed. THEORY BUILDING: A PRACTICAL GUIDE TO THE CONSTRUCTION AND TESTING OF THEORETICAL MODELS. New York: Free Press, 1969. ix, 298 p.

1768. Duncan, Hugh D. COMMUNICATION AND SOCIAL ORDER. New York: Bedminster Press, 1962. 475 p.

1769. _____. SYMBOLS IN SOCIETY. New York: Oxford University Press, 1968. 262 p.

1770. Etzioni, Amitai. THE ACTIVE SOCIETY: A THEORY OF SOCIETAL AND POLITICAL PROCESSES. New York: Free Press, 1968. xxv, 698 p.

1771. _____. A COMPARATIVE ANALYSIS OF COMPLEX ORGANIZATIONS: ON POWER, INVOLVEMENT AND THEIR CORRELATES. New York: Free Press of Glencoe, 1961. 366 p.

1772. Faris, Robert E. L. CHICAGO SOCIOLOGY, 1920-1932. San Francisco: Chandler, 1967. xiv, 163 p. Bibliography.

1773. _____, ed. HANDBOOK OF MODERN SOCIOLOGY. Chicago: Rand McNally, 1964. 1088 p.

1774. Friedrichs, Robert W. A SOCIOLOGY OF SOCIOLOGY. New York: Free Press, 1970. 429 p.

1775. Garfinkel, Harold. STUDIES IN ETHNOMETHODOLOGY. Englewood Cliffs, N.J.: Prentice-Hall, 1967. xi, 288 p.

1776. Gittler, Joseph B., ed. REVIEW OF SOCIOLOGY: ANALYSIS OF A DECADE. New York: Wiley, 1957. 588 p.

1777. Glaser, Barney G., and Strauss, Anselm L. THE DISCOVERY OF GROUNDED THEORY: STRATEGIES FOR QUALITATIVE RESEARCH. Chicago: Aldine, 1967. x, 271 p.

1778. Goffman, Erving. BEHAVIOR IN PUBLIC PLACES: NOTES ON THE SOCIAL ORGANIZATION OF GATHERINGS. New York: Free Press of Glencoe, 1963. viii, 248 p.

1779. _____. ENCOUNTERS: TWO STUDIES IN THE SOCIOLOGY OF INTERACTION. Indianapolis: Bobbs-Merrill, 1961. 152 p.

1780. _____. INTERACTION RITUAL: ESSAYS ON FACE-TO-FACE BE- HAVIOR. Chicago: Aldine, 1967. 270 p. Bibliography.

1781. _____. THE PRESENTATION OF SELF IN EVERYDAY LIFE. Garden City, N.Y.: Doubleday, 1959. 255 p.

1782. _____. RELATIONS IN PUBLIC; MICROSTUDIES OF THE PUBLIC ORDER. New York: Basic Books, 1971. xvii, 396 p.

1783. _____. STIGMA: NOTES ON THE MANAGEMENT OF SPOILED IDENTITY. Englewood Cliffs, N.J.: Prentice-Hall, 1963. 147 p.

1784. _____. STRATEGIC INTERACTION. Philadelphia: University of Pennsylvania Press, 1969. 145 p.

1785. Goode, William J. EXPLORATIONS IN SOCIAL THEORY. New York: Oxford University Press, 1973. viii, 449 p.

1786. _____. WORLD REVOLUTION AND FAMILY PATTERNS. New York: Free Press of Glencoe, 1963. 432 p.

1787. Goode, William J., and Hatt, Paul K. METHODS IN SOCIAL RE-SEARCH. New York: McGraw-Hall, 1952. vii, 386 p.

1788. Gouldner, Alvin W. THE COMING CRISIS OF WESTERN SOCIOLOGY. New York: Basic Books, 1970. 528 p.

1789. _____. FOR SOCIOLOGY: RENEWAL AND CRITIQUE IN SOCIOLOGY TODAY. New York: Basic Books, 1973. ix, 465 p.

1790. Hare, A. Paul, ed. HANDBOOK OF SMALL GROUP RESEARCH. New York: Free Press, 1962. xiv, 512 p. Bibliography pp. 416-96.

1791. Hare, A. Paul, et al., eds. SMALL GROUPS: STUDIES IN SOCIAL INTERACTION. Rev. ed. New York: Knopf, 1965. xvi, 706 p.

1792. Hertzler, Joyce O. A SOCIOLOGY OF LANGUAGE. New York: Random House, 1965. xii, 559 p.

1793. Hinkle, Roscoe C., Jr., and Hinkle, Gisela J. THE DEVELOPMENT OF MODERN SOCIOLOGY: ITS NATURE AND GROWTH IN THE U.S. Garden City, N.Y.: Doubleday, 1954. x, 75 p.

1794. Hollander, Paul. SOVIET AND AMERICAN SOCIETY: A COMPARI-SON. New York: Oxford University Press, 1973. xx, 476 p. Bibliography pp. 451-71.

1795. _____, ed. AMERICAN AND SOVIET SOCIETY: A READER IN COMPARATIVE SOCIOLOGY AND PERCEPTION. Englewood Cliffs, N.J.: Prentice-Hall, 1969. xviii, 589 p.

1796. Homans, George C. THE HUMAN GROUP. New York: Harcourt, 1950. xxvi, 484 p.

1797. _____. SOCIAL BEHAVIOR: ITS ELEMENTARY FORMS. New York: Harcourt, Brace & World, 1961. viii, 404 p.

1798. Horowitz, Irving Louis. THREE WORLDS OF DEVELOPMENT; THE THEORY AND PRACTICE OF INTERNATIONAL STRATIFICATION. 2nd ed. New York: Oxford University Press, 1972. xxx, 556 p.

1799. _____, ed. THE NEW SOCIOLOGY: ESSAYS IN SOCIAL SCIENCE AND SOCIAL THEORY IN HONOR OF C. WRIGHT MILLS. New York: Oxford University Press, 1964. xiii, 572 p.

1800. _____, ed. THE RISE AND FALL OF PROJECT CAMELOT: STUDIES IN THE RELATIONSHIP BETWEEN SOCIAL SCIENCE AND PRACTICAL POLITICS. Cambridge, Mass.: The M.I.T. Press, 1967. xi, 385 p.

1801. Hughes, Everett C. THE SOCIOLOGICAL EYE: SELECTED PAPERS. Chicago: Aldine, 1971. 584 p.

1802. Kunkel, John H. SOCIETY AND ECONOMIC GROWTH: A BEHAV-IORAL PERSPECTIVE OF SOCIAL CHANGE. New York: Oxford University Press, 1970. xvi, 368 p.

1803. LaPiere, Richard T. SOCIAL CHANGE. New York: McGraw-Hill, 1965. vii, 556 p.

1804. Lazarsfeld, Paul F. QUALITATIVE ANALYSIS: HISTORICAL AND CRITICAL ESSAYS. Boston: Allyn & Bacon, 1972. xvii, 457 p.

1805. Lazarsfeld, Paul F., and Henry, Neil W. LATENT STRUCTURE ANAL-YSIS. Boston: Houghton Mifflin Co., 1968. ix, 294 p.

1806. Lazarsfeld, Paul F., et al., eds. THE USES OF SOCIOLOGY. New York: Basic Books, 1967. xl, 902 p.

1807. Lenski, Gerhard E. POWER AND PRIVILEGE: A THEORY OF SOCIAL STRATIFICATION. New York: McGraw-Hill, 1966. xiv, 495 p. Bibliography pp. 447-67.

1808. Lindzey, Gardner, ed. HANDBOOK OF SOCIAL PSYCHOLOGY. 2nd ed. 6 vols. Reading, Mass.: Addison-Wesley, 1968.

1809. Lipset, Seymour Martin. POLITICAL MAN; THE SOCIAL BASES OF POLITICS. Garden City, N.Y.: Doubleday, 1960. 432 p.

1810. Lipset, Seymour Martin, and Bendix, Reinhard. SOCIAL MOBILITY IN

INDUSTRIAL SOCIETY. Berkeley: University of California Press, 1959. xxi, 309 p.

1811. Lipset, Seymour Martin, and Smelser, Neil J., eds. SOCIOLOGY, THE PROGRESS OF A DECADE; A COLLECTION OF ARTICLES. Englewood Cliffs, N.J.: Prentice-Hall, 1961. 635 p.

1812. Lundberg, George Andrew, et al., eds. TRENDS IN AMERICAN SOCIOLOGY. New York and London: Harper & Brothers, 1929. xii, 443 p.

1813. Lynd, Robert S. KNOWLEDGE FOR WHAT: THE PLACE OF SOCIAL SCIENCE IN AMERICAN CULTURE. Princeton, N.J.: Princeton University Press, 1939. x, 268 p.

1814. MacIver, Robert Morrison. ACADEMIC FREEDOM IN OUR TIME. New York: Columbia University Press, 1955. xiv, 329 p.

1815. _____. POLITICS AND SOCIETY. Edited by David Spitz. New York: Atherton Press, 1969. 571 p. Bibliography pp. 533-43.

1816. McKinney, John C. CONSTRUCTIVE TYPOLOGY AND SOCIAL THEORY. New York: Appleton-Century-Crofts, 1966. xiii, 250 p. Bibliography pp. 217-39.

1817. McKinney, John C., and Tiryakian, Edward A., eds. THEORETICAL SOCIOLOGY: PERSPECTIVES AND DEVELOPMENTS. New York: Appleton-Century-Crofts, 1970. 538 p.

1818. Marsh, Robert M. COMPARATIVE SOCIOLOGY: A CODIFICATION OF CROSS-SOCIETAL ANALYSIS. New York: Harcourt, Brace & World, 1967. 528 p. Bibliography pp. 375-496.

1819. Martindale, Don Albert. THE NATURE AND TYPES OF SOCIOLOGICAL THEORY. Boston: Houghton Mifflin Co., 1960. xiv, 560 p.

1820. _____. SOCIOLOGICAL THEORY AND THE PROBLEM OF VALUES. Columbus: Charles E. Merrill, 1974. x, 246 p.

1821. Mead, George Herbert. MIND, SELF, AND SOCIETY, FROM THE STANDPOINT OF A SOCIAL BEHAVIORIST. Edited by Charles W. Morris. Chicago: University of Illinois Press, 1934. xxxviii, 400 p.

1822. Merton, Robert K. SOCIAL THEORY AND SOCIAL STRUCTURE. Enl. ed. New York: Free Press, 1968. xxiii, 702 p.

1823. Merton, Robert K., et al., eds. SOCIOLOGY TODAY: PROBLEMS AND PROSPECTS. New York: Basic Books, 1959. xxxiv, 623 p.

1824. Miller, Delbert C. HANDBOOK OF RESEARCH DESIGN AND SOCIAL MEASUREMENT. 2nd ed. New York: David McKay, 1970. xiii, 432 p.

1825. Mills, C. Wright. THE SOCIOLOGICAL IMAGINATION. New York: Oxford University Press, 1959. 234 p.

1826. _____, ed. IMAGES OF MAN: THE CLASSIC TRADITION IN SOCIOLOGICAL THINKING. New York: George Braziller, 1960. 534 p.

1827. Moore, Wilbert E. ORDER AND CHANGE: ESSAYS IN COMPARATIVE SOCIOLOGY. New York: Wiley, 1967. viii, 313 p.

1828. Moreno, Jacob L. WHO SHALL SURVIVE? FOUNDATIONS OF SOCIOMETRY, GROUP PSYCHOTHERAPY AND SOCIODRAMA. Rev. ed. Beacon, N.Y.: Beacon House, 1953. 763 p.

1829. Nisbet, Robert A. THE SOCIOLOGICAL TRADITION. New York: Basic Books, 1966. xii, 349 p.

1830. Oberschall, Anthony, ed. THE ESTABLISHMENT OF EMPIRICAL SOCIOLOGY: STUDIES IN CONTINUITY, DISCONTINUITY AND INSTITUTIONALIZATION. New York: Harper & Row, Publishers, 1972. xvi, 256 p.

1831. Odum, Howard W. AMERICAN SOCIOLOGY: THE STORY OF SOCIOLOGY IN THE UNITED STATES THROUGH 1950. New York: Longmans, Green, 1951. vi, 501 p.

1832. Ogburn, William F. SOCIAL CHANGE: WITH RESPECT TO CULTURE AND ORIGINAL NATURE. New York: Huebsch, 1922. viii, 365 p.

1833. Page, Charles H. CLASS AND AMERICAN SOCIOLOGY FROM WARD TO ROSS. New York: Dial Press, 1940. xiv, 319 p.

1834. Parsons, Talcott. ESSAYS IN SOCIOLOGICAL THEORY. Rev. ed. Glencoe, Ill.: Free Press, 1954. 459 p.

1835. _____. POLITICS AND SOCIAL STRUCTURE. New York: Free Press, 1969. xvii, 557 p. Bibliography pp. 523-38.

1836. _____. THE SOCIAL SYSTEM. Glencoe, Ill.: Free Press, 1951. xviii, 575 p.

1837. _____. SOCIOLOGICAL THEORY AND MODERN SOCIETY. New York: Free Press, 1967. xii, 564 p. Bibliography pp. 531-32.

1838. _____, ed. AMERICAN SOCIOLOGY: PERSPECTIVES, PROBLEMS, METHODS. New York: Basic Books, 1968. xxii, 346 p.

1839. Parsons, Talcott, and Smelser, Neil J. ECONOMY AND SOCIETY: A STUDY OF ECONOMIC AND SOCIAL THEORY. Glencoe, Ill.: Free Press, 1956. xxi, 322 p.

1840. Parsons, Talcott, et al. WORKING PAPERS IN THE THEORY OF ACTION. New York: Free Press, 1953. 269 p.

1841. _____, eds. THEORIES OF SOCIETY: FOUNDATIONS OF MODERN SOCIOLOGICAL THEORY. 2 vols. New York: Free Press of Glencoe, 1961. Vol. 1, xix, 682, xiv p.; vol. 2, xix, 1479, xiv p.

1842. _____, eds. TOWARD A GENERAL THEORY OF ACTION: THEORETICAL FOUNDATIONS FOR THE SOCIAL SCIENCES. Cambridge, Mass.: Harvard University Press, 1951. xi, 506 p.

1843. Riesman, David. THORSTEIN VEBLEN: A CRITICAL INTERPRETATION. New York: Scribner, 1953. xv, 221 p.

1844. Roucek, Joseph, ed. CONTEMPORARY SOCIOLOGY. New York: Philosophical Library, 1958. xii, 1209 p.

1845. Schermerhorn, Richard A. COMPARATIVE ETHNIC RELATIONS: A FRAMEWORK FOR THEORY AND RESEARCH. New York: Random House, 1970. xviii, 327 p. Bibliography pp. 302-15.

1846. Schwendinger, Herman, and Schwendinger, Julia R. THE SOCIOLOGISTS OF THE CHAIR: A RADICAL ANALYSIS OF THE FORMATIVE YEARS OF AMERICAN SOCIOLOGY (1883-1922). New York: Basic Books, 1973. 573 p.

1847. Shibutani, Tamotsu, and Kwan, Kian M. ETHNIC STRATIFICATION: A COMPARATIVE APPROACH. New York: Macmillan, 1965. xi, 626 p. Bibliography pp. 591-96.

1848. Shils, Edward. CENTER AND PERIPHERY: ESSAYS IN MACROSOCI-OLOGY. Chicago: University of Chicago Press, 1974. 560 p.

1849. Smelser, Neil J. ESSAYS IN SOCIOLOGICAL EXPLANATION. Englewood Cliffs, N.J.: Prentice-Hall, 1968. viii, 280 p.

1850. _____. THEORY OF COLLECTIVE BEHAVIOR. New York: Free Press of Glencoe, 1963. xi, 436 p.

1851. Sorokin, Pitirim A. CONTEMPORARY SOCIOLOGICAL THEORIES. New York and London: Harper & Brothers, 1928. xxiii, 785 p.

1852. _____. FADS AND FOIBLES IN MODERN SOCIOLOGY AND RELATED SCIENCES. Chicago: H. Regnery, 1956. 357 p.

1853. _____. SOCIAL AND CULTURAL DYNAMICS. 4 vols. New York: American Book Co., 1937-41. Vol. 1, xxi, 745 p.; vol. 2, xvii, 727 p.; vol. 3, xvii, 636 p.; vol. 4, xv, 804 p.

1854. _____. SOCIETY, CULTURE, AND PERSONALITY: THEIR STRUC-TURE AND DYNAMICS, A SYSTEM OF GENERAL SOCIOLOGY. New York: Harper & Brothers, 1947. xiv, 742 p.

1855. _____. SOCIOLOGICAL THEORIES OF TODAY. New York: Harper, & Row, Publishers, 1966. xi, 676 p.

1856. Stinchcombe, Arthur L. CONSTRUCTING SOCIAL THEORIES. New York: Harcourt, Brace & World, 1968. xv, 303 p.

1857. Timasheff, Nicholas S. SOCIOLOGICAL THEORY: ITS NATURE AND GROWTH. 3rd ed. New York: Random House, 1967. xiv, 350 p.

1858. Tiryakian, Edward A., ed. SOCIOLOGICAL THEORY, VALUES, AND SOCIOCULTURAL CHANGE: ESSAYS IN HONOR OF PITIRIM A. SOROKIN. New York: Free Press of Glencoe, 1963. xv, 302 p.

1859. Zeitlin, Irving. IDEOLOGY AND THE DEVELOPMENT OF SOCIO-LOGICAL THOUGHT. Englewood Cliffs, N.J.: Prentice-Hall, 1968. x, 326 p.

1860. _____. RETHINKING SOCIOLOGY: A CRITIQUE OF CONTEM-PORARY THEORY. New York: Appleton-Century-Crofts, 1973. vii, 263 p.

1861. Zetterberg, Hans L., ed. SOCIOLOGY IN THE UNITED STATES OF AMERICA: A TREND REPORT. Paris: UNESCO, 1956. 156 p. Bibliography pp. 131-56.

INDEXES

Author Index
Periodical and Serial Title Index
Title Index
Subject Index

AUTHOR INDEX

Index entries refer to entry numbers rather than page numbers.

This index includes 1,300 names of first and second authors and editors; where there were more than two authors or editors, only the first is listed.

PERIODICAL AND SERIAL TITLE INDEX

Index entries refer to entry numbers rather than page numbers.

Periodical and Serial Title Index

TITLE INDEX

Index entries refer to entry numbers rather than page numbers. The titles listed are book titles only.

B

Title Index

Title Index

Title Index

Title Index

Title Index

K

L

M

Title Index

Title Index

Title Index

Title Index

Title Index

Title Index

Title Index

SUBJECT INDEX

Index entries refer to entry numbers rather than page numbers.

A

Abortion 370, 1074, 1076, 1079, 1486

Abstracts of journal articles, books, and papers 13, 37-50

Academic freedom 1814. See also College and university administration; College and university faculty

Achievement 15, 17, 307

Activism. See Black activism; Student activism

Addiction. See Alcohol and alcoholism; Drug addiction

Administration of justice. See Justice, administration of

Adolescence 15, 210, 650, 1071, 1129, 1131-46, 1537. See also Youth

Afro-Americans. See Black Americans

Aging 207, 208, 339, 394, 1664, 1669-91

Agriculture. See Farm life; Migrant workers; Rural studies

Alcohol and alcoholism 216, 1310, 1422, 1471, 1495-1510, 1706. See also Skid row

Alcoholics Anonymous 1496

American Indians 674-83

American society 41, 251-326

Amish 827, 828

Anti-intellectualism 278, 326

Anti-Semitism 652-65

Antiwar movement 1417, 1423, 1431, 1432, 1443, 1444

Appalachia 358, 401-6

Arab-Americans 687, 826

Armed forces. See Military life

Art 1302, 1303, 1309. See also Popular culture

Asian-Americans 684-93

Subject Index